DoveTales

"Nature"

An International Journal of the Arts

Published by Writing for Peace

DoveTales, an International Journal of the Arts
"Nature"

DoveTales is published
by Writing for Peace
P.O. Box 270908
Fort Collins, CO 80525.

Email: editor@writingforpeace.org.
www.writingforpeace.org

A note on photographs and art: Unless otherwise indicated, photographs and art are independent of writings published in DoveTales. Photographs and art do not illustrate incidents, events, or characters depicted by writers; writings are not intended to describe incidents, events, or characters depicted in the photographs and art.

Front Cover: Pd Lietz, Writing for Peace Artist-in-Residence

ISBN: 978-0-9891206-3-0 Print Edition

Printed in the United States of America
by McNaughton & Gunn

Sponsored by:

Colgate University Research Council

DoveTales

Contents

Artwork

na·ture

: the physical world and everything in it (such as plants, animals, mountains, oceans, stars, etc.) that is not made by people

: the natural forces that control what happens in the world

: the way that a person or animal behaves : the character or personality of a person or animal

~Merriam-Webster's Online Dictionary

This DoveTales is uncharacteristically large. Our journal includes the most imaginative, beautiful, and challenging of hundreds of submissions, so clearly the "nature" theme struck a chord.

Our natural world is under attack by corporate interests. As artists, we see the evidence all around us, and feel that pain acutely. But we also feel the insidious presence of another kind of assault, an attack against our private natures. We are only now beginning to comprehend the oppressive qualities of this near-omniscient surveillance state. As Glenn Greenwald put it:

> "The mere existence of a mass surveillance apparatus, regardless of how it is used, is in itself sufficient to stifle dissent. A citizenry that is aware of always being watched quickly becomes a compliant and fearful one."

As writers, artists, and activists, we make a decision to stand when told to sit, and to cry out when silence is expected. Artists speak truth to power. That's not to say that we are fearless, just that fear is irrelevant.

In this edition of DoveTales, our contributors explore the meanings of nature. We lift up their vision, and thank them for their courage.

Pax,

Carmel

A Global Effort for Our Young Writers

Andrea W. Doray

"Words have the power to spread awareness, hope, and inspiration to people who would have otherwise despaired."

Is this wisdom from Mahatma Gandhi? Albert Einstein? Martin Luther King, Jr.? No, these words are from Jordan Dalton, a 16-year-old high school student from Indiana, USA, one of the 2013 winners of the Young Writers Contest conducted annually by Writing for Peace.

Writing for Peace, headquartered in Colorado, USA, is a now-global organization that began with a local Young Writer's Contest in 2011, holding its first nationwide contest in 2012. By the 2014 contest, Writing for Peace has received submissions from students in 24 countries, including India, the Netherlands, Bangladesh, Great Britain, and the Philippines, as well as Vietnam, Pakistan, Malaysia, Macedonia, and the United Arab Emirates. Sponsorships from educational institutions such as Colgate University help produce "DoveTales: An International Journal of the Arts," which attracts literary submissions and student writing from around the world.

Along with other Board members of Writing for Peace, we act to cultivate empathy through education and creative writing to develop a worldwide foundation of compassion on which to build a more peaceful world. Our goal is to inspire and guide young writers so that their literary focus can be part of bringing nations closer to nonviolent conflict resolution and into societies that value human rights.

If we are to hope for a more peaceful world, we need such future leaders with vision and clarity ... and empathy. The Writing for Peace Young Writers Contest challenges these students to develop global and cultural awareness while refining their writing skills. In my own work with student writers, I am inspired by the tough topics they tackle and their deep commitments to following through on their words, as advocates as well as activists.

Young people like Cassidy Cole from Denver are confident that they too can change the world with their words. Cassidy, an 8th grade student when she took third place in the 2014 Young Writers Contest fiction category, says she uses her empathy as a compass, "wishing to understand a bewildering world."

Nneoma Ike-Njoku, then 18 and a second-place finisher in 2013, describes her writing as an idea that "becomes a daughter cell, actively dividing into legion." Nneoma hails from Mararaba, Nasarawra State, Nigeria – a country where kidnapped schoolgirls still remain missing, and where at least 50 students were recently killed by a suicide bomber during a school assembly.

Violence like this is one of the reasons why it's so important, so urgent for organizations such as Writing for Peace to inspire and guide young writers so that their writing can work toward bringing nations closer to nonviolent conflict resolution and into societies that value human rights.

Does this sound too optimistic, too naïve? Without these ideals, we can never hope to accomplish peace, and without the voices of the world's young people – bold, questioning, and "dividing into legion" – we cannot move forward in empathetic leadership that will effect real change in the world.

This kind of leadership is best expressed not only in the words of Gandhi and Martin Luther King, but also in those of Janani Venkatesh, 19, of Chennai, Tamil Nadu, India: "I learned many wonderful, bewildering, and shocking things about the world during my research," and in those of Jordan Dalton: "I've come to realize that my work really can make a difference in the world."

White Dove
Christopher Woods

Three Poems
Hélène Cardona

How God Thinks is Surprising

My mother and I are two swans intertwined.
We show the world, on stage, our connection,
our closeness. The bond never goes away.
God is the director of the play.

We're part of the other,
a continuation of movement, dance, beauty.
Together we form a whole, a heart, an angel.
Our core holds a plate to be filled

with what life brings.
We create a celebration for no reason in particular,
the symmetry of our truth a vision, an offering.
We invented time.

The more we make it disappear,
the closer to God we grow.
I know what it's like absorbing the nature of plants,
living off the land and rain.

I used to be a flower.
I like transforming into an animal,
devouring who I was.
The earth never fails me.

Unveiling Jean Couteau

I step out of painted panels, touch
the pulse of time, ride
a panther, rapacious illusionist, ripple
onward in the mist, sensual robe.
The cinnamon sun weaves whimsical
unicorns, soaks cardamom
clouds, quickens the skin,
illuminates the moon in the world
access, melts the snow in great shafts,
reminds us it's a wild place we inhabit.

Hélène Cardona

Spellbound

Fall asleep at the lake
tonight, no boundaries, like a fairy.
I'm the eagle song, a calling, light
defying gravity, someone you could steal
horses with, case of mistaken identity, tears
transforming into fish in the air, force
that propels forward, surrenders, proclaims
who I am with the kind of passport God
has, Her will an explosion, words
for bullets. I'll bring you everything I have
to offer: stardust, silence, grace from heaven
and flutes like wind, impish, mischievous,
good and bad, pulled out of myself into
the spell. I'll ask anything, the unthinkable.
I move so fast, breathless, delicate
craftsmanship. I must've walked
on all fours, elongated, neither human
nor animal, creature you only see in magic.

Two Poems
Ben Gunsberg

Audubon Exit

Wading birds gone south, fiddler crabs
burrowed deep beneath the reedy tidal slosh,
our guide says new moon tides transform
that little copse into an island, tells of finding
sharks' teeth, sea stars, and this—a turtle shell
she pulls from her burlap pack and passes
so we can thumb pale barnacles
locked against the shell's humped keel.
I want to know more about this shell,
the gulls who glide and plunge above
the gray Atlantic shelf, the seal who bobs
like a black buoy. What type of algae
banks red against the sandbar's edge?
Then the sun drops behind a cloud,
and the sea, having lost its sequins, becomes
a field of slate, and I feel I should escape
all prior knowledge, wander shore, turning
shells over in my hand, deciding for myself
about why we're whirled and thinned by time
then strewn across the beach like pieces
of a shattered clock. It feels fine to wander
from my body and my body's guide, the mind
hurled breathless onto shore, hungry and unfurling.

Ben Gunsberg

What to Do with Minnesota

What to do with muddy fields in fall
besides study the strange loyalty of geese
as they pass disguised as a necklace
over all that missing corn, the last beets
guarding their sweet magenta. You feel
sorry for naked trees, also for yourself
because you know this isn't March
when geese return like seeds,
proving life begins

                                                again.

Remember when you weren't sure
what to do with muddy fields last fall
and like a beet buried yourself
in memory, the strange loyalty of geese
disguised as seeds blown over earth,
all pasts planted in the present
like new grass curtained by rain.
Forget the prophecy of leaves
torn apart by a hard wind.

Ross Knapp

A Few Years on Lake Minnetonka

The memories make me shudder when I am in this place
Too many scars sliced raw onto my heart and face.
Yet this pitiful place of mansions sitting
Mockingly atop formerly sacred Indian shores
Holds a strange allure, a repugnant beauty for me.
I drive daily over the old historic roads.
Smaller narrower and quainter than I remember
Winding gently around swerve of shore and
Bend of bay leading to forgotten sacred streams.
Ancient mixing slowly with new
Resisting like a desperate youth becoming a reluctant whore
Out of necessity, but not yet-
Here the pace is still habitual
Here the tone is still traditional
Here the neighbors still know one another a little
Here the trees still watch comfortingly
Here the birds still beckon pleasantly
Here the sands still speak Earth's mysteries
Here the waters still whisper of eternity
I hear the silent rumbling of the waves on the rocks
I smell the scent of the fresh water
I see the auras of the animals
I taste the music of the wave crests rhyming back and forth
I touch and feel it all
Nature calls out to me
Introducing me to her Native daughters and sons
Who did not seek to control and conquer,
But sought simplicity, harmony, and to speak nature's tongue.

Ross Knapp

Country Fields

I drive away from the commotion
The constant motion fades slowly

The ticking city within me stills
Like a mystic or a Buddhist
To silence for a few sacred seconds

Its siren still wails within
Flailing its restless working hands
Fight or flight, flight or fight, figh...or...

Quiet. Peace. The noiseless fields
Whisper soothing voices,
Melodies. Simplicity. Negation. Nature.

I grasp the soil in my hands
Aromas of ancient grain
Daily animal rhythm
Rituals of millenniums
Wind winds its way into my ears
Stars stare into my eyes
Crop kernels seep into my blood

My mind elevated fleeting
Streaking though endless epiphanies
There is no country
There is no morality
There is no God
There is no you
There is no me
City and country are one
Good and evil are one
Justice and mercy are one
Faith and reason are one
You and I are one
The base of all action—
                    Inaction

Annual Spring Renaissance

New life rushes forth
From soil to soaring sky
Death's scythe banished for short time

Plants burst forth from their pots
Trees bud and bloom wafting
Intoxicating fragrances of fresh life

Battalions of birds return
Bringing music in their wake
Buzzing chatter of another Resurrection

Sun wins the upper hand
Stretching herself farther and farther
Longer and longer, diminishing her dark sister

Warmth lights up the world, wiping away the scorn
Catatonic cold compartmentalized into distant memory
Spring strikes her match, summer fans his flames

The Phoenix of Heat reborn, crescendoing slowly out of
prison to climax
Former glory finally restored
Final grip of frost shattered, melted to a pathetic puddle

It lifts its wrathful wings in triumph
Purging the world of imperfections
Its fires ascending to the heavens

Its euphoria engulfing every nation
Wonder and ineffable mystical joy
Frenzy and revelry our Apostolic tongues

All men Transfigured to David, all women to Helen
The short lived time when nihilism no longer feels natural

United Pride
Eve Gaal

My eyes focused and refocused on hundreds of pink flamingos standing tall in wild, yellowing grass. We were sitting on a slow moving tour bus with oodles of ogling tourists staring at the delightful spectacle unfolding in front of us. Strange, light-green cacti in various formations rimmed a small lake, busy with activity. A natural fence, the colors blended into running watercolors—vivid—yet slightly blurred like a Monet painting. In the distance, violet hued hills brazenly sat under poofy clouds of white and gray. Wet drops on the bus windows mixed with the excruciatingly uncomfortable bus ride. We were on a rustic road, creating this lasting memory, this painting in my mind where blush-colored birds frolicked peacefully among swaying and contrasting reeds. The long beaks, the slender legs and the model-esque poses made the flamingos look proud and superior--almost vain-- yet immensely elegant. Some were standing on one foot, next to baby flamingoes and they all glanced left and right at the noise of the bus under the general excitement of summer rain. They stretched their long necks towards our caravan and slowly moved away, heads bobbing up and down, stepping deliberately and cautiously in unison—a symphony of movement—a painter's palette.

Hard to imagine but our bus trip was called a 'Country Drive in Curacao' and everything would have been just fine if it wasn't for the bus with a broken air conditioning system. With high humidity and insane heat, the driver didn't allow anyone to open the windows, putting passengers near the precipice of passing out. Sweat dripped down our temples, stinging our eyes and soaking our shirts. The fogged up windows, the breath of gasping travelers, coupled with the smell of perspiration, accompanied the bumpy dirt road and generally hellish ride. Next to us sat a priest who inadvertently reminded me of acceptance and humility. Yet, while on a rather expensive vacation, the idea of self-sacrifice didn't seem appropriate. Didn't a vacation guarantee comfort? Didn't I pay for air-conditioning? After seeing the wild flamingos, we took tours of rock caves where we disembarked for a short while. The rain had subsided but gray clouds still lurked above. Rarely have I wished for a dreadful bus trip of such gorgeous proportions to be over. There we were on a long arduous bus trip, testing our deodorants, while we zipped past cool beaches full of coconut palms hemmed with romantic lagoons.

When the sun popped out the bus temperature rose, and we felt like boiled peanuts. Salty drops kept blinding me and fogging up my contact lenses. Father James himself looked a little hot under his clerical collar. He smiled as if everything was fine and, of course, on some strange level of reality I suppose, everything was absolutely fine. We were still alive and the following day would be Palm Sunday where we were going to read The Passion of Our Lord. That same priest had honored both of us by inviting us to read at mass the following day. There was a message here in the midst of our luxurious vacation and perhaps that reality, that beauty is an analogy for happiness. It's the swirling Monet instead of the pristine and perfect photograph, where we typically pose in front of landmarks or proudly model our swimwear.

I think back to that humbling vacation seven years ago and recall the image of those birds perched on one leg. In my memory, I see pink and various shades of green dripping down the windows in one massive sopping, throbbing human cage, but I also see art. Under those waving palm fronds, we are one for a few moments--all of us. Thousands of dancing flamingos seem to be part of a baptismal ceremony under a consecrated blanket of rain. As unwilling parishioners and even more unlikely godparents, we had transformed from our guise of weary, sinful travelers into a blended passion play. God had united us at that moment into a masterful impressionistic portrait consisting of a stunning island filled with tall grass, tropical birds, reptiles and exotic plants. Though uncomfortable at the time, I still remember a mandala-like creation spanning from the center like wet tie-dye.

Finally disembarking, we held the rail and jumped to the ground. Our backs ached and we stretched while glancing around and inhaling deeply. My legs felt numb but I stood on one and then another. We wanted to make sure we didn't leave anything behind. Nothing but drops of sweat lingered in the old coach, waiting for the next group of unsuspecting travelers. We waved to Father James. It didn't take long for us to get back to our extravagant holiday--back to the posh excess of freezing cold air-conditioning and pride.

Early Morning in Trawangan.
Pratima Annapurna Balabhadrapathruni

One morning, before sunrise,
 as the purple of dawn turns to blush
and ushers me into a deeper state
of relaxed observation:

The koi in the pond splash around
a Bolshoi ballet gone berserk
to the tune of a dog:
Time seems a series of yelps
until it tumbles to stop
even as the sun ripples a thousand
brush strokes on the calm and restless sea
and dallies out a sienna red
into the swift shadows of deep night,
a moment stretches in the womb of turtle
and births introspection.

Somewhere birds harness the present
under the span of their wings

with the wind as
an accompaniment to their song

Dawn tethers itself to the spindle of daylight
and spins a world of ochre and gold

until
    the tarnished brass of unfamiliar voices
    trespass the solemn reverie.
    The turtle backs to its citadel,
    an enraged sun floods the sea.

Poet's note: Last year, while holidaying in Bali, we decided to stay in the rather quiet island of Gili Trawangan, which is the natural breeding site for the green turtle and the Hawkbill turtle.

On that particular dawn that I mention in the poem, I stood ready with my camera, waiting for the spectacular sunrise. I stood in the Bali sea, my ankles submerged in water. There was a soft splash. I looked down to see a turtle stare back at me.

We looked at each other, each of us trying to see what kind of animal the other was. It was as if time stood still.

It was a strange communion, neither threatened by the presence of the other, the sea singing softly to both of us.

Then the sun began to rise, and the turtle swam a little closer, I almost ran back onto the beach, but stood my ground, and smiled at its insistence to get close, until some people chose to come out of the resort with loud blaring voices, breaking our reverie.

The turtle swam away. The sun rose in haste and painted the sea red and orange...and then all too bright gold, way too brilliant to see which direction the turtle had headed.

Three Poems
Yuan Changming

Another Seascape

A dolphin jumping high above the horizon
A gull charging down right towards the ocean

A double focus of nature
But a single moment of anti-self

Yuan Changming

Seasonal Stanzas

October

Burning, blooming
Like spring flowers
All tree leaves
Giggle, guffawing
With the west wind
In their fierce defiance
Against the elegy of the land
Recited aloud
In blood-throated voices

November

Most monotonous month:
Each passing day is depressed
Into a crow, its wings
Its body and tails
Newly glazed in the mists
Of thick dusk
Though its heart still
Lingers in the memory of
Summer's orange morning glow

December

As the sun sinks deeper every day
Into the other side of the world
The shadow is getting longer, darker
Making our lives slant more and more
Towards night, when nature
Tries to balance yin and yang
By covering each dark corner
With white snowflakes
Ever so softly, quietly

As each twig frowns hard at twilight
Why not give it smile and thus
Book a space in heaven?

Natural Confrontations

Crow

A baby raven
Popping up from nowhere
Tries to
Establish itself:
one dark truth
On the skeletal tree top
Yawing fiercely
Towards the sky, the wind, the buildings
The fields and the entire afternoon
All so fluffily white
In jade-toned snow

Plum Blossom

Without a single leaf
Grass-dyed or sun-painted
To highlight it
But on a skeletal twig
Glazed with dark elegies
A bud is blooming, bold and blatant
Like a drop of blood
As if to show off, to challenge
The entire season
When whims and wishes
Are all frozen like the landscape

Eddy

A gossamer-like breeze
Left far behind
By a running dog
Tries to strike
The stagnated twilight
Hanging above the whole city
Before the storm sets in

Beach
Carl Scharwath

The Explorer Returns
Dean K. Miller

Last night's fog, which shrouded the street lights, had descended to hug the ground. The sand was damp and cold against the soles of my feet. The distant sound of breaking waves, unseen through the brume, cast an ominous mood. Undaunted, I proceeded toward the ocean. Looking behind me, the hotel was obscured, swallowed by the gray moisture. Moving nearer the salty surf, my footsteps exposed dry sand hidden under the wet, thin-crusted, top layer. I walked into the enveloping mist, welcoming the solitude and grateful to be heading home.

Dressed in only shorts and a t-shirt, the cool morning breeze met little resistance. A chilled shiver coursed up my spine. Droplets of moisture collected on the hairs of my arms. The constant crashing of waves grew louder. The scent of oceanic decay filled the heavy air. With a final check from where I'd come, I saw the sun's deep, muzzled glow, its heat unable to penetrate the gray. Continuing on, I reached the hard-packed sand, remnant of the receding tide. My feet sensed another drop in temperature. The sea drew me nearer.

And then I saw her. My pace quickened; the first shallow rush of water, chilled from unfathomable depths, covered my toes. I spiraled back in time, memories washing through me as quickly as the wave receded and then another took its place. The frigid liquid wrapped around my shins as I waded deeper. It released its grip and proceeded inland. The brief meeting of old friends complete, we both had more to do. We would meet again.

With gentle relentlessness the waves continued to

oppose my direction of travel. The cry of a lone gull, unseen in the thickening fog, signaled a warning; I had ventured far enough. Foaming waves crashed mid-thigh. The morning sky, a pale blue along the horizon, became visible through a small portal in the fog. I looked into forever and the vastness of beyond, seeing every possibility of life. I understood what the sailors of yore had felt and possessed the knowledge of their ship's captains: Another world was out there, waiting to be discovered.

A second cry from the gull signaled my time to return. I retreated from the sea, taking with me its lessons. Each passing wave guided me inland and then returned to its source, accepting its journey as complete and welcoming its new direction.

I reached the hard-packed sand, a traveler from a distant time and yet, from not so long ago, and discovered a new world inside of me.

Crown for Rivers
Wang Ping

Joy as I welcome you and the gift, acorn of small things
Light on the river's tongue, and long day of a mayfly
Who gives us the power to judge which poet is more sublime?
Who, returning from the deep, still remains the same?

And yet…the heart is made to keep going at her own pace
Sacred, this memory from the fountain of youth
A prayer begins at the edge of void, the edge of no shame
What arrow points us to a possible grace, here and now?

 The river runs through us—our kin, our blood
As the ghost returns home as the warrior of peace
Look at this beauty--so simple and perfect in this agate seed

This is my eye—blindly—in the river wild and fast
With a hearts bleeding and pounding till it breaks free

Three Poems
Stephanie Noble

Crossing the Stream

Crossing the stream, arms akimbo,
I teeter on one stepping stone while testing
for solidity of the next before giving over,
yet again, full reliance to a rock that may wobble.

With information, too, sometimes I lose balance,
stumbling upon Wikipedia discussions
where opposing rocky facts are hurled
and I duck and dodge getting hit in the crossfire --
like which side of the Nepal-India border
is Lumbini, the birthplace of the Buddha?

Now I shed my shoes to walk the riverbed.
No need to test, tentative, or teeter, tensed.
Instead, I sense the river pulsing my ankles
as I wade in the cool clear rapids.

Then I slowly let myself go, and sink up to my shoulders
in a quiet pool in the shade of an alder tree.
Dark buoyancy holds me lightly.
The point of my chin softens in wavering circles
spreading out from the dappled dance of water skates.

Yes, rocks may give water a course to run,
and the interplay of the two is a glory to behold.
But, truth be told, water runs, rocks or no,
along the path of least resistance,
flooding fields and lapping shores.

Just so the dharma dances beyond idea of borders,
sweet and bracing as clear water
beneath verdant boughs on a sweltering summer day.

Ever So Slowly

The Earth is a restless rotisserie sleeper
-- shifting, snorting and flailing about.

We may accept our own fleeting nature
yet still trust that this rock is eternal.

But rock breathes too, albeit slowly
so that my whole life and the lives

of my children's children's children
ride the wave of one languorous exhale.

Stephanie Noble

What It Is

The soul's not mine to name or claim.
Yours or his, it's all the same:
A densely-crammed attic of a packrat fanatic,
a honeycombed catacomb, an old folks' home,
where nothing's measured ounce for ounce,
and earthly wealth no longer counts.

Sounds abound like a babbling stream
and every dream of every sleeper,
every thought and even deeper in the heap
are untold riches and unscratched itches,
ravines of gold and offal ditches.

All of a piece absorbed unjudged,
sweet and sour, sludge and fudge.
The repository of every story, tall or gory,
ever told within the fold of creatures bold
and critters shy, how they lived and how they died,
what they felt, how hard they tried,
when they laughed and why they cried.

Held forever in a vast embrace,
beyond all limits of time and place:
Every sigh, every season, every excuse
and every reason, every joy, every despair,
every curse and every prayer.

And underneath each fallen leaf,
each lost belief, each sigh of relief,
each hollow heart trapped in its grief,
are earthy odors rich and moist
of every word still left unvoiced.

Laura Grace Weldon

Overheard Calls

The ordinary is mysterious to me.
How plants breathe out
what we need to breathe in
and how their leaves eat sunlight.
How radio waves careen
through buildings and bodies
making invisible fields speak.
How songs play
over and over in our heads,
a gift of memory
from ancestors who heard music
only as it was performed.
How we argue over eternity
because what's living
grows old and dies,
while styrofoam cups
and car tires persist beyond us.

It's mysterious
we can call one another
trusting our voices carry
exactly to the ear we seek,
as we'd like prayer to do.
If, before the phone's invention,
we'd sought out
a stranger or two from history,
a man laboring in the fields,
a woman weaving cloth,
telling them there would come a time
when anyone, anywhere
could speak to anyone, anywhere
and they'd hear close up
sorrow and delight in far off voices
that farmer, that weaver would rejoice
in the blessed device, seeing it
spread wisdom and compassion.
What a time to live in, they'd imagine.

Laura Grace Weldon

I hear us come into this fullness.
On crowded streets I walk by
as people speak to distant ears
of seven billion selves.

Voices connect
across trembling waves.
It sounds mysterious
as quantum entanglement,
ordinary as love.

Earthbound

Are we supposed to settle for a planet
lagging behind our expectations?
We want reversible time,
admission into past or future
easy as changing our minds.
We want teleportation, so we can
zip anywhere for the afternoon,
maybe Iceland or Argentina,
where we'll make new friends,
agree to meet up for lunch
next week in Greece,
on only an hour's break.

We want to get past
greed and suffering and war,
enough already.
And death? That's awfully primitive
for souls with so much left to learn.

That said, this planet does a lot right.
Birds, for one.
Water in all its perfect manifestations.
Those alive poems called trees.
The way a moment's glance
can reveal a kindred spirit.

Which we all are, really.
The oneness between self and everything
is this planet's secret, kept imperfectly.
That's more than we might expect.
Although time travel would be nice.

Guardian

He's drawn outside to stand,
back to the house,
sensing more than thinking.

A woman calls him in
but he doesn't answer.
Doesn't move. Watches.

His skin reads the wind's narration,
lungs gauge icy breaths,
a whole being alert to
darkening smoke-gray clouds
over the box of peace he calls home.

His father and before him, grandfather,
did what he does now. Watched
and waited, small mortal men
backs to a doorway's open mouth,
facing the sky.

Bad, but not too bad,
the body tells the mind.
He lingers. Hail spatters
dust awake. Gusts
tango with tree branches.
Rain polka dots his shirt.
He won't turn around just yet.
There's a rightness he can't explain.
Within it he feels completely alive.

Three Poems
Bredt Bredthauer

K-Street Community Gardens, D.C.

The collard seeds sprouted overnight,
small petioles emerging from black
six-packs filled with Arabica
coffee and buffalo manure.

First frost, I watch
a doggedly persistent crowd
of seeds rise on stalks no larger
than a single strand of angel hair.

Each day ends like the one before.
My fingers look like tuning forks
as they remove weeds from the bed.
I spread my arms like a scarecrow.

A man walks by with a gas-powered
leaf-blower attached to his back
He's clearing away the dead leaves
and gradually erasing our footprints.

Bredt Bredthauer

What gives Life Must Endure Burning
– After Victor Frankl

By spring you will be buried
beneath the oaks.

I never expected to survive
your absence.

They say that morning forgives
the night her infidelities,

but the world is not divine.
It waits to decompose,

misshapen by the hard
midwestern frost.

Out of this, we rise.
Before the spirit must surrender

to the body's cold fire,
the heat of flesh

undoes what no smoke
sufficed to do.

Election, 2016

It's mostly when I'm hunkered down
among the rows of endive and escarole,
probing for thrips, aphids, and earworms
while the fusty muck and moist peat
partially obscure each fingerprint
that I think of the president.

Showerside Economics
David S. Pointer

Bathtub monsters swim as invisible chemical couriers to show up through a plugged-off drain

Bathtub monsters use misdirection to trickle down the nozzle-head spray

Mothers would jump through public illness hoopla-hoops to assist clean up

Mothers would scrub every oceanographer's oily animals to demilitarize police

Mothers would dance through punji-stick strip-pits for world peace, but

Foot-shooters anonymous refuse to leave their financial districts to start a top-down environmental debris self-help group

Foot-shooters anonymous refuse to admit their powerlessness over their own monetary system's seeping lagoons or leaking groundwater

Superfund free market mirage teams up with untreated toxins to discover friendly-fire environmentalism and fiscal conservatism double as one and the same

Superfund free marketeers scoop up profits here while depositing poisons there like ever melting Easter egg observatories or hatcheries

Bathtub monsters can embed inside ever expanding chest measurements sometimes misidentified as bi-products of more nutrious non-food diet as whistling others objectify sanctioned insanity

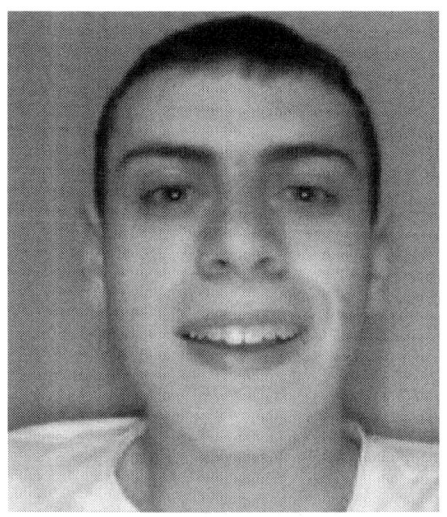

Ben Gershenfeld
2014 Young Writers Competition Nonfiction Contest
First Place

Cultural Obstacles

Voorhees, New Jersey, United States
Eastern Regional High School, Grade 11

*I admire how the author combines the personal – holiday
schedules at his school – with the wider view, such as his
father's workplace, the corporate world beyond, and the
US House and Senate, to reveal deeply ingrained inequity
in how we treat religions and religious holidays.*
~Dinty W. Moore

Cultural Obstacles
Ben Gershenfeld

While many people in the world believe that Anti-Semitism was eradicated after the Holocaust, it is very prevalent in our society today. Even in towns where secularism is preached and supposedly practiced in the school system, Christianity is still strongly favored. There are many examples of a lack of religious equality that I have experienced.

The school administrators think they are doing the right thing by giving students days off for Jewish holidays. But there are still school-related athletic functions that carry on those days. The coaches claim that these practices are "optional," but we all know that playing time will be significantly reduced if practice is missed. Is there optional practice on Christmas or Easter? The contradictory argument is that many people do not know the timetable of Jewish holidays, and that may be true, but ignorance is not an excuse.

The government is guilty as well. Congress goes home for the Christian holidays at the end of the year, but there is no recess during Rosh Hashanah and Yom Kippur. There are currently 45 Jews in Congress, which comprises 8.4% of the total members. Across America, Jewish employees are forced to work during their holy holidays while Christians always get the day off.

Why is winter break in schools always centered around Christmas and not Hanukkah? Why is spring break always centered around Easter and not Passover?

These are questions that administrators at public schools fail to answer. Jewish students just like me are forced to give up school lunches during Passover and instead resort to eating crushed Matzah.

Thinking that perhaps the corporate world might demonstrate a more fair and equitable approach to this issue, I asked my dad to share his experiences with me. He works for a Fortune 500 company and has so for many years. Because he interacts with many other companies in his role, he also has knowledge of how those organizations work. It has been his experience that the corporate world shows even less consideration for those that practice Judaism than do the public schools.

According to my father, Christmas Day, Christmas Eve, and Good Friday are all corporate holidays at his company. And while always Easter falls on a Sunday and is not considered a company holiday, it is understood that no meetings requiring travel are ever to be scheduled on the Monday after Easter. There are no Jewish Holidays observed my father's company and he tells me he is unaware of any company he has ever worked for or worked with that have done so either. In order for my dad to observe holidays such as Rosh Hashanah or Yom Kippur, two of the holiest days on the Jewish calendar, he is forced to use all of his allotted personal days. This, of course, leaves him no personal days should he want to use them for any other reasons.

When I asked my father how this makes him feel, he tells me this inevitably leads him to build up feelings of resentment towards his company, as it does for most of his colleagues put in the very same position. Additionally, he said, it is more than just the days off that trouble him. It is the fact that meetings and conference calls are scheduled during these Jewish Holidays, which he is forced to miss. Just like those "optional" practices the Eastern athletic teams hold where players who choose to miss for religious reasons are not penalized, he indicates that missing company meetings when he takes personal religious days certainly makes him feel as if he is being put at a disadvantage.

There has been a tremendous amount of debate over the past few years that the liberal government has waged a war on religion. What most of the people are really complaining about, both the politicians and non-politicians making most of the noise, is not a war on religion, but more so a war on Christianity. They are worried about Christmas and Easter being threatened, but seem completely unaware of the silent war that has been waged against Judaism and other non-Christian religions. I believe this has been a war of ignorance, which is where most prejudice and discrimination comes from.

Our country and, in fact, the entire world, has a long history of religious persecution which has been born out of ignorance. We have spent a lot of time and energy in the United States attempting to separate Church and State. However, the truth is religion finds its way into everything we do – school, work, politics, etc. Maybe if we spent more time learning about every religion we would gain a deeper understanding of the importance religion plays in every culture. Hopefully that deeper understanding would allow us to appreciate why levelling the playing field for all of us is simply the right thing to do.

Bio~

Ben Gershenfeld is a 17-year-old student from Voorhees, New Jersey. Ben is involved in both his school and his community. He plays soccer and volleyball for Eastern High School, where he soon hopes to win a state championship. He also participates in Model United Nations and loves learning about the world and different cultures. Ben is an intern for Jewish Community Relations Council and is interested in government and international relations. He is also an employee at Wayback Burger, where he cooks hamburgers and makes milkshakes. Ben plans on attending college after graduation from high school and aspires to one day be a top business executive.

2015 Progress Report~

After being rewarded first place in the Writing for Peace contest, my confidence and appreciation for writing was elevated beyond its previous point. The next major phase of my writing came in the form of college essays. I carried the same lessons I learned from Writing for Peace— incorporating personal examples, evoking pathos, and writing with passion— into my college essays. The consummation of my college writing/application process occurred when I was accepted into Cornell University, where I will be writing the next chapter of my life.

What W4P means to me~

As young students, there is much expected of us, but we still don't have the capabilities to make significant change in the world. We can't vote. We do not have radio shows or television shows to use as platforms. There are myriad injustices in the world, so how can we promote change? Writing for Peace gives us great opportunities to broadcast our voices and listen to each other. I know that I learned about different cultures and struggles from reading my peers' works, and I hope someone learned something from mine.

Three Poems
Jennifer Clark

John Chapman, 1774-1845

To sow hope, slip into a burlap sack.
Cut holes for arms and legs. With a tin pot
on head for hat set bare feet to soil and go forth
into the wild frontier.

Head west, following streams and their tributaries.
Search for a clearing in the woods. Stoop, then
furrow soil with finger. From a satchel, pull seeds—
salvaged from pomace—and one by one press down.
Cover lightly with loam. Build a fence to allow work
to take hold—gather the scattered, the fallen branches
and vines; weave together while singing. Move on.

When hungry, eat cornmeal mush and swallow coffee.
When tired, sleep on the forest floor.
Return each year to tend the saplings, pinch off
any misplaced buds before they swell to stray branches,
mend sections of fence destroyed by deer and cattle.
Remember to bring bits of calico to offer tan-faced
children whose parents now lodge near.
Accept cast-off clothing of any kind. Move on.

Continue along the stretch of Maumee River,
leaving a trail of thirsty pioneers, drunk now
on the sweet juice of sermon.

John James Audubon (1785-1851)

At 27, he becomes a still life of despair—
discovering that a brood of Norway rats

had chewed through 200
birds of America.

He'll sketch his way out,
render them again, only finer

after he forges through forests
comes upon rose-breasted grosbeaks,

blue jays, and birds no longer here,
like the passenger pigeon, notes of one

*seen gliding through the woods
and close to the observer, it passes*

*like a thought, and on trying to see it again,
the eye searches in vain; the bird is gone...*

Reassures his dear, kind readers *that nothing
but the gradual diminution of forests*

can accomplish their decrease. He'll tie
silver threads around the legs of Phoebes,

fling them into the sky, await their return,
his mind, his world and its thick carpet

of trees, brimming with birds.

Jennifer Clark

The world and everything in it, a laboratory for the soul

The stone is like a fact. Hard and cold.
Answer the damn door.
Welcome the stone into the house.
Set a table place for wind and tree.
Wonder why rivers are prophets.
Walk out the damn door.
Notice dirt, a book in the Bible.
Turn the page with your foot.
Read.

Annette Marie Smith

Come Spring

The air is filled with tiny white umbrellas
spinning as they fall
and interspersed between them
are raindrops cold and shaped like tears.
They coat the tips of trees in chrysalides
beneath the falling snow.
Such glass cocoons will bud with leaves
which unfurl their wings like butterflies
to flutter in the breeze,
come spring.

Annette Marie Smith

Forgiveness finds me

For you
Have been seeking me out
Hard on the scent of my betrayal
Like a hound you set on me.
Faithful and undeterred
Forgiveness followed me
Saw through my every ruse and trick
And me
Thinking I am a clever fox
Running
Doubling back and hiding my tracks
Crossing the most barren land
And the greenest flecked bog
To shake you.
Here you are anyway with your
Hands on me soothing my ruffled pride
That wouldn't let me see
How fine your fingers
Combing out the brambles would feel to me
And forgiveness, your faithful hound
Has been shut outside the door
Because we don't need him anymore.

Flags are birds

and they are the only birds
that do not raise their young
but promptly bury them,
consign them while enshelled
to die for the 'greater good'
of their flock-nationality
in flights
of war.

The Reflection of the Flag at the Y

Danny P. Barbare

In
the
light
of
things

stars
and
stripes
are
reflecting
in
the
window

as
if
to
say

and
quite
squarely
so

this
is
our
country.

Arlington

The morning air feels fresher here.
All at once, next to a mound
of newly dug earth, rifles appear
to salute a cloudless sky. And while

they do, somebody's choked-back tears
are muted by the blanks sounding
until each barrel descends,
and six young soldiers, three to a file

each side of a tri-colored bier,
one by one, fold then bend
its flag into a perfect wedge.

While a boy who used to play "War" near,
camouflaged by some neighbor's hedge,
no longer plays. Today war ends.

Mark Mansfield

Au Balcon

All the world's houses will vanish
Except for one balcony.
                   — Jules Supervielle

As if from nowhere, maybe very soon,
we'll both arrive past midnight at a ball
in time to hear its last waltz down a hall
which opens at one end on a small porch
where we will rest, both gazing at the moon.
The only other light, a golden torch,

will rise and fall with each breath from our lips,
as dark waves crash against cliffs far below.
And while we whisper, shapes will come and go,
seeming to know our thoughts and all we say
before we do, although our fingertips
by then, as always, will have found their way.

Then soon two more shapes, gliding across the porch,
will dance away before the moon will say
something about a ball that long ago
with fingertips like flames formed a great torch,
while a waltz that down a dark hall used to play
called millions of others, all lost below.

How Still We See

Every Tear from Every Eye
Becomes a Babe in Eternity.
                    — William Blake

His tiny body scarcely moves
on this now-silent night,
born again into a world
where more peacemakers fight.

No manger for a bed, he's curled
by shepherds' corpses where
a "smart" bomb, traveling too far,
flared then burst midair.

Near death, her face deformed
                    and charred,
his mother's blank eyes stare.
His tiny fingers press the wet
dark warmth matting her hair.

Droning steel wings silhouette
the moon through blasts of snow,
while from an unseen star -- a light
shone down here long ago.

Three Poems
Mark J. Mitchell

Villanelle on a Theme from Samuel Ha-Nagid

War begins like a pretty girl
dancing, skillful, shy and alone.
When she stops she can end the world.

She waves her flag, makes it unfurl
then smiles. What's done is done.
War begins. Then a pretty girl

gets wounded. Her too-pampered curls
are shorn, her face scarred. Her low moans
will stop soon. She ends like the world:

Broken, dark, silent and no pearls
from presidents to help. To atone
for war, we offer pretty girls

to soldiers. They use them and hurl
them away, and we're on our own.
It comes to a full stop. The world

spins on, spins out its endless whirl.
The dancer's become a toothless crone.
War begins like a pretty girl
who can't stop 'til she ends the world.

After a War in the Middle East

So Hector's body left the field at Troy
And Achilles' followed down that low road,
Their swords left to rust, to be found by boys

Unschooled in arms, their war some episode
To study later. The boys make up games
Without Greek glory and no warrior's code.

Hecuba is dust, Priam lost. The names
Of those great ones are hollow as the earth now.
Just this bare hill's left, below it a plain

Where weapons appear while they tend dull cows.
They don't know a blind man will make a song
About how their fathers fell, about how

Their mothers were carried away as toys
For strangers just as long vanished. Wild toads
Hold more interest for these orphans. The fame
Of warriors can't be cooked. And boys, somehow,
Must eat—to grow proud, grow vicious, grow strong.

Mark J. Mitchell

Home Front

In green light just before the evening wash
of blue comes out of the east, songbirds play
tag in a magnolia tree. A cool bath
of marine air pushes mist on its way.
The streets are quiet and a meal simmers
on my stove. The hair on my neck quivers.

I ignore the war but it won't ignore me.
Even with the news off, I know that bombs fall
while I crush garlic. Tea steeps. People die
half a world away. We all feel too small
to end it. How did we let it come to this?
We're dumb fingers on an ignorant fist.

Dashiell Yeatts-Lonske
2014 Writing for Peace Young Writers Poetry Contest
First Place

A Pashtun Girl in Northern Pakistan

Rockville, Maryland, United States
Richard Montgomery High School, Grade 10

This poem is deeply intelligent, with stanzas arranged in order of the daily calls to prayer. The writing is clear and unaffected and subtle in its irony and grief. The work of a real poet.

~David Mason

A Pashtun Girl in Northern Pakistan
Dash Yeatts-Lonske

Last night a man was murdered in our clan;
according to Pashtunwalli,
we must kill someone in theirs
for the sake of justice

But as I conduct my Dawn Prayer
I pray nobody shall
because that isn't justice
not in this century

I go to school;
many people try to stop girls like me
from attending school
for the sake of Islam

But as I conduct my Noon Prayer
I pray nobody shall
because that isn't Islam
not in this century

I don't wear a burqa;
many people try to force girls like me
to wear a burqa
for the sake of decency

But as I conduct my Afternoon Prayer
I pray none shall
because that isn't decent
not in this century

I eat my favorite, pulaw, for dinner;
I look forward to Eid-al-Adha;
we give a nomad a place to stay for the night
for the sake of hospitality

And as I conduct my Sunset Prayer,
I thank God for everything
that makes my life so great
in this, the best of centuries

I hear the drones flying overhead;
they target suspected terrorists,
but innocents sometimes die
for the sake of security

But as I conduct my Night Prayer,
I pray nobody shall
because that isn't security
not even in this century

And as I fall asleep
I think of tomorrow morning

Bio~

Dash Yeatts-Lonske is an 11th grader at Richard Montgomery High School, near Washington, D.C. In addition to writing poetry, he enjoys reading, playing ultimate Frisbee, and discussing the geopolitical future. His favorite map projection is Waterman Butterfly.

2015 Progress Report~

Over the course of the past year, I've continued to write and perform poetry and was published in the print edition of Teen Ink. I hope to continue to explore issues of current events and global citizenship through my writing.

What "writing for peace" means to me~

To me, Writing for Peace is a vessel for empathy between people who have little in common. It strives to break down barriers which we've erected over millennia, and I'm thrilled to be a small part of it.

Cassidy Cole
2014 Writing for Peace Young Writers Fiction Contest
3rd Place

Face Me

Denver, Colorado, United States
Girl's Athletic Leadership School, Grade 8

*"Face Me" is a portrait of a very young woman living un-
der the Taliban regime who feels unseen, faceless, power-
less, because she was born female. It is a uncompromis-
ing, harrowing depiction of the kind of rage that being
treated like offensive "lesser" property engenders, a
glimpse at societal abuse, and worse, through the eyes of
one hidden girl who has not given up a dream of power,
whatever it takes. A painful and deeply moving piece.*
~Robin Black

Face Me
Cassidy Cole

There is something about a face that I want. I want a
face that you can see on a skull of a person. Their cheek-
bones perched amongst the crevice in their lips. I want to
smile to see the dimples settled on my temples, but why
would I smile? I don't have a face of my own. I am disal-
lowed to uncover my face, for no other man should see my
beauty because beauty is corruption. Beauty is a sign of
hope and we have no hope. I have no hope. I have birthed
two babies from a man I don't know.

I am married to a man. He is the man I don't know.
I am to take the punches from the man I do not know. I
am to accept the welts upon my back but still love the man
I do not know. I don't love him, and I never will. I am to
cry blood, but wipe it away before anyone sees me. I am
to accept the dust cloaking my throat, and I am simply
invisible. I am not to use my voice, for no stranger should
have to hear the sound of a woman's voice, no man should
have to hear my story. If the Taliban had their way, we
would all be dead. The women like me who rip the insides
of their burqua in anger. The women like me who silently
curse every man who lays their hands on their own bod-
ies. The women like me who speak loud inside their own
isolated minds. The women like me who want a face. The
Taliban want them, like me, dead.

I am unwelcome in my family. I am sin. I know they
wanted a boy, and then they got me. They must have
considered me their own little piece of Jahannam. I was
eleven years old when my father sold me to a man who my
family was in debt to - and by sold - they called it mar-
riage. Faceless girls like me get poisoned. Faceless girls
like me get bombed. Faceless girls like me get burned. My
windows are blackened, but not by the ashes of my own
burning skin. But no, I can't be seen from the outside. I
am forbidden to let the sun dance on the absent dimples
on my face. Though, my mind is screaming through the
walls. These walls look like the smoke of a bombed city, its

people, and myself. Everyone thinks these extinguished walls must be quite strong to keep a person inside of them, but maybe they don't know that the person inside of them is dying from the inside, out. I am thirsty. My nose finds its way to the dirty light. I scan the light along my eye's iris and watch my eyes glimmer. I watch the pores of my skin inhale and I watch my chapped lips burn. I am to see light. I am to be light.

My feet are drowning in dust now, and my words are trying to swallow themselves. I won't let my words go unheard. Sometimes my body and my mind dwell without one another. My mind is isolated into blackness and exhaled out through the mesh in my burqua. Everyone tells me power is not real. My father, the man I don't know, and the Taliban. Only they have power. They have the power of the whip. They have the power to cut the tips of women's fingers. They have the power of hurling stones. They have the power of metal bars against brittle bones. They have the power of my light, but suddenly they don't have the power of me. I let the dry wind tickle my fingernails. I let the angry dust rise up my arms and I let my veil get caught around my wrists and I allow it to peel off my face. I strip my veil of all the power it had over me. I rip away the future it had for me. The confinement, the abuse, and the torture of being imprisoned within my own mind. The sun caressed my face, and my skin grew chills. I will be powerful. I am powerful. I will not be constrained to something I will never seep low enough to be. I never was my own, but now I am my own. Now there is nothing that can stop me. I will be beaten. I will be killed. The faceless women thirsting for a face who did what I just did were killed. But I feel as though I have power. I will not leave because I was nothing. I will leave because I was something. I was something everyone feared. My father, the Taliban, the man I don't know.

I was change.

I was powerful change.

Bio~

Cassidy Cole, born and raised in Denver, Colorado, is in the 8th grade at the Girls Athletic Leadership School. English has always been her favorite subject. She loves the idea of creating her own worlds or using her language to change the world. She often wonders what life is like in the shoes and eyes of another. She is a dancer, a writer, a thinker, and a yogi. She daydreams about traveling around the world and scribbling out words upon words. She uses her empathy as a compass, wishing to under-stand a bewildering world. She believes that injustice needs to be seen by the outside and that a thirst for justice should live within each and every one of us. She believes everyone deserves a face, a face not and never formed by another.

2015 Progress Report~

Writing has always served as a way to breathe for me; I need it to survive and enjoy the deep ones. Writing helps me think about the hard things, the happy things, and the murky things.

I have always valued the importance of one's story, and I believe full-heartedly that writing is key to one's story: the act of writing it, discovering it, and preserving it.

This year, as many years before, poetry has been a habit to my everyday life. Poetry is "my everything." It is something I cannot live without. Poetry has made me see the world in a brighter light, feel the world as if it runs through my veins like blood, hear the world with a more critical ear, and taste the world with more sensitive taste buds. Spoken word poetry is also a big part of "my writing life" this year - not only do I get to write my story through poetic prose, but I also get to tell it.

Memoir writing is also something of great promi-nence this year personally. Writing about my own life is a very therapeutic process for me and always has been; it has proven to be vital to my survival. In a unit in my

American Literature class about memoir writing, I composed a story *"Somewhere Over That Rainbow, My Little One Dances"* about an unforgettable summer camp experience. I also journal often, which I consider to be memoir writing because it is a great challenge for me to write without even a touch of creativity, so those journal entries always end up into little memoirs here and there.

Writing will always be part of life, for I see myself making a future out of it. The saying, *"Live the life you love, love the life you live"* is something that speaks to me and is my goal for my future, which is now screaming writing and I believe will never stop. I will never stop writing, for its like breathing to me, and one must always breathe.

What "writing for peace" means to me~

[Writing for Peace Mission Statement - Also Known as the Passageway to World Peace:]

An organization dedicated to cultivating empathy through education and creative writing in order to develop a foundation of compassion on which to build a more peaceful world.

See, the thing about this statement is that it, indeed, could solve all the solution-less problems and change the world drastically to something incredible, wonderful, and beautiful.

Writing for Peace and all that it stands for is what this world needs in the light of peace, happiness, equality, and a more desirable place.

Just the pure existence of an organization that aims to create compassion and peace through creative writing gives me easeful thoughts for our future.

Writing for Peace gives me hope and I am utterly inspired by its vision and what the organization does.

This organization is the light of not only what lays on the other side, but the light that guides all us writers there.

Picking Up The Pieces
Sandra McGarry

Before her hands kneaded bread,
raised to kohl her eyes,
chose a dress for her brother's wedding,
the missiles came.

The mountains flowered into light,
desert heated, sandgrouse
came to a watering place,
around them voices
gathering in this day,
bartering for this and that
but never for the telling
of the head found on a rock,
dark hair parted down the middle,
brown eyes stuck open, lips seared.

On the sand scatterings:
A left foot forgetting which way to go,
four-fingered hand cupping the sky.

Her name passed around like hot bread;
tongues lost in the mouth's cave
when someone asks for a bag
to pick up the pieces.

Going to school in Gaza

We take our lessons in the open air
and sometimes death flies by, just overhead.
We've learned to stand our ground and not despair.

We send our grateful thanks to all the dead
who tried to save us. From our prison here
we honour them, and follow where they led

towards a world of freedom, without fear
as one by one they showed the way. Our land
is living history. We hold it dear

and blossom with the flowers in the sand
that spring from missile craters. Find us there
and teach us how to better understand.

We take our lessons in the open air,
we've learned to stand our ground and not despair.

Mercedes Webb-Pullman

Let love in

Fimbriate, the first
tentative tendrils of love
twist blindly, searching
for sustenance.

Let them in,
and be ready
for renewal.

They bring life:
hope to the forgotten,
honey to the hungry,
peace to the oppressed.

More precious than roses,
rarer than red diamonds,
as common as grass,
as awesome as stars,

this is your proper food,
and your only real task.

Harvest in Gaza

When harvest time arrived we all joined hands
and set to work like one big family
but that's before the wall divided lands.

Together we made busy minstrel bands;
our routines were deserted happily
when harvest time arrived. We all joined hands

and stripped the trees of olives; harsh demands
on muscles we endured, sang happily
but that's before the wall. Divided lands

and checkpoints keep us stuck on empty sands
while dozers clear our homes and fell our trees.
When harvest time arrived we all joined hands

and celebrated life. Who understands
our need to follow seasons faithfully?
But that's before the wall divided lands.

A thousand years we shared. Now contraband
our olives, and our homes and lives it seems.
When harvest time arrived we all joined hands
but that's before the wall divided lands.

Three Poems
Zeina Hashem Beck

Inside Out
For Gaza, July 2014

people inside out
on the streets in their loved ones'
arms people screaming
in football stadiums
my friend's mom in Gaza is cheering
for Brazil and Holland
all that orange
burning almost
a sunrise all that
smoke
there's an old woman
who dies holding
her spoon waiting
for *Iftar*
which comes but so do
the rockets
and the news
Brazil loses to Germany 7-1
ABC News confuses
Israel and Palestine
the whole dichotomy
occupied/
occupier inside
out
out
Holland loses
a girl not yet
one
wrapped in a flag
flags wrapped
around cars necks shoulders heads
in Gaza God
is the eyes
of a little doll kicked

among the rubble
eyes follow a ball
kicked in mid-air
a roof collapses
houses inside out
one bride postpones
her wedding
the game goes into
extra time
shelters there are no shelters
shield yourself with
your hands your voice
i haven't slept since
yesterday writes Anas *go ahead*
and bombard july 13th
he dies the next day
a player kisses a trophy
his wife his son
a mother
kisses a dead child
grief inside out
is resistance
the crowds wave
at the victorious team
a whole family stands
on the roof waving
at the enemy's planes

Zeina Hashem Beck

Gaza mothers soothe their kids
Found poem for Gaza, based on an article in Baraka Bits

by telling them fireworks   are beautiful

be brave and laugh   it's the TV I am going to turn it off

when there is bombing   I hug them and cry

in one room without windows   playing cooking watching

cartoon movies on TV   if there is electricity

my oldest Ahmed he's old enough   to understand

not fireworks or the neighbors   cleaning the rug

Maysam

Ten-year-old Maysam from Gaza speaks
in English on YouTube, says, *I'm still
alive and I'm not
terrorist.* She smiles,
recites her lines in a sing-song manner
as if rehearsing for a school play
with the word *kill* in it,
shakes her head on the word *not*,
waves on *hello!* and *bye!*
as if waving to her mother
who is watching in the audience,
as if she could persuade
young Israeli women who tweet
*stinking Arabs may you
die amen.*

Matthew Rice
2014 Writing for peace Young Writers Poetry Contest
Second Place

Milk and Honey

Buffalo Grove, Illinois, United States
Adlai E. Stevenson High School, Grade 11

The poem is vivid in its writing, with wonderfully specific touches about life in a divided land. The poet shows real structural intelligence in the movement between two columns of verse, and the verse itself is strong.

~David Mason

Milk and Honey
Matthew Rice

I.

The nomadic trash, flecked with splintered glass,

gleamed—just a glint; he could only hope—as

the boy in the navy knit kippah peddled

past the waste heaps in lucid silence, the

hungry kind that echoes boundlessly

from generation to generation.

> The girl in the cotton quilted hijab

> a stone's throw across cobbled cement,

> must have caught a glimpse of it too—for just

> a moment; maybe?

He could no longer pause. The girl faded

into the millennial grooves and ridges

of Old Hebron. There is no voice,

no gesture he could have given to her as

> *Shalom aleikhem,*

> *As-Salaam-Alaikum,*

feel a world away, ripped apart

in the great resting place of Abraham.

The valley's fog dusted the dented land.

II.

For both of us, sweeping catenaries

lie in the lines of the Devine. A chain

branching from the samak and sea bass baited

at the brink of a Red-Sea-dawn,

through our curled-up covers,

the sun ceding on our corner of the globe.

From the olive fields to the markets, the

mensches and marabouts bartering in

universal may-peace-be-upon-you-

lingo to mothers, fathers, blissfully

ignorant offspring gathering supper-bound

for a day of rest and a month of fast.

Dancing nightlife folk, rabbis in prayer

undulating—shockeling, in the old country—

for a new era, un-stodgy avengers

amongst sticks of thorny bougainvillea

in strike-a-nerve-fuchsia, the hue of youth.

A walled garden in a strip of sand. A

Mediterranean alcove guarded,

the prickly nature of politics burning

like the sea salt bursting our fathers' wounds.

> *We must think differently, look at things*
>
> *in a different way. Peace requires*
>
> *a world of new concepts, new definitions.*
>
> —Yitzhak Rabin

The land rooted in milk and honey where

Milk and Honey do not mix, will not mix

without new cuisines, new provisions.

Bio~

Matthew is a junior at Adlai E. Stevenson High School in Lincolnshire, Illinois. He has a spark for the social sciences both in and out of the classroom and warmth for writing whenever he gets the chance. As a research captain for his school's Debate Team and a state champion in the Illinois Youth and Government Judicial Program, he would like to thank Writing for Peace for the opportunity to infuse both of these interests into one poem. His poetry can currently be seen in the 2014 edition of Teen Ink magazine.

John Vernaglia
2014 Writing for Peace Young Writers Poetry Contest
Third Place

Shalom, Salaam

Medford, Massachusetts, United States
Cambridge Friends School, Grade 8

*With its ironic formal symmetries, this poem simply
and beautifully underlines the absurdity of a situation
in which people who are culturally tied become enemies
because of bigotry and mistrust.*

~David Mason

Shalom, Salaam
John Vernaglia

Shalom

Salaam

I'm Israeli

I'm Palestinian

I live in a land filled with history

A wondrous land filled with fruit

A land that's rightfully mine

It belongs to my ancestors

the Jews

the Muslims

My people are right, they are wrong

But we come together to learn about peace

I start to see their perspective

The land belongs to us both

the Muslims   and

the Jews

History can be changed

If we can learn to live in peace

Salaam

Shalom

Bio~

John Vernaglia lives outside Boston, Massachusetts. He is an incoming freshman (Class of 2018) at Concord Academy, Concord, Massachusetts. John was inspired to write "Shalom, Salaam" by his experiences at Kids4Peace, an interfaith youth group that brings together children from Israel/Palestine and the United States to educate and inspire Jewish, Christian, and Muslim kids to be peace leaders.

He is also on the Advisory Board for Creative Kids magazine, where he has published a number of poems and book reviews. John's poetry has been recognized in a variety of regional, national and international refereed contests, resulting in more than 25 publications and awards. Outside of reading and writing, John enjoys playing sports with his friends including: baseball, soccer, basketball, and golf. He is an avid Red Sox fan.

2015 Progress Report~

This year, I tried my hand at co-authoring an historical fiction as well as experimenting with different styles and themes of poetry. My poems have taken a more personal focus, ranging from issues around my grandmother's illness to being a teenager and starting high school. In the future, I plan to continue writing and using this art form a mechanism for spreading messages of peace.

Thank you for this opportunity.

IDF Gaza Training
Hadas Parush

To the Soldiers I See
Cory Lockhart

When I see you leave the safety of your guard post, canisters of unspent teargas dangling casually from your hand, I want to scream, YOU WERE MADE FOR MORE THAN THIS. Instead the words play in my head.

When you shoot round after round of gas as children try to reach school, I know *you were made for more than this.*

Eyes sting. Throats burn. Noses drip.

Maybe a few boys threw a few stones. Yes, maybe a few 10-year-old boys threw pebbles. Maybe some 12-year-olds. Maybe some young men threw large stones. I know. But —

The teargas stings my eyes, too. It stings the eyes of the father walking his daughter to kindergarten. It burns the throat of the infant startled awake from her daddy's shoulder. It stings the eyes of the street cleaner who faithfully sweeps the candy wrappers and chip bags, who sweep around you as you check the IDs of teachers you see every single day. Some of the teachers, the young ones, you check *every single day*. Because today they might be dangerous, even though they weren't yesterday or the day before or last year.

Try to live as they live, passing through your checkpoints daily, sometimes having to take off a belt, empty their pockets, wait 20 minutes or more to get their IDs back. And you with your semiautomatic weapon slung over your shoulder, you with your finger resting close to the trigger, you who control whether they're on time or late or make it to their destination at all. You who decide if they will have a good day or a bad one.

Try watching the harassment, the beating, the arrest of fathers and brothers and uncles and friends over and over again. Try being harassed or beaten or arrested yourself. Repeatedly. Simply because of where you were born. Try watching your little brother cry, trembling while your mother screams, clutching him as the soldier pulls him from her grip. They, those fathers and brothers and uncles and friends and mothers, were made for more than that.

I read in Ha'aretz that three more soldiers who served in the Gaza slaughter committed suicide. They knew they were made for more than what they saw, what they were ordered to do, what they did. They could not face the chasm between what they did and what they were made for. It was too far a leap from dismemberment to embodiment. And so they plunged to their own death, more lives wasted. They were not made to destroy.

You were not made to destroy.

You were made to create, to affirm life, to be alive!

Maybe you know that. Maybe you even think you are doing that. That's what they told you as you prepared to come here. They tell you: you are protecting life.

Dear One, look around you. Your teargas, your stun grenades, your skunk water, your rubber-coated steel bullets, your live ammunition don't affirm life. Your actions don't create. You were made for more than this.

You greet me sometimes with the word shalom. *You were made for shalom.* You were made for peace, for love, for joy. You were made for kindness. That night you asked me for water for the man who came gasping through the checkpoint. You were made for *that.*

That day you followed orders, allowing no one through the checkpoint for hours. You were not made to keep people from their families. For no good reason. Deep sorrow brewing, you said you wanted to be in your room. With your girlfriend. Reading comic books. Watching *Lord of the Rings.* You were not made for severing relationships, but for building them.

Baby Face, I want to talk to you, not as adversaries, but human to human. You look so much like the boys I used to teach. If you took off the gun, the uniform, the glare, I'd mistake you for one of them. Your arrogance, masking fear, is familiar.

I want to tell you: you have the power to create, to live expansively, to love widely, to change the world. You are brimming with potential. Preserve it.

Try to make it through your service without forming a shell around you so small that only a few can reach your tender heart.

I know it's so hard to be tender here, but please, *please* protect that deep place within you that loves. Please use your eyes to *see* the ones whose lives you now control. Let them burrow into your soul.

When you can, break the shell; let your memories drift out into the light of truth. Beware: they may not drift out gently. They may explode.

Use your truth, quietly released or burst wildly, to change the world. You were made for truth, for justice. For mercy. Forgiveness. You were made for love.

Sweet Boy, take this candle. Carry it with you always. Let it be your light of truth.

You were made for more than this.

O Charioteers

This green country
armored in camouflage:

broken streets,
shards of civilians.

How long has it been
since they owned us,
The Troubles?

The sweeping chill
of a gun's flaring breath
through 3,622

spreads
more bad news

like ointment
for an incurable disease.

Lauren Kessler

Stained

Come to me
in a thousand paper words
drenched by a rainstorm—
rivulets of ink
colliding into one
incalculable color.

Let me read you
in the spaces
between clouds,
through the torrent
that was droughted
for so long.

With ink-stained fingers,
let me play you on
my off-tune guitar,
strum your chords,
and dance
delightfully careless
with your closed-lip smile.

Come to me
when there is nowhere
left to go, when there is
no reason to run
because no one
is chasing—except
hearts and breaths,
a million of them
pounding in the violent rain.

Canoe

Blue knows
only the world
beneath her rippled stillness.

Gray finds the flattest stone
on the shore, skips it,
startling Blue out of sleep.

A cold cocoon of sheet metal
follows his lead,
leaves a soft wake of Blue.

Above the expansive world
White tries to conquer sky
with thick awnings of shade.

Black's plastic soul –
sturdy, inconspicuous, cruel –
breaks Blue into millionths

each stroke

Three Poems
Sharon Goodier

PTSD of the planet

Earth has no memory centre
to shrink, no way to forget
the abuse that imprints
its legacy on
        mutated cells
        arctic creatures drowning
        in melting ice
        droughts, floods

Winds stir oceans to madness
        every disaster a cry to stop
        but the abuse goes on

A game of musical chairs is played
        to a syncopated rhythm
        all chairs removed
        save one in which we all sit

Earth has no feeling centre to stretch
accommodating overwhelming
emotions
        fear, anger, desperation
        no capacity for blaming itself
        for the abuse of others

The ultimate victim
Earth is a child
in the arms of psychopaths
        begging all of us
        to make it
        stop

The Nature of War

Even a baseball cap can't totally obscure
the downcast eyes
lids weighted heavily with shame

A beard or make-up can only pretend
to obscure the boils of war
the scarred skin of silence
in the face of atrocities
       the twisted lips of ambivalence
       on the faces of those forced to wield
       various tyrannies

The brain's memory centre becomes
a prison cell confining fear
regret   anger   self-hatred
       cockroaches of conflict
       crawling over everything

Civilian suits come with seams that can be
let out under stress but army uniforms
leave no wiggle room
       Orders are orders

Conflict rages in the gut
       squeezes lungs
       pounds the heart

There is no kidney to detoxify
a soul forced to hang its basic values
out to dry
       integrity shriveling like a prune
       the mirror of the mind revealing
       the original face we have betrayed

in order to survive the "system"
and that nothing can hide

Sharon Goodier

Soldier Wrestling with Suicide

The rigid protocols of military life
act like a straight-jacket confining
my flailing arms, my torso exploding
in rage, my head like a Halloween
jack o' lantern carved with eyes, nose
mouth   a fabricated grin

No candle flickers light from these
orifices; they lead instead to
the darkest caverns of my mind
where my former self is only an echo

Once home, jacket comes off
muscles scream for pillows   walls
windows   seeking an outer pain
to overpower the inner

Once home, intense camaraderie gone
loneliness burns like a match held
against frayed nerves

And nightmares with surround sound
projected onto the screen of my mind
deny me the consolation of sleep

I want to die, to live, to cry, to laugh
every possibility morphing into its opposite
and back again

Friends, family, veterans swim around
my head like ghosts of a former life

My heart is a stone I sometimes throw
at those I love

Celtic Cross, A Symbol of Faith, Change, and Hope
Sylvia Freeman

Two Poems
Don Hogle

Genetic Switch

I've heard no matter where
we live or who we are –
Bedouins, Inuits, Bulgarians,
or socialites from Bel Air –

put pencils in our paws,
ask us to draw the ideal
landscape, and we all will
sketch it much the same:

a broad and partly shaded plain,
gently grading down to water –
an image of the African savannah
from which our species sprang.

The memory sings out,
the old familiar melody
contained in twisted strands
of DNA. Amino acid

strings stay tuned to retain
what we've forgotten otherwise.
The little ditty's filled with clues –
how we managed to survive.

Like when our world was washed
away. The same old story surfaces –
whether Noah, Manu or the tale
of Utnapishtim: an angry god displeased,

one man is told to build a vessel,
the endless rains, the flood, the way
a chosen few survive to see
the sun break through one day.

Today, a plague of rain plays
deluged fugues on the roof.
The gutters gush. Rills course,
unbound, to meet in teaming streams.

Schools of ripped leaves swirl
in pools that flood the sodden
ground where, mirrored, the sky
gives up the ghost and drowns.

I sit on the porch and try to read,
but a feeling of doom intrudes,
until, lickety-split, some
genetic switch gets flipped.

Like light flooding a darkened
room, a message bursts into
my brain, and this simple,
saving thought splinters the gloom –

Build a boat, float and hope
until the sun shines.

Don Hogle

Driftwood

Count me among the driftwood
cast onto this valiant band of sand
clutching the canyon wall.

I lie on my cot, naked
as a Christmas turkey –
even a sheet is excess in the heat
retained from the day, radiating
from the red rock behind me.

Air moves, but without relief,
as though the whole of Arizona
has opened their ovens in unison
to check the roast. I bake
to sleep, self-basting.

Suddenly I wake. Where am I?
I see trees, a rock wall, I hear
the rush of water through the pitch.

And what strange sky is this? What
a quiverful of arrow-shafts of light.
I'm Sebastian, supine, pierced
by stars I never knew existed. How
they crowd about in their ink-dark sea!

And through them, the Milky Way
winds, a current so brightly opaque,
I could jump in and ride it to be
tossed onto even more dazzling shores.

Qumyka Rasheeda Howell

The Silent Still Point in the Water

If I could find
Just for a moment
the still points in the water
I would change the world.

Hold time in nature's looking glass
and see the Divine in you.
Tipping your face to meet the axis of the sun
I see the earth move in your stillness.

But when I see it
in the silent still point in the water
I fail to leave it
the echoing thoughts.

Those thoughts will not allow you to see yourself
tempting the silence that insist on doing.
Remembering, again
the ripples of the dark shadow

To be rid of it you must watch it
sit with the echoes within.
Wrap your arms around it
burrow into the psalms.

Placed in chapter and verse
placed where you are aware
placed where there will be no thoughts
placed in the moments of dimming rays

When see the silence.
That still point in the water
and certainly when you find it
you will have changed the world.

Qumyka Rasheeda Howell

The Sun Kisses the Stone Yellow

The will of the stone
is a manifestation
an imagination
of personal will.

It holds space for the sun
the warmth, the comfort
the sovereign immortals.

Protecting life
sheltering little creatures
harmonizing winged beings
bantering with four legged friends .

Pendulum offerings of direction
clearing the mind and stirring the soul
like the sunlight of spring
encouraging fullness of life.

It awakens the creativity and imagination
holding on to dreams deferred
wishes of tangible formation
filled with stories of loved ones.

Eavesdropping on the wind-songs
melodic tales of
remains left in the cravats
of time's rounded edges.

Grounded, waiting patiently
welcoming the rebirth of season

as the sun greets the stone
and gently leaves a kiss in yellow.

Three Poems
Howard F. Stein

Evolution

Who speaks for the earth,
that ocean blue speck
in the spiral arm
of an unremarkable galaxy?

Why are we so eager
to find life elsewhere
in the universe
that we squander the gift
we have here been given?
Will any other planet
offer us sanctuary?
Would we spoil it, too?

With what gratitude
do we spew our contempt
for earth's frailty
into the air and into the seas?
What hatred have we come
to have for our nest,
as we anxiously prize
over all else
the next quarterly report?

What animal have we become
who makes this blessed home
into our accursed tomb?
Is the choice only between
incineration and suffocation?

Originally published in *Anthropology Now*

A Time to Stop

a time to stop –
a time to put
time's relentless arrow
in *pause* –
a time without punctuation

echoes of the *Big Bang*
will still be there
in the farthest galaxy –
the universe will
continue to expand

a time when Alpha and Omega
are invisibly joined
in a Möbius strip
of one continuous plane –
a surface that turns
in on itself and closes
to start anew –
a pause to quiet
the driven heart

a time to stay in one place
long enough to taste eternity –
a Sabbath to the workaday
time to redeem time –
when even the ordinary
is sacred
and history and fulfillment
are one

Before Sandia Mountain, New Mexico

Mysterious mountain,
sacred to Pueblo tribes,
towers above the desert.
Forested on the east side,
its sheer drop on the west side
glows iridescent red
when the sun sinks low.
It draws me near
as I pass it by.
An ancient aura surrounds it –
there is power in this place.
Its power flows
to anyone who will receive it.

Alien
Alan Semrow

Opening night at the Italian restaurant next door was the night my business began to leave my weary grasp. We had been alive and running for almost fifteen years. Our customers told us we had the best Mexicana food in the city. They said our chips were *the shit*. They said our salsa was the best salsa in the city. The recipes were all as mi madre had taught me when I was a young girl growing up in Mexico City. Mi madre, tough, a provider, a nurturer—she was all I had, and she spoke kindly of mi padre. She told me it was love at first sight. She told me he had to leave, because his love was too strong.

Mi madre brought the seven of us up strong as she could. She taught me her ways. And when she passed away—me, the age of sixteen—I knew I would have to find my way to America.

I opened the restaurant after meeting Jorge. It was with him that I birthed mis niños. I had mi familia and I had my restaurant. Everything in life at that moment seemed to have reached its sweet spot. Our regulars tipped us well. They ordered many margaritas and said they could die for my chimichangas.

Mis niños still work here for me and, as the business has begun to dwindle, we often spend hours waiting for something to happen. The satellite has been disconnected. The food has grown stale. The electricity alone is more than we can pay. I watch them show each other that unconditional love that I have always shown them. They sit at the tables and munch on tortilla chips and the salsa, thin and perfectly spiced. On occasion, they'll ask me what will happen when we lose the place. And I always assure them that nothing in this whole world could be lost, because I would still have them. I, after all, am the creator. I created this, this dedication. And this familia, so warm and so understanding.

I close up shop by myself every evening now. Not much clean-up is required, so I tell mis niños that they must go home early and put their own beloveds to rest. Tonight, as I close up, I think of them.

We had four sets of customers today. We wasted more energy than we made in money. I pray often. I pray I can make this work. I clean the bar and the kitchen. I clean the bathroom, and turn off the lights. I lock the front door and stare up at the red and green fluorescent sign that reads, *Mi Madre*. I smile and begin my walk home. It is seven blocks. I pass the Italian restaurant. It is midnight and they still have customers. The customers seem happy.

When I walk, I do not think of much at all. It is my quiet time and I look forward to it each evening. It is my time to simply take in the beauty of the night. The beauty of this world, the beauty of this moment when I am not concerned. The city, it seems quietest in the summer months, when the air is warm like the Mexican air of my childhood. Right now, I am only a person walking down the sidewalk.

I climb the stairs to our three bedroom duplex apartment. I unlock the door and enter. Mi hijo, Hector, is asleep in the living room next to his wife, Pilar. There are no sounds coming from the other bedrooms. Everyone is asleep. I walk quietly to my bedroom, where one of my grandchildren, the baby, sleeps in her crib. I get down on my knees in front of my full size bed, which is covered in a quilt mi madre made me when I was young. I take the time to pray to Jesus Christ. I mumble, "Dear Lord, please give mi familia the time in this life to have a break. We are struggling, but I rely on you, dear Lord, to keep us safe and to allow our business to keep running. I need this business. I need this business because it is my livelihood. It is mi madre. In the name of Jesus Christ, Amen."

I climb into bed and fall quickly to sleep.

I wake to the sound of the baby crying and banging

on the front door. It is loud banging, yelling. Telling me to open up my home. The baby cries harder and harder. I shoot up out of bed and look at the clock. It is three in the morning. I have slept less than three hours.

I run out into the living room and tell mis niños, "Hide! Hide! Get in the closet! Go! Go! I love you, mis niños. Now go!"

They run past me, whispering, crying, hugging me. Mi hija, Maria, tells me, "No, mi madre. No. No. I must help. You hide. I cannot!"

"No, no," I whisper. I kiss her on the lips, but the banging, it continues—haunting me, taunting me, scaring me half to death.

I run to the door and open it. I am ready. I am ready for the next chapter. The men in black storm in. One grabs me, holding me against the refrigerator. The others run past me to the back rooms, where mis niños are hiding. I scream out, "Hide!" And I hear yelling and more screaming from the baby. I hear terror and I can feel mis niños tears.

And I listen. I listen so carefully as I hear the one word I always feared more than any to hear in my life. The one that suggests we are some extraterrestrial forms from Mars. And I cry and I cry as the man in black places the handcuffs around my tired, wrinkled wrists.

Three Poems
Shannon K. Lockhart

Radioactive

the memories
are radioactive
toxic, glowing in the darkness

they snake themselves around my heart
and pull tight
stab the muscles of my neck and back,
squeezing the air out of my lungs

they want to escape
and sometimes i want that too,
but
they have been given to me

to hold sacred
to remember

it's the only thing asked of me....

"listen carefully,
wear our clothes,
to show that
you are willing
to be one of us,
to take the risk of
being killed like us"

and so i put on my huipiles [1]
i tighten the faja [2]
and i carry these stories everywhere,
tenderly wrapped up into a bundle
woven from a fuchsia and turquoise
cloth

---

1 A huipil is a woven blouse used by indigenous women in
Guatemala
2 A faja is a woven belt or strap

Shannon K. Lockhart

i use the very same mecapal [3]
that was used to carry my water from the river
in the jungle
it is frayed now
and i worry that it will break
spill, and
cause a nuclear reaction
a meltdown
that contaminates
other people's lives

most days i can't even stop
the memories, they
radiate from my body
in the form of images and dreams,
snapshots of
bones, pools of blood,
roots nourished by rotting flesh
and that sound i can't erase,
the AK-47, reverberates in my body...

i see those little bodies
i see the twisted boots,
melted with the bones inside
the bits of hair
the stained and ripped clothes
ropes
i see dead eyes
a cheek blown away
a head cut off
i see soldiers surrounding us
snipers
men in dark suits
outside the door
listening to us in their headsets

i burn
i am engulfed
my whole body pounds

3 A mecapal is a headstrap used to carry objects on one's
back

i desperately
want to pause along the road,
to sit down and kick off my boots
patch my blisters

i want to let someone else
put on the mecapal
and carry this burden
for just a little while

and yet
i feel protective
i don't want the images to flood out
and destroy everyone in their path
it doesn't seem fair
it doesn't seem real

because they can be poison
when you don't know how
to handle them

they multiply over time
not everyone can carry them
i see this in your face
when i start to share the pictures
in my head

i have almost forgotten how heavy
this burden feels
the first time it is shouldered

i just need a space though,
just a little while,
to rest my heart
and cushion it with
some tears
to wash away the toxicity
bandage my blisters

before i can continue down my chosen path

Shannon K. Lockhart

Smoke

The smell of smoke
pungent, penetrating,
evokes strong memories

campfires
sticky charred marshmallows
a damp canvas tent
fall leaves
mountains, lots of mountains
guitar notes and stars;

the plas-plas-plas sound of two hands
shaping tortillas, before they
are flipped onto the comal,[4]
bubbling beans set to the side
in a clay pot;

elaborately woven hüipiles,[5]
bought at the market,
which I inhale first, just to
smell the hearth
where each one was woven into life;

the taste of river water, boiled
over fresh-cut leña[6], sweetened with
green cane juice to make it easier to swallow;

candles and Maximón
agua ardiente[7], cigars and incense
and the mix of herbs used for healing
broken hearts;

---

4 A comal is a large flat pan placed over a fire and used to
cook tortillas.
5 A hüipil is an elaborately woven blouse worn by indigenous
Guatemalan women.
6 Leña is firewood.
7 Agua ardiente is moonshine or homemade liquor.

the little wooden box,
containing the umbilical cords of my two sons
and the ashen remains
of a fervent Mayan ceremony
asking for a family,

that is now buried in the jungle

Shannon K. Lockhart

Tocaya[8]

last night
amidst the droning
ebb and flow
of the cicadas,
in the silent shifting of
the seasons,
in the quiet of the night,

you gave me a gift-
perhaps you
weren't even aware
of it

you let me rub your feet,
take care of you,

you gave me that dignity,
allowed me
that purpose,
that vulnerability

you let me
heal us both
by offering me
your trust

by letting me love you
freely
in my own way

the truth is,
you leapt into my heart
and soul
unexpectedly

---

8 Tocaya is the Spanish word used when two people share
the same given name.

making a nest
in my darkness,
and settling into
our friendship
with the spark
of your own light

Butterfly
Chrystal Berche

If She Were A Butterfly
Patty Somlo

On a bright, warm afternoon in late October, Miriam Larson, Ph.D. from the University of California Berkeley, stood surrounded by turquoise, yellow and chartreuse green one-story buildings in the central plaza of Anguenguero. High in the Mexican mountains, bordered by once-thick forests that had come dangerously close to disappearing, Dr. Larson waited. The previous year, she had stood in this very same place, and every year before that, going back a good three decades.

She had on a large, floppy canvas hat with an overdeveloped brim, knotted under her chin as a precaution against an excessively forceful burst of wind. The beige khaki hat was frayed, and what hat wouldn't have been after three decades? Dr. Larson had worn the broken umbrella-shaped hat for every one of the more than thirty butterfly migrations she had witnessed. Never in a million years would Miriam Larson have revealed this fact to her department colleagues or experts tenured in other universities. But she fervently believed that the velvety black, yellow and white butterflies strained their tiny eyes in search of her hat, the last thirty minutes of their remarkable journey.

The hat normally sat centered on Miriam's head. Today, though, the cotton khaki material tipped ever so slightly to the left. The brim was crumpled, like a sheet of paper headed for the trash. If this didn't indicate that life was not as it should be for Dr. Larson, she also had on two left-foot sandals. The pink flesh of her right foot was leaking over the outer edge of one. Both sandals were brown, since the professor tended to buy shoes of the same color and style, for no reason other than that it made life's choices a great deal more simple. Equally revealing, she had neglected the last hole when buttoning her blouse. As a result, the light blue cotton sleeveless blouse hung diagonally across her torso.

Until this past spring, butterflies had been Miriam

Larson's all-consuming passion. She had researched every
aspect of their annual journey – the remarkable fifty-mile-
per-day rate during their thousand-plus mile flight from
Canada to Mexico; the internal compass that kept them
on course, even on days when clouds hid their normal
guide, the orbit of the sun; their winter hibernation in the
Mexican mountains and mating pressed softly against
warm tree bark; not to mention the births and deaths of
several generations on their return flight north. When
the first evidence surfaced that, like so many species, Dr.
Larson's beloved butterflies were becoming endangered,
she found it hard to concentrate. Some days, she had to
remind herself to eat.

But it was an event in Dr. Larson's immediate life
that rattled her equilibrium and sent a crack squirreling
through her once solidly work-obsessed life. Dr. Miriam
Larson, whose butterfly studies and field trips comprised
the passion and purpose of her life, had tragically begun
to lose her eyesight.

Like her increasingly waning vision, the die-off of
the butterflies had not happened overnight. For years, the
forests surrounding Anguenguero had been cut, leaving
bare swathes with little protection from the cold and wind
for those heavenly creatures, whose wings looked as if
they'd been brushed by a master Japanese painter. More
butterflies died. Only three years before, limp, dark wings
had fallen from the trees into hopeless, frigid clumps. The
sight forced Miriam to crouch down and vomit, right there
on the ground.

Of course, her beloved butterflies and her eyesight
weren't the only things that had quietly begun to expire
in Miriam Larson's life. So too had her ability to sit long
hours in the lab, peering through a microscope, or to
stand on her feet presenting papers at academic confer-
ences. From the bunions on her big toes to the fallen
arches, her feet ached at night. Her eyesight failed her in
low light.

It was at night when she'd first noticed a darkening
around the outer edges of her eyes. The doctor performed
a quick laser surgery that seemed to help for a time. But
the darkening returned and now affected Miriam's vision

even in the daytime.

She began to appear in the hallways of the science building wearing an oversized pair of oval tortoiseshell glasses. Whenever students spoke to her in class, they felt as if they were looking through a series of prisms sitting on top of her eyes.

Miriam stood in the plaza shielding her eyes. This was the moment for which she waited. She turned her gaze from right to left. The little turquoise *tienda* where she bought cold lemon-lime sodas, the bottles thick and heavy in her hand, sat to her right, which meant she was facing north. The questions arose. Would they arrive? How many would come? And, once here, would they survive?

Dark walls circled the outer edges of her eyes. To see better, she needed to swivel her entire body from left to right.

The sky was a deep blue, empty of clouds. Empty too of butterflies, so far.

She chewed on her bottom lip, a habit she'd tried to cure but which lately had begun to resurface. She searched the sky another time. In that moment, she let herself imagine things were as they had been the year she first came to Anguenguero. She pretended that she suddenly saw a darkening, not caused by her narrowing sight, but by the butterflies eclipsing the sun and the bright clear sky.

Her breath caught and she felt the lump that had started to appear too often in her throat. She dropped her head down, as she fought back the tears. What bothered her most was that all these years she had been fine, perfectly fine. Of course, it had been hard to watch the trees surrounding this village disappear. She had gone with the scientists and young environmentalists as they met with villagers in the neighboring towns. They had told stories of poor peasants like themselves being murdered, their mutilated bodies hung from the few remaining trees, as a warning from those who came in the night and illegally chopped down and hauled out the trees. She had watched, year after year, as the ranks of butterflies returning to Anguenguero thinned. She had even let the thought enter her mind that one day not a single butterfly might return.

Yes, Miriam Larson had had her moments of grief and despair. She had wrestled with a fierce hopelessness that everything beautiful and mysterious was on the verge of disappearing. Perhaps, if her beloved butterflies had still been cheerfully mating and reproducing, her heart might have been able to accept her shrinking sight.

But then she managed to straighten her back and lift her eyes to the sky.

Miriam had never been a religious woman but those silken wings propelling infinitely millions of fragile creatures down the North American continent caused her to believe in a force that could only be described as holy. She, herself, migrated to Mexico like a homing pigeon, because those fluttering wings made her spirit flush with a hopefulness she couldn't construct sentences to adequately describe.

In some recent years, the bright blue mountain sky had refused to darken with clouds of black, yellow and white wings. Butterflies eventually sputtered in, but only in sparse, bedraggled groups who came to die.

Miriam studied the sky with a cautious optimism but knew something in her heart at the same time. Even if the butterflies returned in clouds so black and huge they blocked out the sun, the ecstasy she had felt every year for the past thirty would never return to light up Miriam's life.

Moments after the sun set, light was instantly swallowed by a startlingly dark sky. Miriam twisted her neck, to relieve the stiffness from leaning back too long. Scattered street lights were flicked on. Miriam took slow careful steps, her fading eyes fixed on the ground.

She had waited for three days, surveying the sky. Not one single butterfly had arrived. She refused to believe this might be the end. If it was, whatever would she do with her life?

Even though she'd eaten only a handful of sunflower seeds and a small box of raisins for lunch, Miriam had no appetite. Her room in the *hospedaje* had such low light, she found it impossible to read, even though the print in her book was several inches larger than normal. Better to walk carefully in the dark, than to return to close her eyes and wait for sleep that wouldn't come.

Miriam raised her head for a moment, just as a terrible wave of self-pity washed over her. Why had she made so little of her life? Yes, she had produced a few unimportant books and articles. But no great discoveries. No groundbreaking research that would live on, once Miriam completely lost her sight or, eventually, when she was gone. Worst of all, there had been little she'd contributed to save her beloved butterflies.

As if that wasn't distressing enough, Miriam began to wonder what she'd missed by never falling in love. And would her life have been more fulfilled if she'd had a child? Why, until these last few months with her ever-shrinking field of vision growing narrower, none of this had entered her mind. Her father, a busy cardiologist, had raised Miriam after her mother died. Miriam had grown up assuming that being occupied day and night with her own thoughts was a perfectly normal life.

Miriam suddenly looked up and noticed the lights. She walked closer, for some reason drawn to that spot. The cemetery was lit with flickering candles and the white glare of flashlights. People were gathered in small groups around the gravesites.

Sprigs of purple and pink bougainvillea spilled from vases set atop colorful tablecloths on the ground. One young man strummed a battered guitar and sang a mournful tune about butterflies and lost love. Children ran laughing amongst the graves and people smiled. The air smelled of corn tortillas and burnt wood.

"*Señora*," a voice said, and Miriam turned in that direction.

It was the owner of the little *tienda* where Miriam bought bottled water and sodas. "Come, sit with us and have something to eat," he said.

Miriam stepped over to where the man was standing surrounded by plates of food. Several women wrapped in blue, red and yellow blankets sat on the ground with the children. One of the women nodded to Miriam, then piled some chicken smothered in a dark sauce, rice and beans on a plate and handed it to the professor, who was still standing off to the side.

The food was heavenly and Miriam realized that she was starving. For the first time in days, she felt all right. Every so often, the store owner, Gilberto, smiled at her, then looked at his children tumbling on the tablecloth.

"The butterflies," Gilberto suddenly said.

"Not yet," Miriam answered, though the question hadn't been raised.

"I believe they will come," Gilberto said. "They are our ancestors. We have food for them and are here, all of us, waiting. Any moment now, they will arrive."

Miriam didn't respond but thought, *I wish I could feel so hopeful.*

Gilberto looked at Miriam and nodded.

"They have always come back to us. Yes, some bad people have taken advantage but we are guarding the trees now. What would we do, we say to one another, without the visits from our loved ones? They help us to be brave and strong, to fight those who only look out for themselves."

Miriam smiled and nodded, glad to be in such warm company. If she were a butterfly, she thought, she would certainly want to come and be here with these kind people.

The guitar player stopped strumming and the chatter in the cemetery suddenly quieted. Children quit giggling and wrestling each other to the ground.

The first butterfly dropped onto the gravestone of Gilberto's grandmother. A second came down on the head of a small child. In moments, the cemetery was filled with wings, fluttering so fast, a person watching couldn't glimpse more than a blur of yellow and black.

Miriam stayed very still, while bathing in the fleeting rapture of the butterflies' return. Then she felt the wings dust her eyelashes. She, of course, could not see, as they brushed her nose and cheeks, her chin and finally her lips. Eventually, the little creatures settled themselves, in the narrow crevasses, to the left and right of her eyes.

Of Nature
Pilar Rodríguez Aranda

Because we have named you we believe we own you
Language seeming to separate instead of bring us together
We write books, thesis, poems...
But such attempt at closeness only seems to drift us apart
We label the visible as well as the invisible
Because we think we understand it or perhaps because we don't
Big Bang, Worm Holes, Soul...
And we classify it all and divide it in dualities
Children of "father" god yet not of "mother" nature
We have grown to be judges, hardly witnesses
Too blind for that
And we live and act as if we had birthed ourselves
Orphaned and feelingless
Half inhabited
Keeping you on the "other" side
Dark, ignored, afar...
Out there, to be conquered and submitted
Violated and exploited
Vanished
We continue destroying
Bit by bit, war by war, poison by poison...
And we remain
Intact, we think
With solitude and aloneness
Our treacherous treasures
While in truth you are us, genesis and end
And we are you, flesh and thought and grace
Unbridled form and process of the unnamable mystery.

Clean Water
Darlene P. Campos

Humans can be dirty beings. It might be hard to be-
lieve this now that we live in such a modern, technological
world. In recent years, we have become fanatical about
cleanliness. Almost everywhere you go, there's a hand
sanitizer dispenser. We bathe every day, sometimes more
than once. It's not unusual to receive fancy soap, bubble
bath, or a terrycloth robe as a gift. But there were days
when hand sanitizer didn't exist and neither did clean wa-
ter for an evening bath. In some parts of the world, clean
water still isn't the norm.

I am Ecuadorian. I was born in Houston, Texas, but
I was the only member of my family to be born outside
of our home country. My birth certificate holds both U.S.
and Ecuadorian citizenship. Spanish and English were
spoken in our house. We visited Ecuador to see relatives,
bring back foods we couldn't find in the United States,
and just to relax.

Despite the rich natural resources of Ecuador, it
remains a third world country. Several services and goods
in Ecuador are cheap, but people don't realize the reason
for that. Last time I was in Ecuador, I went out for dinner
with my brother and a family friend. The three of us or-
dered entrees with drinks and a dessert to share. Our bill
came out to a little under five dollars. Everything is cheap
in Ecuador because if the prices were any higher, nobody
would be able to purchase anything, the economy would
crash. You can buy ten oranges for a dollar or less in an
Ecuadorian supermarket, but you might also see a woman
digging in her purse for one more coin. To an American
tourist, Ecuador is a bargain. To native Ecuadorians, the
country remains way too expensive.

A third world country is defined as an underdeveloped place with extensive poverty. Many Ecuadorians experience poverty. At one point, I did as well for a short time, but compared to what happens in Ecuador, it wasn't so bad. After my parents divorced, my mom collected unemployment for a few weeks until she found a job. We didn't have much to eat and we were worried about the bills. But the community where we lived at the time did not charge water usage. We were anxious about our electricity being cut and about being hungry. Knowing we would still be able to take hot showers helped us cope. Water, especially clean water, is rare in malnourished neighborhoods. Toilets, even in places of greater economical stages, can take a few minutes to flush because there simply is not enough water pressure. I can remember visiting a relative's house in Ecuador as a young girl and having to flush the toilet ten times or more before the water finally pushed through. When that didn't work, I had to squeeze out water from the bathroom sink into a paper cup and toss the water into the toilet tank until it was sufficient for the toilet to work.

Drinking water in Ecuador is another issue. Taking a bath, brushing your teeth, or buying a drink from a food truck all pose great risks. Parasites like to lurk in the dirty water, causing diarrhea and severe stomach pains. Depending how well medical attention is in their area, they may live or die. I didn't know about the parasites when I visited Ecuador in 2004. I drank juices from food trucks, ate in rural restaurants, and bought homemade sodas from local convenience stores. But I was lucky. I caught a cold, but Felipe caught the parasites. I watched him quiver in pain and he could hardly walk. I was certain he would die like many others who acquired parasites in their stomachs. A friend of our father's was a doctor, and he injected Felipe with a medical solution. Whatever the solution was, Felipe's health returned to normal in two days.

According to UNICEF, Ecuador's water still suffers from contamination. In 1990, 79 percent of homes in urban areas of Ecuador had indoor plumbing. In the same year, 100 percent of homes in the United States had clean, pipe distributed water. Since 1990, indoor plumbing has gone from 79 percent to 91 percent in urban Ecuador. In rural Ecuador, the percentage changed from 37 percent to 72 percent between the years 1990 to 2012. Change is happening, but it's taking too long.

Water supply interruption is common in Ecuador. You might be taking a soothing, hot shower when the water suddenly becomes cold and then shuts off. When this happens, Ecuadorians are unsure when the water will return and, when it does, there isn't a guarantee that it will be clean. During Hurricane Ike's presence in Houston, my mom boiled gallons of tap water to prepare for a water shortage. I asked her why we couldn't just buy bottled water from the supermarket and she told me all of the water at the store had already been taken.

"Don't worry about it," she told me. "Boiling kills the parasites."

Even as a child, my mom boiled water. In her home, there was a large pot strictly reserved for boiling water. Around the same time she found out she was pregnant with me, cholera swept through Ecuador. Over 46,000 Ecuadorians were affected, and 697 died. Cholera outbreaks continued during the 1990s and steadily declined as the Ecuadorian officials advised the public to boil their water.

John Snow, an English doctor who paved the way for anesthesia, is probably the key reason we have clean water in much of the world. Before modern medicine, the idea that disease could be passed through dirty water was seen as ridiculous. In John Snow's adult home of London, cholera claimed the lives of thousands. But until John Snow proved otherwise, medical professionals were adamant cholera was spread by bad air, or miasma, which means "pollution" in Ancient Greek.

John Snow was born in 1813 and died at age 45 in 1858 following a stroke. As a child, John lived in York, England, alongside the River Ouse. Only poor families lived near the river because the neighborhood flooded, resulting in large amounts of mud and other kinds of filth. Like almost any English child, John was baptized at his local church at a young age. Considering the putrid water during John's time, this must have been frightening.

When John was 14, his mind became set on medicine. He moved away from his family to work as an apprentice for the surgeon William Hardcastlein in Newcastle upon Tyne. During John's apprenticeship there, he witnessed a cholera epidemic for the first time. The population decreased before his eyes. Historians estimate that cholera was responsible for over 140,000 deaths in Great Britain from 1830 to 1850. At age 18, John Snow worked as a physician treating coal miners with cholera. While contemporary doctors in John Snow's time were convinced cholera was a miasmatic disease, John Snow doubted this because no matter how much bad air he breathed in the coal mines, he never caught cholera. He came to the conclusion that cholera was not airborne, but waterborne. However, before any other medical professionals would listen to him, he first had to prove his theory. By 1854, John Snow had moved away from Newcastle upon Tyne to practice medicine in London. Cholera ravished Londoners once again, particularly at the intersection of Broad Street and Cambridge Street. John was determined to find the cause of this terrible disease.

Cholera is an infection caused by the spread of the *vibrio cholerae* bacterium which affects the small intestine. Common symptoms of cholera are diarrhea, extreme vomiting, dehydration, and blue or gray skin tones. Without any treatment, these symptoms end with death. Before John decided to explore cholera, nobody knew their own water supply was the culprit. Cholera is spread by drinking water or eating food with traces of feces. A person affected with cholera produces anywhere from three to five gallons of diarrhea per day and during the 1854 outbreak, most people used rivers as toilets. When Londoners were thirsty, they would go to their neighborhood water pump supplied by the river to drink, and then either survive or die days later.

While cholera isn't as threatening now as it was 150 years ago, but it still shows up in third world countries. The most well-known recent outbreak happened in Haiti in 2010. Cholera continues to kill more than 100,000 people worldwide each year.

John Snow's cholera examination was centered on the notorious Broad Street Pump. He created a map of Broad Street and Cambridge Street and their surrounding neighborhoods. Then he went door to door, asking each household if they had experienced any deaths from cholera. He noticed that the closer people lived to the Broad Street Pump, the more deaths from cholera occurred. But, church officials at the nearby monastery remained unaffected. In the 19th century, the most common drink was not water – it was beer. These church officials drank only beer which they made themselves. People residing in the Broad Street neighborhood who often visited the pub were also unaffected by cholera. Beer was safer than water due to the fermentation process. Getting drunk in 19th century London was a better idea than being sober.

In my family, drunkenness has never been a major problem. My dad claims to have never touched alcohol in his life, which I don't believe, but considering he is a doctor, he might be telling the truth. My mom rarely drinks and when she does, she complains about how bad alcohol is. I had a margarita for the first time about three weeks ago, took one sip and spit it out in a nearby trash can. I assume aversion to alcohol is in my genes. My boyfriend David comes from a family with alcoholic members. His father got his half-brother, Glenn, into drinking, and he became addicted. Glenn drove drunk, lost control of his car, and drove straight into a ditch. He was killed upon impact. When Glenn died, David was seven years old, but David swears he'll never drink alcohol because of what it did to Glenn. He doesn't remember much about Glenn, but he still misses him.

Though most of my family moved to the United States from Ecuador, some of the old ways are still present. For example, I drink habitually from the kitchen sink tap. My mom does not. No matter how many times I tell her tap water is safe, she refuses. Instead, she purchases many gallons of water from the supermarket. My grandparents came to Houston in 2001. They both refrain from putting ice in their drinks. Whenever I visit them, they always offer me juice or soda. Sometimes I prefer water and my grandfather will bring me a cold bottle of Ozarka. Neither he nor my grandmother has ever given me a glass of iced tap water.

Once John Snow pinpointed the direct source of cholera, he went after the Southwark and Vauxhall Waterworks Company. At the time, the company got its water supply from the River Thames. The River Thames was infested with sewage and completely filled with waterborne bacteria, causing four cholera outbreaks from 1832 to 1865. With John Snow's advocating, the handle of the Broad Street Pump was soon removed. People living on Broad Street and surrounding areas could no longer use the pump as a water source. Henry Whitehead, a clergyman for St. Luke's Church, was John Snow's detective partner in the cholera mystery. When the Broad Street Pump's handle was removed, Reverend Whitehead recorded the number of cholera deaths. There were 142 deaths on September 1, 1854. On September 7th, John Snow publicly gave his theory of cholera's waterborne characteristic. The Broad Street Pump's handle was removed on September 8th and, on that same day, Reverend Whitehead recorded 14 deaths. As the days passed, the number of deaths went down. After a few weeks, nobody on Broad Street died from cholera. John Snow's ideas were rejected by medical professionals, but decades after his death, he was given credit for saving what was left of the population on Broad Street. Today, Broad Street is called Broadwick Street. A replica of the original Broad Street Pump was put in place in 1992, more than 130 years after John Snow's discoveries. A pub named after John Snow sits behind the replica pump. People who visit the pub have a glass of beer in his honor.

Soon after the pump handle was taken away, John Snow made an additional discovery. The Broad Street Pump was built just three feet away from a cesspit. A cesspit is similar to a sewer, but only holds waste temporarily. In the case of the Broad Street Pump, a baby who caught cholera by drinking dirty water had her soiled diapers tossed into the nearby cesspit. Soon, the neighbors on Broad Street were drinking water contaminated with baby feces. As London's population grew, many homes were built right above cesspits. When the 1854 Cholera Outbreak arose, London was home to more than two hundred thousand cesspits. The poor emptied their waste out onto the public waterways. People with cesspits in their homes preferred to throw their bodily waste and trash into the River Thames because cesspits were expensive to empty.

Despite John Snow's findings, London's water supply continued going downhill. Prince Albert, Queen Victoria's husband, died from typhoid, another waterborne illness. The pollution got to be so bad, the time period was given the name "The Great Stink of 1858." The House of Commons on Westminster was moved far away from the foul smelling River Thames. Though the City of London slowly began taking precautions to improve the water supply, no government official ever came forward to say John Snow was right. The theory that water with traces of feces could be the cause of many deaths still seemed foolish to the government and the general public. However, John Snow never died from cholera. He drank alcohol and boiled his water.

Like anyone without direct access to clean water, John Snow understood poverty too well. He knew from a young age that he wanted to be a doctor, but during his childhood, there were only two universities offering medical degrees – Oxford and Cambridge. His father was a laborer in a coal mine and couldn't afford to send John to college, so John Snow became an apprentice. He served as an apprentice for nine years. He probably didn't know how much he would change the world in his later life. John Snow knew the effects of drinking dirty water, but I wonder what made John Snow's determination flourish within him.

My dad has been a practicing doctor for almost 40 years. Just like John Snow, his parents were blue collar workers and there was no way they could send him to a good university. My dad grew up in southern Guayaquil, the poorest section of the whole city. His water supply was rarely clean. Bath time consisted of getting water from a well and then praying for mercy. As my dad grew up, he began taking odd jobs to earn some money for his family. One day, he had to take a bus to central Guayaquil, an area where people of high social status tend to live. His job for the day was to mow the lawn of a house five times the size of his own. He started the mower and slowly made his way around the grass. When he was halfway done, he turned off the mower and left without collecting any money since he didn't finish his assignment. I asked him about this incident and he said he felt that if he had kept mowing, he would be doing it for the rest of his life. He wanted to be a doctor. And he became one, despite several obstacles. There came a point when he had to take his exit exam and the study book was too expensive for him to buy. So, he went to the bookstore at his university, stole it, and passed his exam. He was never caught.

"I was sick of living with dirty water," he told me years ago. "I couldn't do it anymore. I wanted to have clean water like those rich people who hired me to mow their lawn."

Hurricane Ike hit the Texas Coast when I was 16 years old. Galveston flooded extensively. The water reached above the seawall and rose over the 1900 Storm Monument. This monument consists of a man holding his wife and child close to his chest. The man's arm reaches up towards the sky, as if he's looking up to a higher being to take him and his family to safety. The Storm hit Galveston on September 8, 1900. Its winds travelled forward at 140 miles per hour, making it a category 4 hurricane. Back in 1900, there was no seawall to block incoming water disasters, so the storm easily took over Galveston. Historians estimate between 6,000 to 8,000 people died. At the time, the highest point in Galveston was a little under nine feet tall. The storm surge stood at nearly 16 feet. The monument of the man, woman, and child huddled together was probably based on a true sight. There was no escape, and the water was not clean. Until relief arrived from Houston a week later, most Galvestonians lived without potable water. Just hours before Hurricane Ike made its way to Houston, I watched a journalist giving updates of the disaster. As he spoke into the camera, waves of brown water splashed around the 1900 Storm Monument behind him.

Houston lies about 60 miles away from Galveston's coast. When Hurricane Ike came, I admit I was not too worried about it. Hurricane Rita seemed scarier because it came to Houston right after Hurricane Katrina ravished New Orleans. I evacuated, like the majority of Houstonians. Those who stayed behind said there was some rain but it was over quickly. Since I thought Hurricane Ike would be the same, I did not budge from my home and my parents, who were now divorced and lived in different houses, did not panic either. The night Hurricane Ike was due, my mom boiled water for hours on end. When Hurricane Ike approached, our power immediately went out. It would not return for two weeks. We also lost our gas line, which meant we lost heat as well. My mom couldn't use the gas stove to boil water. We could take showers, but it was with cold, strange smelling water. Fortunately, high school was back in session for me three days later. I remember drinking fresh, cool water from the fountain near the main entrance.

Decades after John Snow promoted clean water, the public finally agreed with him. Government officials and everyday people alike wanted to have easy access to clean water, but they were not sure how to do it. Many years before people figured out how to purify water for human consumption, something else had to be done first – the sewage system. Prior to the usage of the modern sewage system, waste was thrown outside into the streets or the rivers and lakes. During John Snow's time period, it was common to smell your neighbor's feces as you walked out of your house to start your day.

Chicago, like all major cities in the 19th century, frequently reeked of human feces and urine. The population of Chicago was growing, meaning more human waste piled high around the city. Similar to London, Chicago rested right at water level, so water and feces quickly mixed together. Thousands of Chicagoans were plagued by cholera, typhoid, and dysentery from 1849 to 1855. This is when the engineer Ellis S. Chesbrough took action. Chesbrough had done work for Boston's water system, so the City of Chicago trusted him to fix their waterborne illness problems. He began his mission by installing covers over manholes in order to keep dirty water from reaching the streets. Using jacks, Chesbrough and his workers slowly raised the city. Eventually, Chicago was no longer at sea level and this allowed for a proper and clean drainage system underneath. But since the sewer system was a new innovation, it was not perfect. While it functioned effectively in the beginning, Chicagoans began to experience new bad odors – fish. The drainage system in Chicago leaked out into the Chicago River and Lake Michigan. The route of the sewer was not appropriately connected which led thousands of dead fish into the bathtubs of Chicagoans.

My mom was born in Guayaquil, Ecuador, but she lived in New York City for a few years and moved back to Ecuador when she was a teenager. My grandfather was a dentist and he opened an office in a small city called Playas, about an hour away from Guayaquil, because it was cheaper to set up a business and home there. The word Playas translates to "Beaches" in English, appropriate for its position beside a long, sandy coast. Unlike Guayaquil, Playas is rural, with dirt roads, tin shacks, farmers, and loose animals, predominately chickens. There are some slightly urban areas, which is where my mom lived. Those who resided in these particular areas did not dare to drink from Playas' water supply. Running water inside homes in Playas was rare. My mom had it in her house, but some of her friends did not. She recalls watching her friends carry buckets of brown water from the beach all the way home. Once they reached their house, her friends used the water to wash their clothes and dishes. She told me this water made the clothes and dishes dirtier than before. My grandparents prohibited use of the local water in their home. Every few days, water trucks from Guayaquil called "tanqueros" arrived in Playas to sell purified water to the residents. My grandparents bought water every time they came. Whenever they bathed, got thirsty, did laundry, or washed their dishes, it was with fresh, safe, Guayaquil water. If they ran low on water, they boiled what they had already used from the tanqueros. My mom never drank Playas' water.

I visited Playas ten years ago. I stayed in my mom's old house which had run down ever since my grandparents moved to the United States. It now had running water, though it wasn't the best. No matter how far I turned the knob for hot water, it was always tepid. The pressure was weak, too. It took me nearly an hour to shower because I had to constantly cup my hands to catch what I could of the falling water. The neighbor, whose name was Juan, lived in a dilapidated shack with his wife and children. He didn't have running water at all. I often saw him dragging buckets of putrid sea water to his shack. Yet, somehow, when the water suddenly started leaking at my mom's old house, he came to the rescue. When he wasn't dragging buckets, Juan worked as a plumber. He took a close look at the pipes and stopped the leak in a few minutes.

"Nothing I have not seen before," he said. "Water can be a pain sometimes."

During my stay in Playas, I visited a pastor named Valdez. Valdez was a friend of my father. He preached at a small church in the rural part of the city. One evening, he invited me over to his house which stood across the street from his church. His house was actually a shack made from crooked wood and tin. It was composed of a single room with a dirt floor, hammocks as chairs, an old, metal television, and a Gateway computer in the center. His bathroom was in the corner of the shack, a large bowl, where he and his wife and their four children did their business and then threw the waste outside. They took baths with water from the sea. It was 2004 when I visited him, and Valdez had a computer, mysteriously hooked up somewhere in his shack, but he didn't have running water.

Four years after John Snow cracked the case of the 1854 Cholera Outbreak in London, John L. Leal was born in the small town of Andes, New York. John Leal's father, John R. Leal, was a physician and treated wounded soldiers during the Civil War. John R. Leal, like the majority of people in the 19th century, drank polluted water. As a result, he was diagnosed with dysentery and died. Being thirsty in the 19th century was deadly. John Leal followed in his father's footsteps and went to Columbia College for a degree in medicine. Once he graduated, John Leal became a physician in Paterson, New Jersey. He was responsible for the opening of the first outpatient clinic at Paterson General Hospital and a few years later, the City of Paterson named him their official Health Inspector and Officer.

John Leal was especially interested in Paterson's water supply. When typhoid fever took over Paterson, John Leal determined contaminated water was the offender. He spent most of his time thinking of ways to clean Paterson's water. He wanted to prevent the population from dying off and find out exactly why dirty water had murdered his father.

As John Leal further studied Paterson's water, he became convinced that chlorine lime could kill lurking bacteria in the water supply. He had already been utilizing chlorine lime to sterilize regions where cases of scarlet fever and diphtheria were reported. In addition, John Leal heard of other doctors hypothesizing about chlorine lime's potential benefit for contaminated water. As Health Inspector and Officer, John Leal was responsible for the safety of more than seven billion gallons of Paterson's water. In 1908, when John Leal was so positive chlorine lime would clean Paterson's water, he secretly began dripping chlorine lime into the water supply. His actions were soon discovered and he was called into court, accused of trying to poison Paterson. When asked by the judge if he really thought water with chlorine was safe to drink, John Leal answered, "I believe it is the safest water in the world."

Luckily, for his own reputation, John Leal proved his theory correct. By 1910, chlorine was officially approved for cleaning water meant for human intake. Eight years later, 33 million Americans were able to enjoy a glass of water without wondering if they would die. Typhoid, cholera, and dysentery in the United States were nearly nonexistent by the 20th century. In 1900, typhoid affected 100 out of every 100,000 people. Twenty years later, only 34 out of every 100,000 contracted typhoid. Currently, it is extremely rare to die from typhoid, cholera, and dysentery in the United States. John Snow might not have been able to figure out how to kill bacteria in large bodies of water, but his curiosity served as a starting point for those who came after him, including John Leal.

Chlorine is ultimately what makes our water drinkable. Before John Snow and John Leal, public water was discolored and smelled unpleasant. With chlorine, we can now clean any type of water for safe usage. Prime examples of this are the swimming pool and the water park. In the era of our ancestors, the idea of going for a swim or building a water park would have been asinine. Presently, swimming in a pool and visiting a water park during the hot summer months is a common pastime.

When I was five years old, I visited Ecuador with my family for vacation. We got together with relatives, as usual, and then before I knew it, we were all at a huge water park. The park seemed to have an endless supply of slides, whirlpools, and spray fountains. I remember being scared of the thick waves. I did not know how to swim, so I kept thinking I would drown. My mom held me close to her body. She assured me water couldn't hurt me if I was brave enough to stand up against it. Within an hour or so, I was able to go down a small slide on my own and my mom caught me when I reached the bottom.

There's an account of me as a toddler, which I don't personally remember. My mom used to be an avid swimmer. She went swimming at our neighborhood pool almost every day before I was born. After I arrived in the family, she would sometimes take me with her and hold me on her back as she maneuvered through the water. But one day, being the toddler I was, I threw myself into the pool when she had her back turned for a second. My brother Felipe went swimming with us that day and he dived deep into the pool and pulled me out before I drowned. I finally learned how to swim for myself during elementary school, but before then, there was always someone to protect me.

I have not visited Ecuador in over ten years. Airline tickets to Guayaquil have risen by 200 percent in the last few years and the flight routes have changed from five hours to sixteen hours. One day in the future, I would like to visit with David at my side. I have told him about the poverty issues of Ecuador and about the water sanitation problem the country faces every day. If I go there with him, I will not let him drink the water. Physically, I am much smaller than him, but I plan to be on the other end of the dirty water slide, should he go down it someday, to catch him.

Water is the most abundant resource in the world, yet it can be deadly to humans if it is not clean. Doctors John Snow and John Leal were pioneers, but one day I believe my home country will be free of filthy water. The spirits of John Snow and John Leal will stand at the other end of the water sanitation slide and they will catch Ecuadorians from falling into the dirty water.

Three Poems
Jasmine V. Bailey

Elegy with Nicaragua

I was always spilling watermelon juice,
stretching uselessly in the millennial heat.
Dust was remaking us—we confused our colors
and forgot whether we had showered under
the cool trickle that failed to penetrate hair.
We were cleaned by the angels of jocote or the Pacific
or tongues too young to realize where to kiss
to greatest effect—we were lousy with mangoes
and uncultivated flowers, sewing thread just holding
our clothes together, Aleman just holding the country
together, the blood in the streets finally old enough
to drink a beer in the United States, unlike us.

•

Then we drove to the sweltering River, walked
through the studio where everything—the windows, the floor,
the men working—were made of clay, turning pots
on kick wheels, cutting Montezuma out of thick sides,
feather-skirt, firebird, ordering the inexhaustible mess
and shipping it to Manhattan. I know
you were looking at this for the only time, even the shanty
city bordering the landfill in Managua, where everyone
was inconceivably poor, poorer than your family,
its house of wood and a single sheaf of tin—these
might have remained unknown to you if not for us, trying
to do something right in looking, which usually
seemed wrong. Your body was a miracle of economy,
so thin you might think the soul would be easier to find,
which it was, and when you used your body
to get out of the country as a dancer, that was proof
of the magnificence of all bodies. You were flown
to Mexico and Argentina, maybe even Florida, and still
never saw more of Nicaragua than we did together.

•

The tinaja and the mask of the fanged bird curse
their abandonment by the country named for the moon
or the sweet sea, and we only added our breath
to the goodbye. Swirling around the world like sugar
in cool tea, kites tangling and loosening. It was possible
for a few cordobas to buy a plastic bag of jocotes,
and sit at a footrace for an hour or two piercing the skin
and rolling the gooey flesh in your mouth, trying
to figure out how to eat them, or not eating them,
but tasting in them the tongue of someone you just now
realize you love, the sweat of the dwindling jungle, the clumsy,
indifferent ocean, the bankrupt lakes, the sweetness—
I do not know if you still eat them, but you remember.

Jasmine V. Bailey

Elegy with Argentina

You had never lost anyone and wanted to see grief,
so we went to Plaza de Mayo where mothers marched
twenty years strong around the fountain, between stalls
that sell flags and the cathedral, white as knuckles that fire
a gun for the first time. They shared their abundance with us
like bread there beneath the palace where Evita lifted her hands,
and Juan Peron braced her against collapse.

.

The Spanish empire was made and remade with silver ingots
and we hear it in the chime *Argentina* but not
in the shuffle of currency distributed at rallies.
In Santa Rosa, we went to the end of a dock on the manmade lake
with a thermos and in the dark I imagined everything bigger,
more complex than it was, the rich richer, each building
more sound, roses lavish. Alone, I began my apprenticeship
in waiting, but never learned to wait forever for the beloved,
for a set of teeth that could be identified, confirmed.

.

Two hours from Neuquen you see the Andes tower
at the end of the road your bus has broken down on,
teaching contrast, how the flag omits the clay desert,
the reddened pampas grasses but preserve snow and sky.
With no distractions, nothing to mark time, the disappeared
scream whether you listen or not. We want to hoist
the white flag over our troubled lives, to give the desert back—
the mothers are albatrosses stranded in the doldrums.
They fold me into their ceaseless work.

Elegy with the Soviet Union

You dreamed you loved a woman and then dreamed
her onto a train bound for Stalingrad. Strangers called out
to your black car from the streets wanting your confession
or your advice on buying fruit. You said, *they talk this way*
in the Ural mountains and I've never learned another way.
There was no electric light and you invented vodka
with nothing but your mouth and your need.
That is how you changed from widower to soldier,
that's how you became consumed.

.

You smolder atop the inadequate cool of ice
and pickled mushrooms—eating caviar to kill
the ocean-hating demons. Sturgeon swim upstream
and you take the train to Bryansk, rocking in fevered sleep,
ordering tea in glass tumblers set in filigree, searching
the visible forest for dachas, proof of one of winter's names—
you see hoarse-voiced angels, house cats crazed with sadism.
You arrive, and in memory departure and return are simultaneous.
Time undresses, fever passes, dreams feast on your mind.

.

Illiterate angels cloud the church with their quarrels, weighing
down the overgrown beards—you've witnessed a tall woman
doubled under the polished boot of her husband, her razor
cheekbones smothered in leaves. You believe the myth, suspect
that a generation was chilled into never appearing,
the living bewildered by the matching streets, hallways,
bedrooms of The Party's deliberate repetitions—you get off the train
and into any bed; the woman in it takes you for her lover, and only
when you touch her wakes, asks herself if this is, then, a man.

Evan Kielmeyer
2014 Writing for peace young Writers Nonficiton Contest
Second Place

The Health Care Struggle of the Australian Aborigines

Smithtown, New York, United States
Smithtown High School West, Grade 10

The author's well-researched and compassionate look at the many obstacles – cultural, economic, geographical – that aboriginal citizens face in obtaining quality health-care is compelling and important.

~Dinty W. Moore

The Health Care Struggle of the Australian Aborigines
Evan Kielmeyer

In August of 2012, I had the opportunity to visit Australia. It was my first trip to the continent. While there were many interesting things about this place, I found myself most intrigued by the Aborigines. The Aborigines are the major indigenous group in Australia and they have a complicated place in the history of the continent. According to 2012 estimates, there were 669,736 indigenous people in Australia. The highest concentrations were in New South Wales and Queensland. As of 2012, 90% of Australia's indigenous people were Aborigines. Upon my first encounter with Aboriginal people in far north Queensland, I noticed that they appeared to segregate themselves from the rest of the population. Social scientists refer to this as self segregation. It caused me to wonder why this might be happening and I became interested in their struggle. I have since discovered that the Aboriginal people have very long held customs and traditions that are neither fully known nor fully understood by many others in Australia. As a result, many Aboriginal people do not completely trust people who are unlike themselves. This has resulted in a disconnect in areas such as education, social welfare and representation in government. One of the main challenges of the Aboriginal people, however, is access to health care.

One of the main reasons that Australia's indigenous people are at a health care disadvantage is their location. This population tends to self segregate in more remote parts of the continent. This makes it challenging to obtain access to quality health care. This is due to the fact that better health care options tend to be available in major cities such as Sydney, Melbourne and Brisbane. Approximately two-thirds of Australia's indigenous people live outside of major cities. While in Australia, I met a guide in the remote town of Cape Tribulation who told me that the population of the area was small due to an interesting Aboriginal connection. He went on to say that many years ago, the Aborigines in the area used to hollow out the trees to bury their dead. When the Europeans arrived, they assumed that the trees were eating the people and they refused to settle there. Misunderstandings such as this have been evident between the Europeans and the Aborigines for centuries. Many misunderstandings still exist today.

Another reason that leads to lack of proper health care for many Aborigines is cost. Many Aboriginal people cannot afford health care. In 2009, the unemployment rate among Aborigines was 18%. That is three times higher than the rate for Australians as a whole.

Unfortunately many doctors in Australia are unfamiliar with how to provide culturally appropriate health care to Aboriginal people. This is yet another reason why Aboriginal people are not accessing health care. The Australian government published an 82 page document entitled: "Providing Culturally Appropriate Palliative Care to Aboriginal and Torres Strait Islander People: Practice Principles." It is a guide for health care professionals and it outlines how to best work with indigenous people. It explains how their definition of family often extends to non-blood relatives. It also discusses the fact that by the time an indigenous person seeks medical help, they tend to be further along in their illness relative to non-indigineous people. In addition, it is important for a health care professional to be sensitive to the familial hierarchy. There are customs related to who can be a decision maker and who can receive information and who cannot. Health care workers need to be very careful not to make a mistake or it could cause a problem within the Aboriginal family. It is also important to note that many Aboriginal people tend to prefer to pass away at home and hospitals and doctors need to be aware of this and help make necessary arrangements for final days at home. The hope is that by being sensitive to the cultural differences and increasing familiarity with these people, they will be encouraged to seek more medical attention.

The Australian government as well as the private sector are working hard to bridge the gap between the Aboriginal people and the rest of the population. The fact is, however, that more needs to be done. The Aboriginal people are very slow to embrace changes and they are slow to seek health care. The belief remains that by encouraging more Aboriginal people to join the health care field and by training and educating others, it will bring Aboriginal people into the fold. In addition, Australians need to seek ways to bring health care to the more remote parts of the continent. The continent is so vast and most of the population is crowed around the coast, but the Aborigines must not be forgotten. They are a vital part of the culture and history of Australia and deserve opportunity and respect.

Evan Kielmeyer

Bio~

Evan Kielmeyer is a 10th grade student at Smithtown High School West in Smithtown, NY. Evan is a member of the English Honor Society and is Vice President of The Red Cross Club. Evan has been playing lacrosse for 10 years and plays defense for his high school team. Evan, along with his younger sister, founded a charitable organization called Stix Together. The organization collects new and used lacrosse equipment and donates it to teams in need. Since its inception in 2013, the organization has donated thousands of dollars worth of equipment.

Evan believes that peace flourishes through compassionate engagement between cultures. He is an avid traveler who enjoys seeing the world through a myriad of perspectives. He will visit his sixth continent by the end of this year. He hopes to study philosophy and law after high school.

Evan wishes to dedicate his essay to his teacher, Mrs. Christina Cone, who inspires her students to be advocates for human rights and guardians of peace.

2015 Progress Report~

Since last year I have traveled to Indonesia, South Africa and Costa Rica for charity work. I wrote about my experiences in blogs which appear on my website stixtogether.com. I have also co-written a paper for my AP US History class which was selected to be presented at our district's AP Conference. I took a class on Human Rights which was taught by Christina Cone who was the teacher who sponsored me for your contest last year.

What "writing for peace" means to me:

Writing for Peace has meant a lot to me as it was the first time I formally put my cultural experiences into an essay. I look forward to making writing a focal point of my college studies and hope to one day make a difference with my words.

Roland Freisler's Gesang
Sy Roth

Woof,
the shepherd barked.
Mein Schatzi, Barry, so true,
Roland's retort.

He did it, didn't he?
Growly woof-bark
in the affirmative.
Wolfish gargle lodged in his throat
Volcanic testimony,
a Vesuvius eruption of assent
reverberates from the bench.
Spectator muddle of mudlicious dithering echoes.

The prisoner
held his pants up
arms out like a flightless penguin.
Beltless,
Shoulders slumped,
Head bent in defeat
eyes glued to his eyebrows .

Growling hound,
and Freisler sang their growling ditty--
Wagnerian tango to the condemned.

Gleeful woof barks follow
Barry's tongue slathering from the side
Sniffing disdainfully at the shuffling prisoner
Swallowed into the conga line crush
of waddling prisoners.

Sy Roth

Barry was right, of course.
Always was.
They had no say.
Freisler proffered his schatzi a biscuit,
Patted his head--
con amore.

Woof, Barry lovingly answered.
Both content to judge,
To devolve into their safer world.

Last Words
Stuart Friebert

To get away for a few days, as things quieted down
when spring break came around of my last semester at
the *Technische Hochschule* in Darmstadt, I went off to
the American Forces Club in town for one last hot shower.
The TH's water, as everyone called it, ran colder than "a
witch's tit," my roommates who'd survived fighting on the
Russian front groused. Wanting to thank the staff for let-
ting me enjoy an American breakfast now and then, I also
hoped I'd run into Ken Silman, the liaison officer at the
American Consulate who'd been supervising my year-long
fellowship as one of the first American students to study
in Germany after WW II.

After all, I owed him a lot, and was quite concerned
about having heard his marriage was on the rocks, which
I hoped was just a rumor. Not only wasn't he around, the
desk clerk said Ken had been reassigned stateside and no
one seemed to know where to reach him. Coincidentally,
the clerk mentioned that someone was on the way to the
TH with my new passport, instructed to leave it with the
administration if I wasn't around. Recently out cycling,
I'd fallen going too fast down a steep incline. It must have
slipped out of my rucksack, but after crawling around
through the gorse, I gave it up for lost. So this was beau-
tiful news, because I wasn't certain my application for a
new passport would clear in time to catch the Queen Mary
out of Cherbourg, as planned, for the journey home.

If a new passport hadn't come through when it did,
it'd have been a headache rebooking and all; but in the
back of my mind I thought I might try to contact the
Kramers one last time. They were relatives of my grand-
mother's friend, who'd welcomed me to their home in
Tuttlingen in Swabia during the fall and winter holidays.
I knew I should anyway, to try to make whatever amends
were still possible to make, even though I deserved to be
written off entirely for my shabby behavior. They'd wanted

me back for the spring break, but I begged off with fake reasons, because I wanted to pursue a relationship with Miriam Pfungsheim, a fellow student whom I'd been eyeing for months, but hadn't had the courage to approach.

Back at the TH, when I'd finished packing, Director Meyers and family invited me to their quarters for something "special to drink" by way of farewell, the note read, and to pick up my passport as well. Leading me into his study, the director said, "Do you approve of our new butler-bartender?"

Professor Breiter, who'd gone out of his way to befriend me outside class – my roommates said he'd lost his family during a bombing raid on Darmstadt in September, 1944, so I was a substitute son of sorts, Martin couldn't resist adding – wore smart white gloves, saluted and bowed. I literally jumped over to him with joy, while the Meyers family stood by, smiling broadly.

"Our specialty for such occasions," the director said, eyeing his new butler, "is tea laced with cognac. Sound all right to you?"

"Never had it but I'm game. Besides," I said, "I've come to value your medical facilities. If anything happens I know I'll be nursed back to health." Professor Breiter started pouring, we started drinking, talking and laughing. Even the children were given a finger of cognac, just in case they developed a toothache, Mrs. Meyers teased. Right before I turned one last time to say thanks for the memories, little Peter, whom I'd become especially fond of, ran to the sideboard to fetch my passport, which we'd totally forgotten about. He'd wrapped it himself in expensive paper he decorated with little white mice on a red, white, and blue background, because we shared a fondness for mice, a sizeable minority population at the TH, majoring in leftovers.

Promising to send Peter an Indian headdress, I helped him slide down the banister one last time, which relieved Mrs. Meyers. Breaking her code for proper behavior, she allowed Peter and me some leeway all year long, which was sure to disappear as soon as I left. Peter sat down on the bottom step, waving the little wave of children, while Professor Breiter called after me that he'd drive me all the way to Frankfurt in the morning to catch the express to Paris, where I'd change to the boat train to Cherbourg.

I decided to walk around the grounds surrounding the TH one last time, finding myself eventually in the cemetery staring down at the graves of Eva Breiter and the two Breiter children. Kneeling to pick a few ugly weeds starting up over her name, I heard a car approach on the little access road beside the gravel walkway. Its lights were off, so at first I couldn't make out who was at the wheel. When the professor himself stepped out, in his signature fedora, waving, I scrambled to my feet, about to apologize for intruding.

"My family's going to miss you and so shall I," he said, putting his arm around my shoulder and turning me to face their headstones. "I've caught sight of you here before."

I was still holding the weeds I'd picked. "Here, let me have those, I should be taking better care of their resting places. The Nibelungs, you know, had it right – one must keep consecrating hallowed ground where loved ones lie. Your President Lincoln also had some words on the subject, as I recall..." We stood for a while, not saying anything, listening to the music of insects in the trees. "I'd offer you a ride to the house," Professor Breiter said, finally – where I'd bunked the second semester as his yard boy -- "but I can imagine you'd rather take the slow road back by yourself on your last night, correct?" I nodded, and he left, calling out through the car window, "I'll be sure to get you up on time if that stupid alarm in your room doesn't go off. It's a Big Ben, after all. No wonder our Swiss industrialist-co-conspirators can make clocks and guns at the same time. That work, alas." I sensed he just wanted to hang that in the air, so I didn't say anything in return.

He had breakfast waiting when I came down into the kitchen. "Americans like pancakes, I believe, so I've made you some from my grandmother's old recipe. Stuffed with cinnamon apples. As a young girl, she was taken to Paris and treated to a fancy meal of crepe suzettes, which made such an impression she begged for the recipe. The chef himself came out in his magnificent hat, huge starched apron, she recalled, and wrote it right out for her then and there on a napkin. And signed it with a flourish, like a great artist. He did tell her mother, my great grand-mother, to withhold the cognac till grandmother's eigh-teenth birthday, which became a sort of family mantra. I'm sorry to say you're getting a bastardized version – no hot orange-butter sauce, but there is a splash of cognac in there somewhere, because I dare say you've past your eighteenth birthday."

Tearing into the tasty cakes, I held back telling him I'd just turned eighteen the past July. He sat there sip-ping his coffee, watching me eat my fill. "My children used to eat just like that," he laughed, "unable to chew one mouthful without stuffing in more. My wife tried making a rule, they couldn't talk till they swallowed, but we soon gave up... God, I wish I'd died with them." Mumbling something about seeing to the car in the garage to make sure it would start, he motioned to leave everything when I finished. He'd hired someone to come in and straighten up as he'd planned, after dropping me off at the station in Frankfurt; to visit a friend, he said, who oversaw the *Goethe Haus*. I recalled Miriam once suggesting we go see where old man Goethe carried on with all those women.

It was still early, so while the professor offered to load my suitcase and duffel bag into the trunk, I signaled I'd take in the trees out back one last time, where we'd sometimes sit and talk about life. He pointed to the sky, which was darkening, threatening a storm. "Don't take too long, the road can turn slippery in a downpour. Where's Goethe when we need him, anyway?" he said. "More light!" He knew I knew those were Goethe's last words.

We'd once sat around with him for a beer after class. He was uncharacteristically jolly and relaxed, I recalled, steering the conversation, stiff with deference to him, toward "famous last words," which he mostly supplied of course, as none of us had made a habit of collecting any yet. "My favorite is Kafka's," he had said. "I pray I'll be up to something as witty and, well, perfectly in character, when my time comes. Now, this may be quite apocryphal, but he said, when the physician attending him refused to administer more morphine – remember, Kafka was in terrible pain, wracked by T.B., I believe, which was killing him – and he said, 'Kill me or you're a murderer!'" Professor Breiter waited for our reaction, but no one had as yet heard of Kafka, much less read him. Promising, if he lived long enough, he'd not only teach a seminar on Kafka if he had to kill to see it approved by the curriculum committee, he'd also see Kafka crowned as the century's most prophetic writer.

We drove along mostly in silence out to the autobahn to Frankfurt, though the professor cursed at a sleek Mercedes that nearly blew us off the road as it hurtled by. In a stretch of a few miles without other traffic, he hummed snatches of tunes I didn't recognize. Leaving the last of the Merck-complex buildings as we left Darmstadt well behind, he said something about them being store-houses for "whoring and healing." It was clear I wasn't expected to add anything . Finally, we pulled into the holding area outside the Frankfurt station, well ahead of my train's departure time. Removing his well-worn driving gloves, he took out a pipe I'd never seen him smoke, tamped in some dark, pungent tobacco and struck a match, only to let it go out again.

Suddenly turning grave, he said, "I'm going to leave you with a serious injunction. I realize you came to us all fired up to continue with your math and science pursuits. And my colleagues on that side of the divide tell me you're not without talent and have some promise – poor old Klarner couldn't get over your solving some equation or other, which even had him baffled for some time." I didn't open my mouth to say I had no idea what he was referring to. "But when it's time to consider graduate studies," he went on, "I think you ought to seriously consider going on in German. Besides, you're smart enough to keep up with math and science developments, at least to some extent I'm sure when you get too bored reading literature, not to mention writing more of those little poems you were wise to show me." He paused to light another match, but it went out as well when he continued. We'd only recently learned that without the help of the Americans governing the Zone that included Darmstadt, he'd never have been allowed to teach the one literature course, which he somehow managed to get required of all science students.

"If I had a few more years to pound more things into your sometimes stubborn head, I think you could actually consider devoting yourself full-time to writing in German, like a few other souls whose mother tongue also wasn't German. Now, I'm not predicting you will turn out to be another Conrad, mind you." I was too glazed, not to say limp, to even nod at that. "But what I've seen is really still quite remarkable for someone your age." He paused to roll down the window to clear the windshield of mist from our breath. "Which is no guarantee of course that you'll deepen and reach the sort of maturity we expect from a real writer. In other words, my friend, it'll be a long journey. You might just fall by the wayside, as plenty of even more gifted young writers have, sorry to say."

When I just sat there dumbfounded, looking more and more confused, he surprised me anew. "I've never told you this and maybe shouldn't even now, but I took the liberty of running a few of your texts past some serious poets in town, who couldn't quite believe you were not only not a native by any stretch, but also just a baby, relatively speaking – no offense. I don't need another dueling scar at this time of my life!" So that's what that dark mark on his cheek is, I said to myself, as in one motion he hopped out and popped the trunk open, hoicking my bags out, without a mention of staying in touch. But I think he knew I'd write him till he begged me not to. He did remove his fedora, waving it like a cowboy when I looked back through the station doors.

I knew I was supposed to feel some sort of thrill that it was the Queen Mary's last voyage I'd booked, without even knowing it. Most everyone was bursting with excitement, signing up left and right for the daily tours ranging all over the Queen's byways, many of which we were told had never been open to the public before. Everything was also high-lighted, from the commemorative salt-and-pepper shakers to the embossed pillowcases. I didn't know a soul, so I didn't have to refuse invitations like those that flew back and forth between passengers, who otherwise would never have struck up a conversation at a bus stop on a snowy day. I did make my way to the railing for a bit of fresh air from time to time, but missed the passing of a whale and sighting of the Queen Elizabeth in mid-ocean on her way back to Europe, which had been announced as one of the things not to be missed. My ears almost came off, however, when they blasted their whistles at each other.

I did manage to save the farewell menu, because a painting of the ship, reproduced in full colors for the cover, said "save me or you'll regret it"; but mostly I buried myself in my bunk, nodding to third-class cabin mates as they came and went, while I pored over every note I'd taken in my courses to reconstruct the whole year before it fell down the well of forgetting. Exhausted from doing so, I had to be jostled awake when we landed. Cabin mates just shook their heads when I didn't rush topside to wave back at the Statue of Liberty.

Clearing customs readily, I made my way through the throng to catch a cab to the airport for a flight back to Milwaukee. I had absolutely no desire to take in the sights of New York, though urged by everyone back home to do so, especially since Wisconsin State's fall term wouldn't be starting for a bit.

My parents could have accused me of withdrawing, because I sequestered myself in the new bedroom they'd added on for me. Mom convinced Dad that I needed to spend my last year at home in relative peace and quiet, given the active lives my younger sister and brother were starting to lead. Basically just showing up for meals, I was still chief dish-washer, but otherwise spent most waking hours trying to figure out what I'd been up to, exactly, and where I was going next.

Professor Breiter's injunction heavily in mind, I made certain I had just enough credits to complete my math and science majors, so I could enroll in as many German courses as possible before graduating to see where they might take me.

To put it mildly, I did less than distinguished work in all my courses. I told myself I was spending so much time on panels to promote international understanding, especially among young people. My exchange year had been widely reported and invitations mounted. Somehow managing to earn a decent enough grade point average by the time it came to apply for graduate work at the state university, I was still facing the nagging question of what course or courses to pursue, inasmuch as I was still totally undecided by the time applications were due.

It never occurred to me to seek counseling, but when Professor Breiter recommended, in a somewhat exasperated letter because I was still hedging, that I talk "to someone with an overview of the American system," I came to my senses. A fellow student happened to mention really profiting from a session with the Director of Career Counseling, so I finally made an appointment, which my mother asked to be in on. He seemed more and more worried that I might be losing my way.

In an initial session, the director reviewed my record with us, asking so many questions I protested I could never afford her. "Just ante up when the Development Office hits you for a donation after you turn into an alumnus," she joked. "Besides, yours is not a run-of-the-mill case. Meanwhile, take these aptitude and assorted other tests along, and do your level best to respond honestly. I assure you nothing you answer will be kept on file, just turn into thin air when we're done." When I returned them, along with some quotes from Professor Breiter's letters, she seemed eager to hear what he had to say about my prospects from his vantage point. "I'll need another week to digest everything here," she said. "The secretary will schedule another appointment for your mother and you."

By the time we arrived, Mom and I both had a case of nerves. Mine, because decision-time was finally at hand; but hers, she suddenly confessed, because of the possibility I'd continue with German studies at a much more serious level. "I keep talking to gramma about things," she said so softly I asked her to repeat, "and of course hope she's not turning in her grave." Startled, I asked her what that was all about. She said she'd tell me later after I finished the dishes and we could pair off to the den.

Waving us into her suite, the director of Counseling let us get comfortable before starting in. "Whatever you decide, please take what I'm going to say as just another opinion. Informed I hope, but I really can't ever be sure. Please think of it as just one more factor among many to ponder," she began. Mom shifted in her chair. I looked over at her hard, because I knew she'd hide her own feelings if possible, and sometimes did so from herself as well. She never gave advice. She just listened, which usually was the perfect antidote to dad's way of dealing with questions in my life. I could count on one thing from her: now as always she'd leave even a momentous decision solely up to me.

"Colleagues who know of Professor Breiter's work, his reputation, have persuaded me to take what he says very seriously," the director said at first, to my astonishment. "Having said that, I can be quite brief it turns out. Even if you do continue with German studies, the best science schools, and medical schools as well, still require grounding in foreign languages, especially Latin and German. So you'd be protected by forging ahead with German, if only for a while." I had had vague thoughts of doctoring, which I might have conveyed to her at some point, though Gramma would tell anyone I'd make the perfect judge to try the evil devils who brought so much misery to the world, not to mention our own flesh and blood, even as she waved off questions about what had really happened to her family after the Germans retreated from their botched Russian campaign. Suddenly awash in that memory, I had to concentrate when the director continued.

"Let me add a complication because of some things I see in your records, as well as the report we received from Director Meyers about your work." She took off her reading glasses to look me straight in the eye. "You can also use your amazing German to pursue a career in the Foreign Service. Do you know they're looking for qualified officers at this time to help ferret out former Nazis, not to mention stabilize the new government? Some contacts we enjoy say our military, along with other departments, are having a difficult time finding out who did what in the war years." Excusing herself for a moment, she let that sink in. Mom looked quizzically over at me, but I could only shrug my shoulders. No one had ever raised that possibility. I searched my mind – had Ken Silman perhaps mentioned anything even remotely like that, given what he was up to? Not that I could recall. My brain began shutting down – too many flavors to choose from – just give me vanilla I kept thinking.

"Well," the director said, when she returned, "that's a lot to think about, I know. But you don't have to decide anything just yet. So why not go ahead and apply for a place in the German Department, as well as in mathematics and, what, chemistry was it, too? And for good measure, why not take the Foreign Service exam when you get to the state university, and let what happens help shape what you wind up doing eventually? In any event, it won't really hurt you in the long run to postpone consequential decisions a while longer."

"Talk about playing into your hands," Mom said when we had thanked the director and left. "Mr. Procrastinator Extraordinaire!" I wondered if most mothers knew their sons as well as she knew me.

"Okay, I'll get dad off your back," she said, when we got home, "you have enough to worry about. We would of course appreciate being let in on any decisions, if you can decide anything at all!" I kissed her smack on the spot on her cheek she pointed to, locked myself in my room after hanging out a sign to keep my sister and brother at bay, put Mozart's third violin concerto on the phonograph, which Gramma had gotten me started listening to some years back, and didn't know what in hell I'd do 'til I did it.

Angela Yoon
2014 Writing for Peace Young Writers Fiction Contest
First Place

The Best of Both Worlds

Gangnam-gu, Seoul-si, South Korea
Seoul International School, Grade 10

*In a sense "The Best of Both Worlds" is itself the best of
two worlds, one the universal coming of age story, a
loss of innocence we all recognize, but in another the
very specific story of leaving a childhood in the Shanxi
Province for a harsh adult reality in Beijing. I admire the
compression and the urgency of this story, the poignancy
of it, and the circular structure, the end and beginning
mirroring one another in this journey of growth and of
loss. A beautiful piece.*

~Robin Black

The Best of Both Worlds
Angela Yoon

My world is the convergence of gold and dust, the meeting point between what I have and what I never will. The fragmented memories I carry now are all shades of lustrous red, tinted with slivers of yellow, perpetual reminders of the land that the blood streaming down my veins stems from. The first gasp of air I inhaled was like any child's first breath in the valleys of Shanxi province- raw and pristine, and little did I know back then that all the tranquility of my life would one day be disrupted.

I was sixteen when I left.

Most people would not understand an adolescent's desire to venture through the heart of the country and into the metropolis, but at the center of my decision were Ma and Ba. It was because every degree that their spines curved downwards while plowing fields paid for my existence. Because every drop of wine-red blood that trickled down their hands from hours of labor had to be paid back, because every effort to stop tears from flooding their past had to be acknowledged, and because the wish they planted into their souls from the minute they created me had to be achieved.

It was the day of the new moon when I told her.

"Ma, it's time for me to leave," I whispered. The utterance of my every word manifested itself into incorruptible silence. "Xiaobei will stay, but you know I must go."

"To the city? But it's so early....you can't go there alone."

"Xiaobei will have to quit school if I don't go. You already know he needs to stay. You know you can't change your mind now."

She knew it was coming. She knew that this day had been edging its way into reality from the minute her son first opened his raven-black eyes; the golden prince had arisen to his throne atop a Confucianist kingdom, and it was my duty to make sure my younger brother never had to climb down. Education was scarce here, and that was something I knew I had to understand.

That was reality. I was faced with the opportunity that had the likes of a double-edged sword, one with the potential to dictate the rest of my life. I had heard of the millions of others just like me, who had no choice but to plunge headfirst into the ice-cold waters of city life and see how long the flame of survival within them could endure the collision of migrant worker life. One of the millions had been my father; forty-nine years in the verdant fields had slapped a warning across his left cheek, telling him that to keep his family alive, he had to do more. What it was like for them, I could only guess.

The midnight train took me to Beijing two nights later, a city that stood majestically among towers piled upon towers 500 kilometers away. Ma had slipped a woven, red silk *qipao* into my bag, hoping the dress would be able to elicit memories of her face and my father's while I was away. They once told me that red was the color of fortune, an emblematic flame dancing away until the night took it for its own. To think that I was already leaving...

The Great Mao gazed into my eyes. Forty years had dissolved since the Cultural Revolution, and he was still presiding over his people, permanently etched into the wall of Tian An Men Square. This was Beijing: the symbol of 21st century luxury that I could only carve into a dirt brick as a lionhearted youngster; the sight of sleek BMW's taking businessmen to adjacent skyscrapers and people wearing perfectly embroidered leathers shoes was all new to me. This was Beijing.

My work was in the packaging industry- eight hours a day with a little less than decent remuneration was sufficient for my daily expenses, so I could not ask for more. Every night, the dorm window opened a portal to the lustrous city lights, twinkling to flaunt their abstract grandeur, and I prayed that someday, the heavens would gift me that same elegance. Nevertheless, nine months had already passed, and my endurance was dwindling for each day I spent incarcerated within the factory walls.

"Why isn't this done properly?" the manager barked. His voice was streaked with a cold stringency that I could not fight. I bowed my head, unable meet his eyes, and the inferno continued.

"*Ni gan ma?* What are you doing? Do you think this job can be tossed around like it's a joke? You should be thankful that I won't be throwing you out."

I wished I could scream, I really did. The gashes on my hands from work throbbed in pain, but so did my heart, which was slowly splintering into ashes from the sorrow it consumed. I felt my oxygen pulsating up my veins, leaving my entire body white and lucid from imperishable deprivation and yet, no sound could escape my throat. I missed Ma, Ba, and the little prince; I missed everything about the unblemished Shanxi valleys that seemed to reach out with open hands, but I was forced to thrust every shard of nostalgia into my past. So I let life proceed as if nothing had ever happened.

There was a time in which I believed in reincarnation. My naiveté told me I would one day let the disproportionate contours of my eyes fade away, and wake up as a princess of a palace. A vestige of that belief still clings onto life within me, though I know that having the best of both worlds can only be an inconceivable dream now. Through the cities I've traversed and the memories I've locked away into the deepest chambers of my mind, I now see that my country will forever be the meeting point between what I have and what I never will.

Bio~

I am currently a rising junior at Seoul International School, my second overseas high school. I was born and raised in the suburbs of Northern California for twelve years, where I was able to fuel a vehement passion for language arts. At the age of 11, I moved to Beijing, China with my family and attended the International School of Beijing for three years, before moving to Korea last summer. Although writing is my main interest, much of my life also revolves around music and political science.

I am Korean by blood, but my character has been molded by more than just a Korean heritage. As a "third culture kid" who has been exposed to a variety of cultures from a very young age, I have come to embrace diversity, enabling me to absorb new cultures whenever I have the chance to do so. By my tenth birthday, I had mastered three different languages and began to explore my own ideas about living abroad. It is precisely the experiences I encountered overseas that have shaped the way I perceive the world around me and the thoughts I incorporate into my writing.

It was definitely a privilege for me to be able to share my writing with the world, and I am grateful that people could grasp the vision of China that I hoped to paint within my fictional essay. I hope that my writing will continue to push myself and others forward on our never-ending journeys.

2015 Progress Report~

2014 and the first half of 2015 so far have been quite the rollercoaster for me and and my writing. After winning the fiction division of Writing for Peace, some of the short stories I have written in my spare time have been accepted for publication by a couple of literary magazines including The Claremont Review and I have recently been accepted to study Creative Writing at this summer's Kenyon Young Writer's Workshop. I have also won an international essay contest that focuses on the concept of world peace and cooperation, but most importantly, throughout all of these writing opportunities, I have been able to explore different genres and content to push myself both as a writer and a dreamer. For me, writing is definitely not always about the result; what matters to me is the process: my idea, how I express it, the questions, and the answers. In the future, I see myself sitting in a coffee shop or library furiously typing away at whatever comes to mind. It may be a serious piece on international relations or it may be a fictional short story on youth. But either way, I would like to use my writing to help others see the world a bit differently.

What "writing for peace" means to me~

Writing for Peace holds a special place in my heart because it's really the first time I had written a fictional piece that digs so deeply into the struggles and wonders of cultural identity. It gave me the valuable opportunity to think about what peace really means, and how to apply the concept to a cultural perspective. Really, Writing for Peace was truly a catalyst for my passion for writing, and I am honored to have participated in it. One of the best things about it is that it is open to the entire world; anybody can submit a piece of writing, and anybody can be encouraged to explore our world's cultural diversity. Some of the most inspirational world leaders have all started out writing pamphlets or articles for a certain cause because to them and to me, writing has always had the power to move minds. Writing for Peace can truly make future world leaders.

Somewhere

Somewhere
in the city's clatter and jar,
a blue ceramic bowl filled
with clear water rests on a table.

Somewhere
in the city's lurch and thrust,
two men sing operatic arias
in a grove of twisted cedars
while sparrows collaborate.

Somewhere
in the city's fumes and gasps,
a grandmother shows her grandson
how to catch dragonflies
with his bare hands.

Somewhere
in the city's press and stifle,
layers of dust and layers of
insect carcasses lie undisturbed
in a temple closet.

Somewhere
in the city's hard rock and roll,
waiting for a train, a young woman
cradles her husband's feet
and begins to clip his toenails.

Elizabeth Schultz

An Outing

In the parking lot of
the Beijing Botanical Garden,
the Tibetan monks
spilled from the tour bus
like bouquets from a cart.

Their maroon and saffron
robes swayed around them.
They juggled words, tossed
Tibetan, Chinese, and English
with laughter into the air.

Clapping each other about
the shoulders, they set out
in search of the Reclining Buddha,
some jogging, some jumping.
They wandered among

pots of truncated bonsai, stooped
to scrutinize the peonies' luxury.
At home with gay extravagance,
they strode confidently
among imported tulips.

Arm in arm, they strolled
up into the hills. Beneath
ancient cedars they reclined,
resting against these trunks,
leaning against each other,

Buddhas all.

Hardly a New Religion

Day and night, the shamans
of industry clang their gongs.
Men lose themselves to such
regularized, metallic rhythms.

Spotlights allow the mesmeric
dance to persist in the dark,
while strings of Christmas bulbs
trim these temple enclosures.

Pulsating, shaking 1000 bells,
iron shafts pummel the earth,
and dust rises up in swirls
as dense as incense.

In the end, men collapse.
They cast off their ritualistic
gear—heavy belts, hard hats—
fall to the ground, spent.

Immense prehistoric cranes
preside over such ceremonies,
swaying, sashaying across the sky,
their long necks gently touching.

Two Poems
Jing Wang

Poem #1
墨落杯中，一片黑云浮琥珀。
梳横枕上，半轮残月照琉璃。 [1]

Ink drips into the cup of tea,
A cloud like darkening amber rises.
My comb lies across the pillow,
A waning moon of lazurite shines.

Poem #2
题 《老妪骑牛吹笛》

玉环赐死马嵬坡，
出塞昭君怨更多。
争似阿婆牛背稳，
笛中吹出太平歌。 [2]

On "An Old Woman Herding Cows"

Yuhuan was given to die at Mawei,
Zhaojun married beyond the Wall.
I long to be the woman riding an ox,
From her flute flows an air of peace.

---

1 Chu, Renhuo (褚人获). *Solid-Guard Collection* (《坚瓠集》), Vol. 6, Section 2, p. 5. Internet Archive. N.p. 2014. Web. 9 Jan. 2015.
2 Wang, Yanti (王延梯). *A Collection of Literary Works by Traditional Chinese Women* (《中国古代女作家集》). Jinan: Shandong University Press, 1999, p. 451. Slight variations in diction in the first two lines show in another collection.

China was a land of poetry in traditional times. The Ming dynasty (1368-1644), one of the periods of unsurpassed prosperity in world history, produced a large number of female poets inferior to none. These two poems were written by a woman surnamed Fan (范氏) – women then, unless already famous in their lifetime, tended to be recorded without their given names. This is the first time these poems are made available in English.

In form the first poem is an antithetical couplet (对联), which is still popular. It consists of two lines meticulously symmetrical in structure. A couplet can be festive, celebratory, motivational, condoning, and what not, depending on the call of the occasion. Written in various calligraphic styles on typically though not necessarily red paper, they are posted vertically on main hall pillars and front door frames, and in sitting-rooms to flank paintings. In English translation, however, linguistic and poetic conventions call for four lines, and some of the symmetry is inevitably reduced.

Following grammatical and logical habits in English, the translator takes two liberties. For one, "the" is added before "cup" and "pillow." Although the Chinese version includes and needs no such a word, there has to be "a," "the," or "my" before these nouns in English for the lines to read fluently. Here the fact that the poet was a widow serves to explain the choice of the definite article - biographical reading in Chinese literary criticism differs obviously from that in English of treating the speaking persona and the poet severally. "The" helps heighten the sense of the poet / speaker being alone, as also conveyed in the image of the solitarily retiring moon. Then, "tea" is also the translator's discretion. In Chinese, it is barely "ink drips into cup." Omission of assumed words in Chinese is common practice. It is automatically understood that the cup contains enough tea to allow the rising cloud of amber. Yet, in English, a "cup" is a cup is a cup; without "tea" the next line simply does not follow.

The role of poetry in traditional China is set off by the fact that this couplet changed the course of Fan's life. According to one source, Yang Shiqi (杨士奇 1365 – 1444) – minister to five consecutive emperors since the founding of the Ming dynasty – chanced upon this piece when visiting a private school of Gan Village (in today's Jiangxi province). Struck by its poetic beauty, he inquired and ascertained its authorship. Yang also learned that Fan was a widow supporting her family by teaching in her own school. He deeply respected her industry and talent. At his recommendation she later became a teacher in the imperial palace.[3]

If again the speaker can be correlated with the poet, the second poem peeps into how Fan felt about being in the palace and expresses her longing for a life in the open country. The first two lines capture the anguish of Yang Yuhuan (719 – 756) and Wang Zhaojun (52 BC? – 15 AD?). Yuhuan was the favorite consort of emperor Xuanzong of the Tang dynasty (reigned 712 – 756). Through her influence, members of her clan obtained high positions in the court and enjoyed unlimited privileges as herself. She allegedly led the emperor to put pleasure before state affairs. Due to complex political and economic problems of the times, two military generals An Lushan (703 - 757) and Shi Siming (703 - 761) launched a rebellion (755 – 763) that devastated the Tang empire. In shock, the emperor managed to flee from the capital Chang'an and headed southwest for Sichuan. On the way, at the town of Mawei, his army refused to advance further and demanded the execution of Yuhuan's cousin Yang Guozhong and then of the consort herself. The emperor had no choice but comply. Whether she was actually executed, however, remains an unsolved mystery due to unexplained excavation findings some eighteen months later and ambiguous, inconsistent official records. The

3 Xu, Xiangyang (徐襄阳). *Miscellaneous Notes from the Western Garden* (徐襄阳 《西园杂记》)".Chinese Text Project. N.p. 2006-2015. Web. 4 Jan. 2015.

other woman Zhaojun was one of the numerous young women pining in the inner palace for the emperor during the Han dynasty (202 BC – 220 AD). In Zhaojun's time, the emperor was Yuandi (reigned 49 BC – 33 BC). At that time, China had troubled relations with the Xiongnu (the Hun), a nomadic people north of the Great Wall. The Han court sought peace in various ways, including giving away princesses as brides. When the Chanyu (Khan) of the Xiongnu, Huhanxie, requested the hand of the emperor's daughter, the emperor looked for a replacement. The disheartened Zhaojun offered herself. Today she is remembered as a hero for helping to bring about peace between the Han and the Xiongnu. These two lines reveal the poet's compassion for Yuhuan and Zhaojun while insinuating her own woe. The last two lines convey the poet's wish for a pastoral life instead of the cloistered and languishing existence in the palace.

This poem is yet another example of the importance of poetry in traditional Chinese society. It is recorded that Fan taught in the palace for a few years. But she was homesick. She was inspired to write this poem by a painting called "A Village Woman Herding Cows." Xuanmiao Xianfei (1397?– 1462), a consort of emperor Xuan Zong (reigned 1425 to 1435), saw the poem and understood. The good consort sympathized and had Fan dubbed a lady, gifted royally, and sent home.[4] Another source tells a similar story but indicates that it was the first Ming emperor Taizu's (reigned 1368 - 1398) empress, maiden named Ma (马皇后, 1332 — 1382) who helped the poet return home.[5]

---

4 Ibid..

5 Lin, Xun (嶙峋). *Blossoms from Heaven: An Anthology of Chinese Women's Literature from Historical Times* (《闺苑奇葩：中国历代妇女文学作品精选》), Beijing: Hualing Press, 2012, p. 116.

Note also that here "ox" (niu) does not mean a male dairy cow. Chinese traditional economy was predominantly based on agriculture, and dairy farming was not introduced to China until early twentieth century.[6] "Ox" refers to a species called "yellow cow" (huang niu) in China, working animals employed to transport goods and plough the fields. The typical image is a young boy riding on a yellow cow, a romanticized notion of rural life as represented in both poetry and painting.

---

6 Gernet, Jacques. *A History of Chinese Civilization*. Trans. J. R. Foster and Charles Hartmen. Cambridge: Cambridge University Press, 1982, p. 27. Zhang, Su (张苏). "Research on the Introduction of Dairy Cows to China" (中国近代奶牛传入与引进的研究进展). *Chinese Agricultural Science Bulletin* (中国农学通报) 29.5 (2013): 1 – 4. Print.

Jia Ce Cai
2014 Writing for Peace Young Writers Fiction Contest
Second Place

Home

Voorhees, New Jersey, United States
Eastern Regional High School, Grade 11

"Home" is a clear, eloquent depiction of the difficulties of living a dual identity, Chinese at home, American at school, lying and covering up in both places. The feelings of shame and of pride that reside inside the narrator are rendered with heartbreaking simplicity. "I changed my name from Xiaofei to Jennifer. . ." The journey to an acceptance of an identity woven of both "homes" is a powerful one.

~Robin Black

Home
Jia Ce Cai

That day everything changed. That day I became someone else. That day I stepped foot into another country.

At the tender age of six, I left my hometown for a new world of mystery. My parents, who were both professors at a local university in the Guangxi province of China, felt as though America contained the answers to their child's future. We left everything, our family, our friends, and our home and went into the new world. During our first years in America, my parents, although college graduates, took on low income jobs. Their college degrees were not accepted in America and thus they could not teach. I went to a local elementary school and started learning English. Even though my parents went to the community college to earn their degrees again, they were unable to assimilate into the American society unlike me. One day, when my mom came to pick me up, my teacher spoke with her about our upcoming field trip. I froze as the conversation started between them. They could hardly understand each other. I became so embarrassed in front of my classmates. From that day on, I decided to live a double life. I would be American in school and Chinese at home. None of the two will mix.

When my parents regained their degrees, we moved to California. I started sixth grade with a clean slate. I changed my name from Xiaofei to Jennifer and I started to wear my hair down instead of a low ponytail. On the first day of school, I blended well with the other kids. Three months past and I started to dress and talk like them. After a year I became one of them. Many times, I was asked if I was Chinese; I just replied that I was American. Every day when I came home, I put my hair in a ponytail, washed off my heavily make-upped face and wore my red and yellow embroidered slippers. I would speak Chinese to my parents at home with some English mixed into every sentence or so and would indulge in traditional Chinese food for dinner. However, after a while, I realized that I started to use more and more English when speaking with my parents. Months past and I almost spoke fully English with my parents. I was mixing my roots with my current life.

However, one day, when my friends and I were talking about what we were going to have on Thanksgiving, I started to realize myself again. My friends were talking about how they were going to have turkey and pumpkin pie on Thanksgiving night. When they turned to ask me, I lied and said that I was having the same thing. My friends seemed puzzled. They looked at each other, shrugged, and continued talking. I felt confused. I have never told them anything about my family, how did they know I was lying? Why did I lie anyways? Why did I pretend that I was going to have turkey when I knew I was going to have roast duck? Why did I pretend that I was going to have pumpkin pie when I knew that I was going to have moon cakes? Why did I lie on a small thing such as food?

The rest of that day was painful. I thought of all of the lies I told my friends and all of the excuses I told my parents for speaking English when they called me on my phone. I became lost in the place I came to call home. Where is home? What is home? I turned the key to my house and walked in looking at the familiar light yellow tone my parents painted the walls because of Feng Shui. Even though our house was built in California, the house looked Chinese. I sat down in the usually sunlight filled living room. Gray clouds covered the sun and soon it started to rain. Like the rain, my tears started to drop. I did not know why I was crying. I only knew I felt a pain deep in my heart that did not seem to go away.

With my head in my knees, I told myself that the only way to save myself from embarrassment was to become American. I reminded myself of that many times, but the warm tears just kept streaming down my cheeks. My mother came back and found me crying over my enigma and quickly came to my side. I looked up and found a warm and kind face like the one I knew as a kid but now filled with wrinkles. The once young and beautiful woman I remembered became a frail and overworked middle aged lady for my sake, and here I was being ashamed to admit my culture. Ashamed to admit I was Chinese. Ashamed to call the people who sacrificed everything for me my parents. I was heartbroken. I turned my head, unable to face my mother knowing that I had cast her aside with my selfishness and stupidity. She hugged me tighter and with more love than I deserved. She turned me around and looked into my eyes and said to me "You are Zhang Xiaofei. Remember who you are." I leaped into her arms realizing that for the past years I have been pretending to be someone I was not and someone who I will never be.

I went to the bathroom to clean myself up. I looked in the mirror to see my makeup washed off by my tears. Slowly, I put my hair back into a ponytail and turned to walk out the door. As I opened the door I became aware that the rain had stopped and the house was filled with sunlight once more.

My name is Zhang Xiaofei. I lived in America for ten years and currently live in California. I am Chinese-American and will always have two homes.

Bio~

Jia Ce was born in the Jilin province of China, but she grew up in three different countries. From China, to Canada, to the United States, Jia Ce experienced the cultures and languages of both the East and the West. A trilingual Chinese-Canadian currently living in New Jersey, Jiace loves to play violin. She also loves reading Chinese literature. She is currently a Junior at Eastern Regional High School and aspires to be a dermatologist.

2015 Progress Report~

This year, as a senior at Eastern Regional High School, I am currently taking AP English Literature and Composition. I have delved into the tragedies of Shakespeare to the ever memorable play of *Pygmalion*. Throughout my journey into British Literature, I have found myself experimenting with a lot more styles and forms of writing. From poetry to writing short plays, I expanded my horizon for both English and writing. With the knowledge and skills I have learned, I see myself becoming more engaged in my literary works.

What "writing for peace" means to me~

Ever since last year when my teacher told me my work would be published, I found a confidence in myself which I never had before. "Writing for Peace" made me realize that my writing has a voice that I never noticed before. Therefore, "writing for peace" is not only a wonderful opportunity for me to share my story but it is also most importantly a medium where I gained the confidence to express my voice through writing. Thank you again for this wonderful opportunity to express myself through writing.

Three Poems
Lisa Rizzo

Morning

Stopping on the side of that hill,
just after dawn and already
miles walked. We breathed deep
to make the final push
and in that moment,
sunlight shone through the trees,
mist curling its fingers
around the spring-pale leaves.

If we had not begun
our journey just then,
if we had not stopped
to rest just then,
we would have missed
that particular moment when,
on a country road winding
among nettles and buttercups,
we were washed in morning light,
cows and sheep the only witnesses.

Interlopers

When the car tires stopped,
only insects buzzed
in the flat-roofed acacia trees –
no human sounds.
I gazed at the unbroken
expanse of grassland
spread out below me - Serengeti.
A Maasai word - *endless plain.*
As I watched scores of wildebeest
with their zebra scouts leading them,
I thought –*heading north toward Kenya* -
a little saddened that I think only
in boundaries,
but thankful that, as yet,
no human fences hinder
their animal migration.

Lisa Rizzo

Serengeti Afternoon

To stand upright,
a wildebeest struggles,
wobbly, his legs broken.
In the thin arms
of a baobab tree
vultures,
ink splotches
across the deep blue sky.
They are waiting
for the wildebeest's
last fall
before they drop
down around him.
I watch stunned
as the first one, brazen,
tears a strip of flesh
from the still-shuddering flank.
Red means only one thing
in the Serengeti.
My silent vigil
is all I offer
the dying.
For the first time
in my life
I wish for a gun.

Yellow Flowers
Christopher Woods

Dandiest of Lions
Tshombe Sekou

there is a flower   in my mouth –
a dandelion   taking root
in my throat
hiding
from
the
mowing man
it hopes to
survive
beheading
long enough
for its downy
tufts to grow
wings –
and should it not
perhaps the world
will now hear
its unspoken
poem.

Tshombe Sekou
Japan

Three Poems
Charles Leggett

Re(dis)cover

I find sweet
mischief in listening, feet
up, dry and ensconced, to this
vigorous rain. Catbird seat,

to be light
of heart inches from what might
otherwise cause one to crouch,
hunch and slouch through such a night.

From the eaves
above, pummeling the leaves
of the maple, large beads dive.
Roiling down the drive it thieves

jiggly sheen
from the street lamps. And its clean,
pattering chatter: of those
sounds that one knows one can glean

only near
water. They're eerie, the sere
maple leaves, glistening wet
in reddish set. In the ear

distant moans
of spinning tread and dry drones
of motors fail to find their
focus; blaring sirens' tones

are drained, or
diminished else, at their core,
of their insistence. The tops
of some poplars, exposed more

to the gray-
lilac, leisurely gusts, sway
like seaweed brushing a tide;
they've a sidelong, fluid play

Charles Leggett

and soft lurch
of vague and robotic search,
tendrils that mindlessly grope,
their trope or to grasp as perch

or to flee.
The trunk of the cypress tree
acquires a lacquer glaze, knur
of texture rather than tea-

shaded sheen,
dark, elegantly gnarled. Seen,
as all this may be, akin
to meditation, this clean

rain *is* thought:
upon everything here, sought,
found, touched, permeated then;
a vast, sensate, bluntly wrought,

flooding-firth
reconnoiter with the earth.
Its worn koan, "What is here?"
My bleeding, sere leaves, my berth

on a rind
of lacquered bark. These have shined
in my voice rising to call
and to fall on what I find.

As Lovers Will

As dogs will do, with rainfall in their pelts;
As athletes will, regrouping from mistakes;
As lovers will; as with old skin, will snakes:
My maple shrugs the snow off as it melts.

Charles Leggett

Ears Cocked in Snowstorm

Stately, collective sleepwalk on I-5:
Hallway of drunks evading picture frames.

The wind a blind, fat whistle through feckless trees.
Occasional low moans from rooftops, spinning

Tires' shrieks and hisses—these had drawn
Pauses from the dog, who'd try to place

The sounds, and fail, but not till then consent
To moving on. The neighbors' chimes a-tattle.

Snow held in cypress palms—even the stuffed
Dinosaur is under corner drifts

Here on the balcony, dead maple leaves
And dog fur gathered round its tail; its posture

Gleans as one of prayer. The glass of dry
Red wine grows cold; the warmth from our sojourn

Down Dexter siphons out; the beef stock on
Since noon reduces, brown and marbly bubbles

Blooming like Creation. Off to bars
Or beds have traipsed the revelers who'd careened

Down hilly streets on improvised toboggans,
Or hurled snowballs, with their happy shouts.

Or: winds would constitute the strings, their heaves
Of thrashing smoothness bowed in unison.

The chimes, then: outposts of melodic inkling,
Vestigial, persistent, near and far,

Embellishment, if fey, if wry, upon
The blanketing harmonics of the storm.

Bella (Spring 1997 - Sept. 4, 2012; rescued November 2001)

174

Kelle Grace Gaddis

Wishes

All the daisies have turned
their sunny faces overnight.
Atop a milky stem charmed
tufts prepare for flight.
That golden youth transformed
into an old lady-do of white.
And the stem, unadorned,
is now nothing more than blight.
I regret I never warmed
to a thousand golden lights.
Now too many have reformed
for me to be contrite.
Upon the wind sojourn
rise-up you little kites.
At least you lack prick thorns,
they, the roses spite.
For if you bore such horns
children would not delight
in blowing 'til they're worn
upon your heads with might.
Away! I am forlorn,
by this end of summer rite.
As seeds set sail I warn,
"Do not my lawn alight!"
My words are quickly spurned
by the daisies that turn tight.
Perhaps someday I'll learn
how to cast my wishes right.
And be without malice or concern,
for the parasols of sprites.

Kelle Grace Gaddis

Open

Alone, I pull the night across my face and let the stars into
my eyes. I dream myself a giant that sleeps between the
ridges of a mountain wrapped in the warmth of the summer
sun. When I wake I walk to the sea in a single step
and swim until the moon sinks into the horizon. There
you'll be in the face of an autumnal moon, laughing with
me. Joyous, we'll warm ourselves through the ephemera
of winter, in a cave of splendor and candlelight. The oceans
dark and night enchant us. The lands where our waterfalls
and flowers bloom give rise to optimism. It is ours, as
certain as another spring. The promise of change is in us,
we that move the banks of rivers, we who journey forth,
unafraid, pausing as we breathe, open and willing to love.

Nature's Song
Edward D. Currelley

The sound of nature, a beautiful song.
The lyrics, the strong will survive
and the weak may fall prey.

Human beings above all,
given the gift of reason,
compassion, understanding,
and conscience to determine
who and what survives.

Fear and poor judgment
not of nature,
just the natural flow of human beings,
navigating a world of promise.
Nature's song, sung out of tune.

Three Poems
Mary Carroll-Hackett

Some Mornings Are Chronic

tenacious in their violence, relentless in the ache that
tastes dark as coffee burnt to the bottom of the pot.

I had dreamt of being deaf, of losing the sounds of birds,
the wishing whir of water, then worse, in the dream,
someone threatened my son, and I, now also mute, found
myself incapable of protecting him. I shivered into the
kitchen. Arms folded, I stared at things, cups, sink, unable
to separate into waking.

A hawk, brown as toast, sat at my window. It was the
morning they blew up Paris. He screeched into the hollow,
and then, into the wind. His ruff, crowned tuft of white
feathers, lifted and fell again and again with each tense
high note. Down the road, I could hear the horses, their
braying, like wailing, like the barbed wire I always knew
would never hold. The hawk screamed for them to stop,
but I knew they would run, persistent in their race against
this insidious sadness, until their lungs ripped with cold
and fire, until their blood left flecked trails on the snow.

Deer, Inarticulated

prone, in my drive, already hurt, already broken out of
body when I arrived, but still warm, my palm on his chest.
This buck, six points and brawny, I knew best as Wan-
derer, the fawn I named for his courage, skittering, last
spring, out from my woods—our woods—brazen on his
new legs like sticks, even while his twin, the doe, clung to
their mother's side in the thick shade of the trees. I'd left
them corn, and apples, bits of broccoli stem that, back
then, he'd nuzzled up from the grass with his wide black
nose, watching me the whole time, not skittish, but bold.
His mother--I'd looked on from my stoop--months later,
had run him off when it was time. Button buck to stag
prime, he'd turned a strong back when she'd risen up on
her hind legs to strike him with her sharp front hooves.

Now, in the cold December dusk, on my knees, I find him,
know him again, but not moving, grown, ripe with his
buck's musk, but yes, gone, body still but not, not the deer
child I'd known, but some antlered arrangement, proud
head, thick hide, but broken free of the frame too frag-
ile, too small ever, for both the freedom and the pain to
simultaneously fit inside.

I stood, walked the black skid marks on the road, tracked
the trail of blood he'd left, gathered up fragments of
ripped fur, shards of bone, one piece near the ditch as big
as my palm, round as a bowl, the crown of his strong hip,
ripped, ragged, raw, a glistening pink hole. I brought it all
back to him, made a small pile there in the white beams
of my headlights, and sat. I had an idea that if I left him, it
would be me who was left most alone, that I'd be stranded
in that eternal half a mile he'd staggered from being hit to
being home.

Mary Carroll-Hackett

Blood Feud in a Place Called Sometime

where they fought over beans, over beans and bread, over
who would be fed, and why, why one and not the other,
why the child and not the mother, why the whys turning
brother on brother, the hunger drawing bloody lines in
the sand, the hands clawing skin man to man, where they
shook their fists at the graying sky, and took up muddy
shovels and picks and swords and sticks, where they
faced off, pacing off to the count of ten, where the how
and when rolled their eyes to blood, turned their bones
to wood, turned their mouths to mud and their hearts to
bread, the bread they wished they had, the need
now so bad, being all they knew, the cry for beans that
would see them through, the hunger for more that made
them run, dropping their sticks, to take up guns, to build
up bombs in parking lots, to move from threats to warn-
ing shots, warning shots that fell like hail while the wom-
en wept and babies wailed, and shouting grew big as their
hollow eyes, and the men with the bombs called them-
selves wise, saying we'll put a stop, an end to all this, the
beans are ours and they flipped the switch, they pressed
the button, they exploded the world, the curling blaze, the
clouds and haze, the slash and fry, they scorched the earth
and seared the sky, incinerating all of it, every bit, they
burned the mothers and babies and sisters and brothers,
the planet itself cracked and split, an end to the feud, at
all costs by all means, boiling it down they showed them
good, til nothing stood, not a single thing, between those
men and a hill of beans.

The Edge
Debra Lynn Turner

Adriana was walking her dog Lucy through the woods near the townhouse she and her husband had lived in since 1995, ten years before the crash. She blogged about how she could be shooing deer away from her tulips and fifteen minutes later driving across the Golden Gate Bridge. The point of her blog wasn't to boast; it was to lobby her readers to salvage green belts, the wooded areas that kept sprawl from taking over.

It was the best time of year to walk the wooded trail. Forget-me-nots were casting a blue glow in the mid-afternoon light, with sabers of calla lilies rising out of the lofting green ground cover. Ornamental plum blossoms turned the air sweet. Lucy, a year-old Jack Russell Terrier, could be trusted off leash unless a deer or a squirrel caught her eye, so Adriana kept her harnessed, dropping the leash from time to time. She'd hide behind a tree and Lucy would race to find her, tail wagging like the windshield wipers on high. Adriana laughed. Lucy's eyes sparked with delight. When they settled into walking Lucy checked back on her human every minute or so and stayed within a ten foot range, just enough distance for Adriana to lunge for the leash if need be.

Adriana pretended the roar was the ocean, with no ebb and flow, just the whir and whine and moan of motors. Through the dense forest of bay and oak, the underbrush of gorse and madrone, wafted the aroma of roasting meat. She wondered if some day Lucy would dash through the woods to the restaurant known for its gourmet burgers and ribs.

Lucy froze and all but pointed like a bird dog at the crows navigating the tightly woven arms of oak and bay, landing on branches like something bigger than a bird, moaning and groaning and clicking to each other. Adriana thought of them as comical and cunning. In groups larger than two she found them menacing, although she enjoyed watching them in flocks as large as thirty fly by her bedroom window in the mornings. She imagined them heading off to San Francisco where they would sell the shiny things they had collected for a healthy profit.

Lucy wandered ahead a little bit too far. She was a skittish dog, so Adriana kneeled down and pushed a foot-tall boulder off the trail, figuring the racket it created would send Lucy racing back to her side. Crashing down the steep embankment, the boulder thundered over branches, stumps, and trees growing sideways. The rock picked up speed and went much further than she'd intended, creating an embarrassingly loud racket. Lucy whimpered and nosed Adriana's calf as if promising never again to venture so far away.

"What a dope I am. Sorry pup. You stay close now." Adriana looked around her, relieved that no one was witness to her prank. From below she heard, "Damn it. Ohhhh."

Adriana felt faint. She'd hit someone. Stupid. Stupid. Stupid.

"Ohhhhhh." A male voice groaned from the tangled woods.

She looped Lucy's leash around an oak branch. "I'll be right back. Right back."

The slope was steep. Fall down, break your neck, and never be found again steep. What would anyone be doing down there? Maybe the chef sends his staff out to gather mushrooms. She navigated her way through so much trash she became outraged as she clung to branches and hoped she wouldn't twist an ankle. She followed the moan, although the thunder of the freeway made it difficult to pinpoint the location.

At sixty-five Adriana had an aging dancer's body, so even though she felt like she was crashing through the underbrush, she wasn't making much noise. Certainly the native Miwok would have heard her, but whoever got slammed in the head by her boulder couldn't hear her coming.

The incline leveled off by 20 degrees. She'd counted five tires, three pieces of coolers and enough plastic bags and Styrofoam bits to infuriate her. She was thinking her next post would be about litter. Litter. Fowl don't foul their nests. What's wrong with us?

She would help the injured man back to the restaurant and surely the staff there would drive her back home. They have insurance. She'll take full responsibility for her foolish prank. But should they really be harvesting mushrooms in what she now thought of as a garbage dump in the woods.

"Did we have a earthquake? God! I'm gonna bleed to death."

She could see him and his small grey tent. His clothes were hanging on hangers from branches. A dozen plastic water bottles were bungee-corded together. The hairs on her neck stood up. He was naked to the waist holding a bloodstained checkered shirt to his temple, leaning against a moss covered bay tree.

She stared at the half naked homeless man whose ribs she could count, whose skin was covered with a grey film. She smelled urine. She turned and clawed and crawled her way back up the hill, accompanied all the way by the deafening pounding of her heart.

She would call the sheriff. It's against the law. They'll have to install alarms. She won't walk through the woods again. They have to ring the property with large no trespassing signs. Maybe they should build a fence.

In her upset she nearly forgot Lucy who sat trembling with alertness. "Sweetheart, I'm so sorry." She kept ahead of her terrier by a leash length until through the unlocked front door. "Won't leave that unlocked again," she said, as she removed Lucy's harness and put two cookies in her dish. "Good girl."

From her back deck she surveyed the woods as she called the sheriff. She explained to the dispatcher that she'd seen an injured homeless person below the path in her woods. Just above the restaurant. She asked that someone check on him. "He's not supposed to be there, right?"

She started and restarted a blog post the rest of the afternoon, pacing through their townhouse, checking on the woods, wondering how much a mile and then some of cyclone fence would cost. Electrified maybe. But she didn't want to hurt the deer.

Spence brought home an herb-roasted-chicken and a large Caesar salad for their dinner. After he poured their Chardonnays she said, "I think we need an alarm system installed and we have to talk with the home owners association about the homeless people living in the woods. There are homeless people living less than 200 yards from here. Do you believe that?" She shook her head. "I had absolutely no idea." Her husband listened to her account and asked, "Is the guy okay?"

"I called the sheriff just before you got home and was told that the man had been apprehended and taken to a clinic. When I asked about the size of the encampment the sheriff assured me it was just the one guy and he promised me they patrol the woods regularly. We need to have someone go through there and take out all the trash. You would not believe what's down there."

Later when she called their son Avery and told him about the experience he said, "You just left the guy there with blood gushing out of his head? That's terrible."

"What should I have done?"

"You should have gone into the restaurant and gotten him help. Geez Mom, you could have killed the guy."

Since Avery went off to college he delighted in finding fault with his parents. They'd gotten along so well through high school, but now that he was majoring in political science and socio-economics he had nothing but criticism of his parents, as if they had eagerly enlisted in the military industrial complex and the first world economic tyranny group. Last time he came for dinner he'd proudly announced that he intended to work for Occupy Wall Street over the summer. When she'd asked how much they paid he'd been indignant about it being a volunteer position and that he couldn't do anything more meaningful than work to fix the broken system that is just enriching the top one percent. When she'd asked him about helping to pay his tuition since his parents certainly weren't in the top one percent he'd had the nerve to tell her that he had a college fund established by his grand-parents. Just before they'd dropped the subject she'd said louder than she'd intended, "And us. Your money-grub-bing parents keep your college fund afloat." She couldn't believe that had turned into the worst kind of entitled twenty-something: ungrateful and biting the hand that feeds him. "He'll grow out of it," was Spence's sole com-ment. Although sometimes Adriana thought she saw a little smile of approval on Spence's face. Admiration even.

The next day she walked Lucy on the loop road, which was paved and skirted the woods. Lucy tugged toward her favorite dirt path, but Adriana couldn't bring herself to risk it. She noticed an unfamiliar mud-spattered black sedan filled with clothes and suitcases, a pillow, water bottles and boxes of energy bars. A sleeping bag was folded up on the front passenger seat. With her cell phone she took a picture of the license plate. As she rounded the low end of the loop she saw a woman in the woods wear-ing a blue fleece over a pair of khakis, a backpack slung over one arm. Adriana studied her. Lucy growled and then began to bark.

"Hi there," Adriana called.

The woman stopped and set the pack down so that she could lean into it.

"Are you back packing? There are several trails west of here a few miles. You can get to them from the top of the road." She pointed.

As she neared the woman Adriana saw that her eyes were rimmed in red. Salty smears ran down her cheeks. "Can I help you in some way?"

As Lucy sniffed her shoes and her pack the woman stared at Adriana.

"I'm looking for my husband. He told me he'd meet me here an hour ago."

"Are you two hiking somewhere?"

The woman so plainly didn't answer, Adriana was certain the lived-in car belonged to her. "Are you okay?"

"I'm not okay. Is that enough of an answer?" Her words were angry, but her voice was flat and soft, as if it wearied her to speak. The pores on her nose and chin were black.

"Can I help in some way?"

"How can you imagine helping me?" She asked as she reached down and let Lucy sniff her filthy fingers.

Adriana imagined proudly telling her son that she let a dirty woman living out of her car bathe in their house, then wondered what she'd be getting herself into. "Do you need some cash?" She could run home and get her a twenty or two.

"My husband needs his job back and so do I, for that matter. Until that happens, yeah, I need some cash. But more than that, I need to find my husband."

"Did he give you an address where he's staying?"

"Yes. Right here."

Adriana had worked as a school counselor before her son was born. She knew how to approach a difficult person so as not to make them feel attacked. "I wonder if your husband is staying with someone in this association. I know most of the residents. Do you know his friend's name?"

"Bay Laurel and Live Oak. Do you know them?"

"Actually they are friends. I work to save them through my blog. I feel so lucky to be living on this edge between development and nature. It's important for us to keep these buffer zones." She sounded like a cardboard cutout to herself.

"We used to give money to the Trust for Public Land and the Sierra Club."

"Really?"

"My husband was doing green building. Got a loan. Was starting to make some really good contacts." Lucy was licking the woman's hand. She whispered to her, so that Lucy cocked her head, "There aren't any good buffer zones when the bottom drops out of your life." She looked up at Adriana, "Unless you're willing to work the system.

Food stamps, disability, all those scams we're too proud for."

Adriana thought that maybe she would offer her a shower and more money.

"From here he can walk to the first commute bus. In the dark people don't notice him much and the bus isn't crowded he says." She looked at her fingernails and made both her hands into fists. "He cleans up at the terminal in San Francisco and applies for jobs from the computers at the main library." The woman squatted and scratched Lucy's backside. "We had to give our dog away. Couldn't feed him." The words echoed in her chest.

Adriana caught her breath.

The woman sank to her knees. "He tried staying in the city, but he was afraid he'd get killed by the street people. I've got clean clothes for him and more food and a little bit of money." Her face grew red and her eyes watered until tears ran down her cheeks. "I think he's been murdered or he'd be here. He's always here."

He isn't here because I hit him with a boulder, Adriana screamed to herself. "Let me call the sheriff and see if I can learn something. I won't tell him you're here or that he's been in these woods. I'll just ask if something's happened."

The woman sat down next to her pack. Lucy sniffed her pants and shoes while Adriana walked to the curb to telephone.

It took a half hour of calls for Adriana to learn something about the man's status. During that time Lucy had curled up in the woman's lap.

"Do you have a cell phone?"

Without an edge of anger the woman said, "What do you think?"

"Well, how do you and your husband communicate?"

"From whatever phone I can find I call him on the pay phone down by the bus stop."

"I think we should wait there for him. The sheriff told me a man had been hit by a falling rock and was released this morning from a clinic in San Rafael. He's fine. It sounds like it's your husband."

"Thank God for falling rocks." She shook her head.

"Our bad luck just keeps coming." As she pushed herself to standing she said, "Thank you for your help. I'll drive down there and wait." The woman hefted the pack to her shoulder and ran to her car. Adriana was struck by her exhausted grace. Maybe she too had been a dancer.

Lucy looked from Adriana to the woman and back, as if to say, "Let's go with her. She's a good dog person. She needs our help. Come on." As they watched the car pull away Adriana decided she'd put together a care package for them and include some money. Maybe a hundred dollars.

Back at home Adriana filled a canvas bag with nuts, apples, soap, a towel, a bottle of wine, a metal water bottle she filled with filtered water, and an envelope in which she place 8 twenty dollar bills. She thought about writing her name, address and cell phone number in the upper left hand corner, like a return address, but talked herself out of the impulse with the logic that she really knew nothing about them. Not really. It could all be a story. They could be dealing in drugs or immigrant labor, or God knows what.

When she drove by the bus stop she saw no sign of the woman or her car or a man with a bandaged head.

Adriana started two blog posts that day – one about litter and one about homelessness. She Googled homelessness and read about free cell phone programs and a bill of rights for the homeless and realized it would take her a long time to know enough about homelessness to write anything of value. Litter, on the other hand, was a simpler issue. Nobody should do it. The blame clearly rested on the litterer, dumpster-diving raccoons included.

When Spence got home he was amazed at the latest installment of his wife's adventure. "You should blog about this. Here we are on the edge in more ways than we're comfortable imagining. I could lose my job tomorrow. A rock could fall on my head. We have savings and investments, but it's not at all out of the question that this nice life of ours could slip away. And fast." He said it as if he thought about their demise often; as if there were things he wasn't telling her.

From then on Adriana stopped sleeping through the night. She got up and paced. Lucy walked beside her, pushing her nose or a toy into her calf. Most mornings at 2 or 3 she poured herself a glass of wine, wrapped up in her husband's long wool coat and drank on the deck, staring into the woods, watching for a light, listening for a voice, a groan.

She stopped blogging. The sheriff refused to tell her to whom the license plate belonged. On every errand she drove by the bus stop then up and down the parking lot aisles. On some days she walked Lucy a dozen times at the edge of the woods. By the middle of June, with Lucy at her heels she walked the trail through the woods again. She sat on a stump and watched the grey squirrels fly from branch to branch. Lucy trembled with restraint, sometimes muttering to herself in a stifled growl, a swallowed bark.

By the end of June Adriana tied Lucy to a tree and retraced her steps to the homeless man's campsite. The bungee-corded together water bottles were all that remained. She snapped open a large black garbage bag and tossed them in and on her climb back to Lucy she picked up Styrofoam bits, more water bottles, candy wrappers, dog poop bags, burger wrappers, a solidified sock, a decomposing flip flop, and the checkered shirt she was certain the man had held to his head when she came upon him. The bloodstain was black now.

Every day for two weeks she combed the woods for trash. By the second week's end she had filled two-dozen 35-gallon bags. She hired two men from Guatemala. The lettering on the wooden sides of their pick up bed read, "WILL HALL JUNK." She paid them well to drag up the things she couldn't – a half dozen tires, parts of a toilet, pieces of terra cotta pipe and three concrete wheel weights they struggled to bring out of the greenbelt.

Once evening when Spence walked Lucy around the loop a neighbor who had watched Adriana's efforts asked him what she'd been up to. He was speechless. "She's been what?"

"You didn't know? She seems a little crazed, I must say."

Over wine Spence studied his wife's face. He knew she wasn't sleeping well, but he was startled to realize how weary she looked, how unwell. "Tell me what's wrong, darling."

Adriana looked at her husband for a long time in silence until the words poured out of her like tears. "I have this horrible case of survivor guilt. Life is so unjust and random and why is it that we are so fortunate? It's not fair. It's never been fair. I know that. I've always known that. But something about the way Lucy curled up in that woman's lap and she'd had to give her own dog away and I don't know what's happened to them and our son is occupying Wall Street and it feels like the sky is crushing me and us and everybody. All the decent little people."

He wrapped his arms around her and pulled a piece of lichen from her hair. "Have you checked for tics? The woods are crawling with them." He undressed her and the two of them bathed together. He loved her body, even and especially as age softened it. They toweled each other dry and he held her until she slept, perhaps soundly for the first night in weeks.

With sun streaming in their window and Lucy snugged up under Adriana's bottom, he kissed his wife's forehead. After he shaved and showered he nuzzled her and softly suggested she see a therapist who might prescribe some medications that would get her through this rough spot. She promised to call a friend for a referral.

After coffee and Lucy's morning walk Adriana found the tent and backpack they hadn't used since Avery was born. She made Spence's dinner and left it in the fridge. She took Lucy for a long, long walk beside the bay after driving by the bus stop yet again. Before her husband got home and despite Lucy's whining and barking, she set out alone wearing the backpack. The weeks of trash removal had worn a few new trails down the slope of the woods. She followed one that led her to the site where she'd hit the man with the boulder. She set up the tent where his had been. Had she been able to figure out a way not to drive Spence wild with worry and still be able to spend the night in the tent, she'd have done it. The best she could come up with was a note that said, "Your dinner is in the fridge. Don't worry. I'll be back first thing in the morning."

Before dark she zipped herself in and watched spiders crawl on the roof of the teal green three-person tent. She imagined that his name was Cole and hers Louisa. The Clevelands. They had a son in the army. Maybe in Afghanistan. Louisa used to work for a day care center. As she knew, Cole was a green building contractor who was just starting out in the field. Had just gotten a bank loan. On weekends they hiked all over Sonoma County with their dog. They had a speedboat and water-skied in August. They went to Mexico in February when they could afford it. Cabo San Lucas. A time-share.

Deer startled her out of her storytelling. What sounded like a dog sniffing nearby was probably a coyote. Raccoons pulled out one of the tent pegs, after the bugs, although maybe it was a skunk. The smell of barbecue made her mouth water and her stomach growl. She ate a granola bar and drank out of her titanium water bottle and knew this was nothing like what he went through. She realized she was acting out in a selfish and self-absorbed way and ultimately punishing Spence. Why would she do that? He was less than five years away from retirement. He'd worked hard for what they had. A paid-for town-house, a time-share in Tahoe and another on Kauai. And a son occupying Wall Street.

The beam of a flashlight fixed on the back of her tent. Her heart throbbed so loudly she couldn't hear footsteps. She hoped it was the man. Cole. She would apologize to him and she would find a way to help him get back on his feet. It was the least she could do.

Three Poems
John C. Mannone

Lilies & Morning Matins

Every sun-filled dawn
  I will steal its colors
    and celebrate until

my throat is crimsoned
  with joy. I will trumpet
    voluntarily your name

to the whole world
  and feel the valley
    fill with fresh light

Your green fields
  washing the sorrow.

Water, Earth, Air, Fire

Water gurgles as the river slurps over rocks,
boulders with hard calcite lines of its gray life
wedge between seams, and moss wanes green,
wet with rush of water's resolve, dissolving
its essence into the flow. And the air, elusive
with scent of rhododendron growing on banks,
washes all memories downstream with the fallen
leaves — mottled black gum and maple, poplar
and pine, the color of their souls. That sweet smell
of your hair. I taste your kiss. And its fire,
even after all these years, water cannot quench it.

John C. Mannone

On a Quiet Walkway

Off Laurel Mountain Road
Great Smoky Mountains

We stepped into a place without clocks.
Where the shadows of leaves and light
Pendulum'd across our faces in the breeze.
By a stream, rhododendron on the banks
Drank laughter. Time gurgled, washing
Over each boulder. I kissed you there
For the first time. Our hearts tossed
with the same laughter, metronomed
Tomorrow. Today only leaves quiver
Keeping time.

Naturally
Jessica Placinto

The cracks of sun
breath lively
The mid-day breeze
shines lightly.
The trickling streams
burn brightly
The natural fires
flow enticingly
Beauty is made in the harshest means.
Her devastations;
bittersweet.

Three Poems
Jeannine Pitas

The Brain Tree

To pray is to reach into darkness and eat it.
To let that bitter fruit be enough for us,
even though a sugar-feast lies within our reach.
"The centre of a poem is another poem,"
a one-celled organism, its world a droplet of water.
Beads of histrionic summer are sliding
down my skin. Water under the bridge, they say.
Is it a human universe, is there really a someone
who takes the time to make us from amoeba
to man, fashioning that cruelly fair process
we call evolution? Clouds, tracheae, trees – all break down
to smaller versions of themselves. We search beneath
the hair, the skull, daring to touch that fractal of neurons,
the trunk and crown we claim to be. The ones who ate
from the Tree of Knowledge didn't know
it was already growing inside them.
To pray is to reach into darkness and eat.
And even in these radiant days, some of us still crave it.

My Compass

I am going to lead you
not along the line of the alphabet
not from the watchtower of A
to the slippery maze of Z
not along golden rosary beads
or the petals of a child's daisy chain
not along a garland of molecules
that sequence of luminous rooms

I am going to lead you
not along the twisting,
crepe-paper river,
each of its rapids
a mouth saying "yes"

not toward self improvement
or joyous cries of "Eureka"
not through the dazzling stoplights
along the number line

No
I am going to lead you
along the path of the teardrop
as it falls into the dry wishing well

to an great field searing with violets
an open flame drawn
between them and the sun

I am going to lead you
deep inside the twisting Mappamundi
down the sinewy path that Dante once
walked, up the hill that hovers beneath

to the centre of the first
November snowflake
just before it touches and melts

Jeannine Pitas

Together we will fly
down the moths' eternal,
perfect path,
around and around
the great ellipse
until all lights
are the moon.

Idyll

I'd like to write an idyll.
Forget tragedies, elegies, solemn odes – I'd like
to write a bland, sentimental, un-ironic idyll

about crepes on Saturday mornings
embraces under soft white sheets
about late-night bus journeys
where the lake is transformed
into a woman's flowing blue scarf
and the flame of the steel plant
is still a hand reaching up toward the moon.

Please, no war this time
no cancer
no car accidents followed by lawsuits
or clandestine affairs leading to
ugly divorces
no abandoned children
no drugs
no pain

Let me write
a bland, insipid idyll
about a family that still goes to church
on Sundays
rides to the country for breakfast
and hikes alongside a swamp.

Let me write of a child who counts
the shiny backs of turtles
rescues them from dump trucks
who traps frogs, stares into their
enormous eyes, then lets them go.

Three Poems
Maija Rhee Devine 이매자

A Headless Plant—in Croatia

You couldn't have
Chosen this—
A gravel bed between
Train tracks—as your home
For life.
From where I stand
And from your scalped face
Blasted by cow catchers, bumpers
Pistons scissoring
From the underbellies of trains,
I couldn't tell what you were:
A thistle, daisy, milk weed?

What must have looked to you like a sky of steel
Lightning overhead samurai-sworded its way
Not once a day, not twice a day, but twelve times
Zyphering between Zagreb and Split
And that line's only a fraction of those that took their
turns
At your body.

You stood beheaded
  Yet, leaves,
   Stems
Bushy, avacado-hued
  Hauled up water
    Drank
     The
     Sun.

A breeze whooshed
You swayed your arms
in a waltz of
"Sweet, Sweet Life."

얼굴 없는 꽃나무―크로아티아에서
(A Headless Plant—in Croatia)

너는 이런 자리를
너의 보금자리로 택했을 리가 없다.
기차길 한가운데의 자갈밭이니
그럴수가.
기차 정거장에서 너를 바라보는
거리 때문인지
아니면 하루에 열두번씩도 더
크로아티아의 자그랩도시와
스플릿 항구까지
쏜살같이 달리는 열차들이
너의 몸에 칼질을해서
너의 머리는 짤려버린지 오래됐기 때문인지
네가 무슨 꽃나무인질 알수없구나.
잡초냐, 들국화냐?

　넌 얼굴도 없는데
　　아보카도색
　　　　잎과
줄기는 마냥 무성하구나.
　물을 빨아올리고
　　　햇빛을
　　　마시고

솔솔바람에
넌 팔을 일렁이며
"아! 삶은 맛있어"라는 월쯔에
춤을 추었지.

(Translated into Korean by Maija Rhee Devine)

Maija Rhee Devine 이매자

Search for a Home
- An American cinquain

Vine shoots

Bean-sprout frail

Three days to find host plant

Or die. I rip, pitch vine, save dill

Sage, rose.

집을 찾아서
(Search for a Home)

바인 뿌리
콩나물 같이 연하다
타고 올라갈 나무를 찾자! 삼일안에
못하면 죽는다. 그렇게 산 생명 뽑아 팽게친다.
장미를 살릴려고.

(Translated into Korean by Maija Rhee Devine)

A Clam's Home Sweet Home
- An American cinquain

A Paul-

Newman-eye moon

Snail saws hole in shell. Clam

Happy, alive. In ten minutes,

Slurp, slurp.

조개의 보금자리
(A Clam's Home Sweet Home)

배우 폴뉴만의
눈색갈의 달팽이가
조개의 껍질을 톱질. 뚫는다.
조개는 집안에서 행복하다. 안전하다. 십분후
후루룩, 달팽이에게 먹혔다.

(Translated into Korean by Maija Rhee Devine)

Yen Nguyen
2014 Writing for Peace young Writers Nonfiction Contest
Third Place

1000 Years

Ho Chi Minh City, Vietnam
Tran Dai Nghia, Grade 10

A fascinating historical look at the ancestors of the Vietnamese people, and how the members of the ancient Au Lac culture thwarted attempts at cultural obliteration to preserve their selves and their society. An important bit of history still, sadly, relevant today.

~Dinty W. Moore

1000 Years
Yen Nguyen

In 179BC, An Duong Vuong –the Lac Lord, lost his country to the hand of Trieu Da – the Han Lord at the time. Over a thousand years, one by one Chinese dynasty took over Au Lac. Chinese attempted to assimilate Au Lac people in spirit and in society which causes a great deal of changes in people's way of thinking and appearances. But still, Au Lac did not succumb. What did Au Lac peasants have to suffer over a thousand years? What did it take to protect Au Lac from being assimilated? All that will be discussed in this essay.

In attempt to assimilate Au Lac, Chinese kings had prepared a scrupulous plan in changing people's belief and way of living:

"They burnt poor citizens under the flames of hell and buried newborn in caves of terror
They deceived Heaven and duped our people, using all sorts of guiles"
-from "Binh Ngo Dai Cao" (proclamation of victory)
Nguyen Trai
translated by Ph.D Vu Dinh Dinh in Traslation and Annotation of
a fifteenth century Vietnamese document

First, they focused on religions and beliefs. Chinese built hundreds of temples and pagodas, making people to worship their God, following their religion –Taoism and Buddhism. They forced Au Lac people to study and to believe in Confucianism, which had a huge impact on Au

Lac culture afterwards. From time to time, Au Lac people had to study Chinese, dress like Chinese, act like Chinese. If not, beheading would be declared. They burned book written by Au Lac people, turning Au Lac into a dirty mud of foolish. Killing and hitting anyone who was trying to restore old traditions. Women were forced to marry Chinese, helplessly sold, traded from one man to another like a worthless good. Because of their violent act and cruel policy, no one dared to flare. The country was once peaceful and beautiful, was now nothing more than a rotten rat-hole.

Moreover, Chinese kings not only wanted to destroy Au Lac's minds and soul but their society and policy as well:

"They levied heavy taxes to impoverish the whole nation.
Miners were led into forested mountain to sieve sand and gold, risked being infected with debilitating diseases.
Divers were forced to dive deep to look for pearls amidst danger of attack by sharks and alligators"
-from "Binh Ngo Dai Cao" (proclamation of victory) Nguyen Trai
translated by Ph.D Vu Dinh Dinh in Traslation and Annotation of a fifteenth century Vietnamese document

They excised hundreds of unreasonable taxes: tax for salt, tax for iron, tax for tree, tax for house, tax for a person.... Many had to sell wives, children, babies for their sake. Mandarins and bloodsuckers wandered the streets to collect money. They exploited men to work for them. Husbands, fathers, brothers had to leave their wives, children, sisters for the sake of their lives, for a piece of food. Men were treated like dogs. Women being raped happened in broad daylight. Babies cried hungrily. Children were sold away to pay heavy taxes. No one dared to voice for fear of being killed. No one dared to fight against the emperor for fear of being punished by the Ruler of Heaven. As the result, thousands were killed. Poverty and hunger preyed on Au Lac's minds and body. The society was full of corruptions and social evils.

A thousand years came and went. Just to assimilate Au Lac, Chinese dynasties had exercised millions of cruel and wicked policies over its people. However, the strong will to protect the native cultures and traditions as well as the aspiration for a united fatherland had turned all the hard work of Chinese kings into a load of rubbish.

Ruthless and cunning as Chinese kings were, in the heart of Au Lac villagers, long-time traditions and native cultures were still preserved. Chinese culture did not make Au Lac people. It was Au Lac that turned the foreign culture into one of theirs. Traditions like blackening the teeth, chewing betel or folk festivals such as buffalo fights, kicking the shuttle cock, swinging, throwing... happened annually.

In family relationships, a beautifully formidable connection between elders and youngsters was formed in the old days. Confucianism along with a great deal of Chinese beliefs, one of which was Male chauvinism, did not change the way Au Lac men saw the mothers, the wives, the sisters in their family. Children respected elders. Parents were responsible for their children: girls and boys alike.

In language and writing, though a large number of books written by Au Lac intellectuals were burnt (some brought to China still remained unfound) and a whole of Han scripts were imported in Au Lac, Vietnam ancestors kept speaking their own language. Moreover, they even combined the two languages to enhance the abundance and diversity of their mother tongue. After generalizations, Demotic script was born as the result of all hard work.

How can they do that you may ask?

Admittedly, over a thousand years living among Chinese, changes in Au Lac culture was inevitable. Keeping a colonized culture from disappearing was difficult. Keeping and enhancing a native culture by combining it with a foreign culture was an even more difficult task. Under the crude rule of Chinese dynasties, Au Lac peasants had to suffer a great deal of pain and hardship. But "Even a worm will turn", hundreds of battles and rises of Au Lac peasants against the kings asking for justice and righteousness continuously happened during a thousand years. Au Lac villages- the home and the hearts of Au Lac people, the place where long-time traditions and native culture were preserved, was where all the rises started.

In the end, the Chinese colonists, crude and crafty as they were, set out to reform Au Lac culture along Chinese lines failed miserably. Au Lac peasants decided who they were, how they lived, where they belonged... and there was nothing Chinese kings could do to change it. Solidarity, patriots and strong will were what it took to fight against the evil side of society. Au Lac peasants -Vietnam ancestors did and had them so they received what they deserved: freedom, independence and the most importance: their own national character.

Bio~

I live in Ho Chi Minh City with my family: my mom, dad, and older brother. I like reading, writing and hanging out with my beloved ones. I love being able to escape into a world I create; a magical world where I can be anything I want to be.

It was my former tutor who brought inspiration to my writing. He taught me how to treasure my life, to make me look at people in a different way, and to believe in myself. He was a dear friend to me. Therefore, his sudden passing away when I was only fifteen, was a huge shock to me. Who would have thought that, while one day he was still a strong and healthy man, still talking and smiling to me, he would pass away the day after? It was then I realized what he really meant by telling me to treasure my life. It was then I realized everything that I thought I could have forever, could be so easily slipped from my hands. It was sad. But his death taught me a great deal.

Other than writing and reading, I also help my mom do housework and attempt to cook. I hope I can study abroad and make my parents proud.

2015 Progress Report~

2014 has been a year full of excitement and happiness. To me, the moment that I was silent with incredulity at the sight of my name on the award-winning essays of Writing for Peace Young Competition, was one of important milestones in my journey to become an international journalist. Writing For peace brings me a great deal of personal experiences and knowledge that at a certain extent dissolves my cultural preconception and at the same time boosts my self-confidence.

I've been quite busy this year with preparations for college but in my free time, I still practice to improve my writing skills. I am now a contributor for Creative Mélange, a special magazine for students across Asia. I hope that in the future, I get a chance to be a part of Writing for Peace, to be able to contribute to the future success of the magazine.

Three Poems
Kevin Patrick McCarthy

Eyeless

At twenty, with a friend,
I climbed a mountain near
a dominant volcanic spike
called Lizard Head

We kicked steps up dazzling
snowfields, smirking for
photos in azure clarity

"Which one's Lizard Head?"
we joked.

Then, having lost sunglasses,
being too callow and cavalier
to retreat, I was blinded

Ocular gravel savaged sleep,
fed desperate meditations
and self-pitiful groans

So I was Lizard Head - a
face-swaddled, ego-blasted
stoker of remorse

As my cheery partner led
me down and out, shambling
through talus cascades,

Glimpses were all I
could manage: boot in
rubble, hand on pack,
distances to fall

Having plunged already,
from cocky conqueror to
careening dolt - eyeless,
helpless in splendor

Reason to Believe

A free rat placed
next to a caged rat
will work tirelessly
without reward to
release the prisoner

When finally successful
the rats rejoice together

Some say it's just dumb
response – a fix for a
squeaky wheel

Dumb response is the
some saying – always
the selling short

The world beseeches

Free every captive

Kevin Patrick McCarthy

Colors to the Mast

What colors might I
strike, if pressed?

Not the maroons of the
Elk Mountains, crisper
and more varied with
each shattering fall

Quaking gold, nervously
knitting saturated hues,
is out of the question

Not white cornices
poised to peel from
mirrored ridges

Never the greens, from
forest to chartreuse of
scattershot lichen

Nor the lapis canopy
itself, breeding
flocks of promise

These set each other
aflame, till you can
taste the smoky Earth
responding

Surging from its
solar creation, we
merely incidental

Yet the primacy pulls
us out and up — each
warm prospect nailed
to twisting spine

Never pressed, but
integral, demanding
only grace

A Cleansing in Colorado
Dean K. Miller

There is a cleansing–
Some might say of evil
in this muddy wash that careened
down the canyon;
a torrent that scoured homes and cars
down a liquid roadway of death.
Unstoppable. Uncontrollable.
Unbecoming of nature herself.
But–

There is a cleansing–
of which we cannot understand.
The hand of God played against
the hand of man. A futile gesture
to believe "we" can contain the unthinkable.
Now not much is left.
But–

There is a cleansing–
in places once deemed safe.
We were wrong or maybe
ignorant; respectful yet cavalier.
"It couldn't happen again.
At least, not so soon." Scars once healed
torn open anew; painful and deep.
But–

Dean K. Miller

There is a cleansing—
As the sun finally parts
the clouds. Too much rain was days ago
yet still they cried their tears into the river
now swollen and brown. What must we endure
except that which we create in concert
or opposition? Only the earth truly understands and
seems not to care.
But—

There is a cleansing
of river and sky, of towns
and homes, of life and lives which
we may never comprehend—or
possibly don't want to. Grief,
despair, anger, and loss; possibly without
ever moving beyond.
But—

There is a cleansing—
in anguish through time
that never heals, like a child's tantrum
ignored, returned with vengeance on
anyone nearby. Now passed—
energy exhausted, but for it's thunderous,
rolling destruction. Landscapes
forever changed, the shadows of history demolished.
But—

There is a cleansing—
of which I hope to never
witness again.

Hangfire
Claudia Putnam

Fuck them, Liza says.

She means our children.

I'm plugging my phone into her charger when she slams on the brakes, skidding for a second before the studs catch. She flips off three blonde women in Lycra and Gore-Tex, pushing jogging strollers.

It's the crack of dawn in late winter and we're heading for the high country, and here we have to slow down at the crosswalk for these young moms. Fuck them too, I say.

Only in Boulder, Liza says.

It's not the jogging or the gear that's bugging us. We've got telemark skis on the rack, backpacks loaded with climbing skins and avalanche beacons. We'd look all right on the covers of the Athleta or the Title Nine catalogs.

I can't believe people are still having kids, says Liza. Isn't this fad over with?

I don't respond. I look back at the moms shepherding their little flock down the Wonderland Lake trail. It can be a little hard to stomach, the whole young mother scene in this town. Those poor women, I think. They really believe their perfect little lives and their perfect little kids are going to work out. And then I think: they probably will. Those women taking it all for granted, with their spiritual workshops, ballet classes, and organic vegetables. It probably will work out just fine for them.

I check the phone now that we're out of the North Boulder dead spot. We're halfway down Broadway by this time and we stop in at the Pekoe teahouse for mate lattes with rice milk and agave syrup, having passed by Starbucks because we disapprove of the way it ran a working-class joint out of business. We try to do what we can, but we're still swimming in the same pond. For example, we're in Liza's SUV. In this town there are so many Hum-

mers on the streets, you can convince yourself that a Jeep
Grand Cherokee is an economy vehicle.

In Pekoe there are more moms, more cute toddlers
in little fleece outfits. One three-year-old cries when her
mother says she can't have any whipped cream. If you
don't stop, you won't be able to have any soy hot choco-
late, either, the mom says calmly. That will be a natural
consequence.

Actually, it's a *logical* consequence, I want to tell her.
A *natural* consequence is when the kid stamps her feet so
hard the ceiling falls down on her head. And then you get
sued and have to take the money out of her college fund
so now she has to work at McDonald's for the rest of her
life. Also, despite what the books say, the girl is probably
too young for either a logical *or* a natural consequence. I
want to tell the mother she should just say no and take her
daughter out to the car. Liza grabs my arm and guides me
to the Jeep.

We drive south to Golden and head west on I-70.
Near Berthoud Pass we park and paste climbing skins to
our skis, saddling up for the long traipse to the Continen-
tal Divide. The only other people in the pullover are men.
They're the kind who still use leather boots and the old
long and skinny skis. If you ask them about their classic
style, they'll talk as though they're remaining true to a lost
ideal, like people who insist on sending letters through the
mail. But they probably just have crappy jobs. They size us
up, both us and our gear, nodding without saying hello.

I pause at the gap in the snowbank where the trail
begins. After the hurl and whirl of I-70, with its fumes
and bumper-to-bumper ski traffic, it's a relief to be here,
in the real mountains, in the silence of the jet stream. It's
not really a silence, but it feels like one, like when you're
swimming with a bathing cap on and all you can hear is
the water parting around your body. Then the wind rattles
my Gore-Tex, and I slide into the shelter of the pines.

Snowy woods. There's no smell like it, bark and clean
laundry and the tang of sap. The occasional skunky musk
of fox. God, I wish there were nothing more to my life
than this.

We stop after about ten minutes to pee in the well of a tree and to remove our top layers. I check my cell phone, but now there's no signal. I didn't really expect one. Liza pushes into the lead, the heels of her red plastic boots slapping against the lifters we use to take the pain out of the trail's steep angle. My lungs gulp, but at a comfortable rhythm. Sweat soothes the crease of my back. I've always loved the motion of cross-country skiing, its grace and symmetry. Every fifty yards or so I plunge my pole down deep, testing the give of the snow.

I'm still not fully back to myself since the surgery I had in late fall, right before the world blew up. It was just twenty minutes under anesthesia, a quick scrape of my womb to remove polyps and cauterize the lining so that I would cease to menstruate. So I would cease to bleed twenty-four days out of twenty-eight. I was in good shape before the surgery, though anemic, but anesthesia takes forever to clear out of my system. My sweat smells metallic. Liza's lead widens.

Having the site of my daughter's incarnation burned out seems apt for what Liza and I are going through, still shy of menopause, but our kids grown up enough sack our hearts. Two of Liza's three sons are heavily into drugs, and Gwen's a runaway.

Atop the ridge we go through our parking-lot routine in reverse. We put on our helmets and our wind shells. We shorten our poles, buckle our boots, snap down the lifters. Peel off the skins, tuck them into our packs, and double-check that our beacons are switched on and turned to the transmit setting in case we're buried. I look at my phone to see if there's a signal up here. Two bars; no messages. I have to turn it off so it won't interfere with my avalanche beacon. We peer over the snow cornice.

Poorman's not the steepest bowl in the world, just your basic expert run at most ski areas, though of course everything is a little different in the backcountry. It's also one of the most aesthetic descents in the central Rockies. I judge a work of art or architecture, such as the new Denver Art Museum, according to whether it makes me feel like this place does. If I get a bolt of energy shooting from my tailbone through the top of my skull. I've skied here probably a dozen times, including last year with Gwen and with Liza's son, Devi, back when our kids would still be seen with us. What a difference a year makes.

Should we dig a pit? Liza asks. And then shakes her head.

I don't think a test column would tell us much, I say. I sink my pole and fling the powder. It feels consistent. It's a perfect go, unless it's not, I say.

There were no avalanches on this morning's report. The danger seems relatively low, though even a lower-angle face like this one always has some risk. The indicators are good. The untracked powder below us is a few days old and has had a chance to settle. There hasn't been any dramatic change in temperature. The wind loading is minimal. And there are no signs of recent slides. I spend a few seconds centering myself, feeling the mountain under my skis, identifying myself to it, asking for permission and protection. It's a routine I have.

I did a few drugs myself in high school; there is no cleaner buzz than the one you get when you jump a curl of hardened snow and land in powder above your knees. The snow stretches and purrs beneath you, snicking against your Gore-Tex. It pours up over your shoulders, biting your chin. I wish Gwen were here with us, with this wind spitting into her face, this view glaring up at God. Sharing experiences like this is one of the reasons I had a kid.

These thoughts are fleeting. The mountain demands my attention and I am glad to give it. I had a yoga teacher who emphasized the *held* breath, the pause between exhalation and inhalation. The place where you discover there is no need for panic. Each turn is a leap into that place, each landing a relief of air. For the duration of the run, my heart is quiet, and even the whoops of the men, lined up along the ridge, don't disturb it. I continue turning past the first line of spruce, following the glades until they tighten around me and I am forced to stop. By then Liza herself is launched and I can't see her through the trees. I busy myself with sticking the skins back on, lengthening my poles, removing my shell. Then there is the business

of trudging back to the skin track we followed to the top
of the bowl. I have to break trail to get there, slogging
up through the glades I descended through so swiftly.
Now there is no sound around me, not even the buzz of a
chickadee.

I reach the packed trail just as Liza emerges from the
trees to my right. She was smarter and stopped sooner.
Her pony tail is coated in snow. At the sight of me, she
throws back her head and hollers. *Sweet!*

I beam back at her. Fuck the surgery, fuck the kids,
fuck the men in our lives or no longer in our lives. This is
sweet. When she catches up with me, I say, How many,
just how many forty-plus women would do that?

We gaze back up at the face bleeding into the chute
we've just skied. We *did* that, I crow. Someone should love
us just for that.

Bindings creak behind us and we turn to see two
young men coming up the trail. The leader leans on his
poles. That was sick, he says. He's grinning. Grabbed
those fresh tracks, did you?

Liza laughs. The sun flashes on her shades. There's
plenty to go around, she says. I don't know why it all sat
here for days, but there you go.

I pull off my helmet and clip it to the back of my
pack. I'm reshouldering the pack when the guy behind me
points up to the ridge. Check it out, he says. Go dudes!

Two of the men on skinny skis have leapt the cor-
nice, skiers' right from where I dropped off. Ancient gear
or no, they float down like synchronized swimmers caught
in a Warren Miller film, and a whoop bunches at the back
of my throat.

Then the whole face lets go.

Slab, says Liza. We're already working to our left,
pushing as hard as we can on our dragging skins, forcing
our hip flexors into the movement, heading for the skin
track. The dudes from the trail are leading, and I just fol-
low their heels, keeping my face turned toward the hill.
I've got the red jacket, I say.

I'm on yellow, Liza responds.

Red Jacket goes under. I mark the spot—it's straight

across from a rock outcropping about halfway down the face—and keep watching. He might surface yet. Yellow rides it out, his arms thrashing. It's a big slab release, which means the worst kind of avalanche. The fracture line stretches out across the center of the bowl, and everything below that crown has let go at once. Think: nearly two feet of settled snow, times about 1200 feet of vertical, and a fracture line maybe 300 feet wide.

We're hardly out of the way when it all floods by. We bend forward with our arms crossed in front of our faces, and still we choke and snort in the plume.

I'm on the yellow guy, Liza says.

Right behind you, says one of the dudes.

No, I got it, says Liza. Search field's too big. You all go look for the other guy.

Did you spot where the other one landed? he asks me.

I point up toward the face, now skinned of snow.

There are still two men peering down from the top of the ridge. They should have had their eye on their friend, and they should know as well as I do where he was last seen. I wave my poles to get their attention, and one of them flashes his pole back at me. I shout and point toward the cliff and they cut the cornice to traverse in that direction.

Are your beacons on receive? I ask the guys behind me.

Roger that, one says, holding it up so I can see the flashing light. He tells me his name is Pete. That's a lot of hangfire up there, he says. He means the snow above the crown line where the slab broke off, and the undisturbed snow on either side of the slide. Any of that could still release.

I pause. Well, I say. Those guys haven't set anything off up there so far. I'll assume we're good if you will.

Pete shrugs. We gesture to section the slope into thirds and then start up.

It's like pushing through a gluey nightmare. The air comes ragged into my lungs; my clothes can't begin to absorb my sweat. It's eight minutes when we pass treeline. Red Jacket's chance of survival is still as high as 95 percent. Assuming he didn't break his neck. I steal a glance over my shoulder. Liza already has Yellow laid out flat on the snow. It looks like she's using her skis to rig a sled. I throw myself at the slope. It's fifteen minutes when we reach the spot where I saw Red Jacket go under. Ninety-two percent now and plummeting. If we don't find him in the next twenty minutes, his chances will drop to 30 percent. I know this from the classes I've taken. Anyone out here ought to have taken them. My daughter took them when she was thirteen.

The other two men in the missing guy's party have traversed down to the base of the small cliff. I meet them there. They're putting on their skins. Their longer, thinner skis will be much harder to maneuver as we begin our search. One of them is pale and shaking.

You guys all know him? I ask.

They nod. It's my brother, the trembling one says.

Shit, I think. Okay, I say. What's his name?

I learn that the buried man is Scott, and his brother is Mike. I size Mike up. Luckily, the old-school purism of this crew doesn't extend to their transceivers, and they all have digital units that you don't need special training to use.

I don't bother asking if any of them has a cell phone. I hand mine to Mike. Climb back up, I instruct. You can get service from the ridge.

I check my watch. Eighteen minutes. The gesture spurs Mike, and he's humping it back the way they came down. I hope to God he doesn't drop my phone and lose it. I see that Liza has left Yellow Jacket wrapped up and has begun searching the lower edges of the debris field. It looks like a giant blender tried to make a cocktail out of ice and trees.

I hike about twenty feet above the cliff, listening to my beacon, just to make sure the roll didn't kick Scott back up the hill. Then I head straight down the middle of the slide zone. Yeah, there's a lot of hangfire still above me, but I decide to take the risk. We're up to twenty-two minutes now. If Scott's alive, it's because he's got an air pocket. It all depends on how long it takes for him to breathe it up.

Got a signal! Pete shouts. He's near the bottom right of the slide. We all head his way. I come in to his left,

picking up the beep too. Pete's moving in my direction. I
call over to the lost guy's friend Ted, but he has his eyes
glued to his transceiver and doesn't seem to hear me. I
shout again. He makes a slashing movement with his arm,
indicating that I should shut up. God damn it. I waste
another minute going after him.

Shhhh! he says when I get close. Shut the hell up,
will you? he says. I think I have a signal! It's around here
somewhere.

There is a faint beep, and the directional is pointing
toward Pete. I grab Ted's arm and jostle him so he has
to look at where Pete has his pack on the ground. For a
second I think Ted's going to punch me, but he pushes off
and skis down so that I actually arrive second. I've pulled
my pack off as I've skied, and flicked my probe out into a
straight long line. How strong is it? I ask when I get there.

Pete's friend says, These are new beacons, we're not
sure.

I drop the probe and check it against my own. I think
it's just a few feet that way, I say. Can you get your shovels
out? Then I lose another minute going back and forth.

Yeah, pinpoint., I say. Pete, grab that probe.

Pete thrusts the probe into the snow, yanks it back
out and inserts it a little more uphill. It's like sewing with
one of those long, sectional tent poles.

I think I have him, he says. Four feet down.

Kevin starts digging, starting about a yard
downslope, while Ted and I clear snow. We're all taking
turns, and it's pretty frantic. It's packed so hard, you have
to jam your shovel in, levering small bits up at a time.
But suddenly the snow beneath Pete's blade gives way. A
patch of red appears. Chest, he says.

We're careful now, scooping snow along the shoulder
line and away from the neck. We chip away at his face.

Unconscious, Pete says. He sticks his gloved fingers
into Scott's mouth. Clear, he says.

Ted and I work our way down the body, brushing
snow from his torso and legs. There's one ski still attached
and Ted pulls the leather boot from the binding.

I yank off my right glove and press a finger on his

carotid. His skin is as cold as the snow around it, but it moves, and I beam the way you do when you touch a baby or a puppy. Pulse!

Pete nods. He's breathing, he says.

Whew, I say. Because CPR never sticks in my head.

Scott's pelvis is twisted in a way I don't like. Though we have no way of assessing the condition of his spine, we pull him out of the hole. Has to be done. One side of Scott's face is raw and swollen; he couldn't open his eye if he were awake to do so.

Liza joins us. How's the other guy? I ask.

Two broken legs, in shock. I didn't think there was a head injury, so I offered him two Vicodin, but there's an open fracture and a lot of blood. We need to get him out. Can one of you come with me?

Kevin goes. The rest of us look down at Scott. We can't ask him where it hurts, so we can't know if his spinal column is intact. Meanwhile, after being buried for so long, Scott's at risk of hypothermia, and he obviously has a head injury, which we have no way of assessing or monitoring.

I glance up to the ridge. Mike is waving his ski poles at me. He points to his hand, which I guess holds my cell, and nods vigorously. Help is on the way.

I turn to Pete. Thoughts?

I got no answers, he says.

I look again at Scott's torso. I can't tell if we made things better or worse by straightening him out.

I don't think we should evacuate without a back board, I say.

Mike arrives. His face his red and swollen with tears he's holding back. I feel sorry that he couldn't let himself take those moments when he was alone to cry, since he definitely won't cry in front of us. He doesn't bend to touch his brother, just stands with his knit cap in his hands. I ask for my cell phone back.

Kevin has finished duct taping Yellow Jacket's legs. They've placed both their fleece sweaters around the leg that's bleeding and made a seat out of one of their packs, which they've lashed to Liza's skis. Yellow Jacket's sitting upright but shaking hard enough to vibrate the makeshift sled. I want to go and put my arms around him, hold him so he's warm and still.

I'll ski down with you, Ted says. Ted I'm glad to get rid of.

Liza and I turn back to Team Scott. If the rescue crew is coming from the resort, it shouldn't take more than a couple of hours for them to get here. We make a bed out of skis and packs. We want Scott up and off the snow, so we can wrap him in our extra clothing. With a person at each end and one in the middle, we log roll him to one side and then slip the padding underneath him.

I really don't like the way his lower spine is flopping around, I say. His legs look wrong to me. Not broken wrong, just *wrong* wrong. If we were thinking of getting him down the trail, we're not now, I say.

What if he dies while we're waiting? Mike asks.

I take his pulse. It's the same at it was before. I think his vitals are stable, I say. But the question sits between my shoulder blades. I feel as though all of us are carrying it, this big globe, we're a football huddle of Atlases around Scott.

I vote we wait for the team, says Liza.

Pete nods. Tough call.

Well, let's just get him wrapped up for now.

When he's bundled up, Liza and I both fall into a silence, looking at him. Unconscious like this, he seems childlike. I'm thinking of his mother, and I'm sure Liza is too.

Did you call anyone else while you were up there? I ask Mike. Does anyone in your family know what's going on?

He just looks at me.

I realize I'm shivering. We've been standing around too long, and my sweat has cooled. High-tech, wicking fabrics or not, wet is wet.

Mike starts pacing back and forth, looking from his brother to the trail below us. He could die, he could die, he keeps repeating. I want to hit him.

Then he turns to me. It's your fault, he says. You should have dug a pit.

I haven't let myself think about that yet.

You weakened the snow, Mike accuses.

It's true I was the first one down. People used to think each set of tracks stabilized the run, but now we know the opposite is usually the case.

Pete speaks up. Fuck off, buddy, he says. This lady just saved your brother's life. If you had a question about the conditions, you could have done your own tests.

And that's true, too. That's the wilderness ethic, especially the guy-wilderness ethic. Band together in an emergency, but make your own decisions. Sometimes you'll see five or six parties strung out along a ridge, each running through his or her little testing rituals.

The rescue team hails us from down the trail, saving me from crying or yelling, I'm not sure which. I'm impressed with how quickly they've climbed to our location. They've even brought Liza's skis back up from below, assuring us that the man she helped is safe in the ambulance. It's a relief to step back and let them take over, sliding the body board under Scott. Before we know it, half the EMT crew, Pete, and Mike have disappeared down the trail. The two remaining crew members introduce themselves to Liza and me as avalanche investigators, and we recount the story to them.

No pit? is the first question.

God damn it, says Liza. Let's go back up and dig one now. I won't be able to sleep.

As tired as we are, it doesn't seem to take half as long to climb the ridge as it did when we were trying to get to Scott. At the top, I turn on my cell, but the message indicator is still blank.

This is the first time I've been out of the range of a cell signal in the five weeks since Gwen didn't come back from a rave she snuck out of her father's house to attend. I get calls from her friends, kids I fed cookies to over the years, drove to soccer games and violin lessons. I'm a step or two behind her, places she's crashed. The kids who call tell me she looks okay. The awful thing is, I'm not sure what that means. How much is there not to know about your fifteen-year-old daughter? She dyes her blonde hair black. Or did. She's pissed as hell. I thought that was normal.

The wind has picked up. The investigators lose interest in digging a pit. They want to study the crown line before the wind fills it in. They take snow saws and show us how the layers don't shift when they load them onto shovels. We all poke our fingers into the different striations. There's one weak line down low, but it's not where the slab gave way. Where is she is she eating has she been raped does she know I'll come no matter what? The investigator shakes his head. I would have skied it, he says. He looks over the cornice. It doesn't even look slabby, he adds. Might as well live on the couch.

A chopper rises from the direction of the parking area. We watch as it tilts and heads southeast toward Denver. Liza presses her gloves in Namaste.

The investigators ask questions about who skied what where. Who went first. They shake their heads when we describe the men skiing simultaneously. Two much weight on the slope. It's not that steep, though, I say, defending them. It slid, the investigator points out. I feel unsatisfied that there isn't going to be a pit. It would take hours, one of the guys says. The slope will be here. We can come back tomorrow if we need more information. But all the info in the pit is right here in the fracture line anyway and look, we're losing the light.

Liza and I glance at each other. There's lower-angle stuff over there, I say, pointing skier's left. If we ski along the ridge, we can drop off through those trees, where it's less likely to slide.

We have to get down somehow, Liza says.

Never say die, one of the investigators says. You girls go on. We'll follow your tracks.

The light is failing when we get down into the trees, but my goggles brighten the snow and the spruce provide some contrast. The snow is even softer in the glades. The shakiness from the adrenaline leaves me. Even the exhaustion flees. I am glad we've taken this one last run, reclaimed our refuge before the return to our real lives.

The final turn whispers against my legs and I come out onto the trail, broad and hard-packed now. We make tight parallel arcs for the remaining distance, cutting to a stop at the snowbank edging the parking lot. It's nearly dusk; the only remaining vehicles are Liza's Jeep and a Toyota Tundra with a door magnet bearing the Colorado Avalanche Information Center logo. I'm kicking off my second ski when a shadow rises out of the Cherokee's wheelbase.

You scared the shit out of me, says Liza.

Nothing scares the shit out of you, says Pete.

That's so untrue, I think.

You waited for us? Liza says.

He shrugs. I wanted to make sure you got down okay.

Was Scott all right? I ask. What about the other guy?

Kevin will be fine, I think. Bad breaks, but they'll heal. Scott. Don't know.

Liza throws her boots into the back, one at a time, really throws them.

Pete looks at me. You made good calls. You were right not to let us take him down without the board.

We were a good team, I say. What a cluster if we'd had to deal with Mike and Ted alone.

Ditto. I'd a pushed that Ted dude right off that cliff.

Perfect crime, I say.

Pete asks about the snow layers and we tell him there was basically nothing to be learned from them. As we drive down the pass, the moon sharpens Bowie Peak. Liza glances at me. I think I still have that CD in this car, she says.

I dig around for it. Neither of us has known where to start with the iPod thing. When you have something like 3000 CDs, are you really supposed to burn each one and transfer them all? So, the years go by and it gets worse. Sorry, this isn't personal, I say to Pete in the back seat, sliding Marilyn Manson into Liza's stereo.

When I was pregnant with Gwen, I played tape after tape of classical music for her. She loved Beethoven and Aaron Copland all the way through middle school, though parallel interests developed. I listened to what she did. We'd have Ministry growling their incomprehensible but probably disgusting lyrics as we drove back from Steamboat, with the Never Summer mountains gleaming on the far side of the valley. Last year, coming down from Poorman's, she'd wanted us to play Marilyn Manson.

Oh, baby, I think. How could you believe I didn't want to understand you?

Now Liza and I play this CD in her honor, hoping somehow she'll hear us, that Marilyn Manson of all people will carry our love to her.

What was that about? Pete asks.

A ritual, Liza says. We've got teenagers. We wish they were here, but they're blowing us off.

Jesus Christ. Imagine having chicks like you as moms, getting to ski this shit on the weekends instead of play video games.

Exactly, Liza says.

I keep my head pointed forward.

We hit the interstate and I check my cell for messages. Nothing. I dial Gwen's phone. The police say it's still active, but who knows who's using it. I leave a message. Hey, I say. It's me. Haven't stopped thinking of you. Liza and I skied Poorman's today and wished you were with us. There was an avalanche, and we could have used your help getting the guys out. I hope you'll be home soon, just wanted you to know.

I flip the phone closed. God. Were those all the wrong things to say?

I'd be happy to ski with either of you dudes again, Pete says.

I almost say, Word. But I can't quite bring myself to. Also, I'm not sure the exact tone you're supposed to use for saying it.

Liza grunts. I assume it's in assent.

Don't your husbands ski?

Mine does with his new wife, I mutter.

Liza's husband used to ski, but now he's home watching TV for some reason. We've analyzed it to death; we suppose it's some avoidance tactic we have no respect for. He's certainly no help with the boys. Liza would buy him a red car and stock it with a co-ed if he would drive off into the sunset and leave her with the rest of their assets.

We drop Pete off at the Park'n'Ride in Morrison. He

wasn't *hitting* on us, was he? Liza says after about a mile. That question about the husbands?

I shrug. How would we even know? I ask. We're so far out of the loop. We wouldn't even recognize it if someone our own age acted interested.

Liza sighs. Did you smell him? she says. I could get accused of adultery just for having him in the car.

I laugh. It feels good to laugh a little, even if the attention we get is from an audience that's irrelevant to us.

We still have another thirty minutes to drive, along what we call the Ho Chi Minh Highway, a horribly banked two-lane with nasty winds out of the west.

Should we have dug that pit? I say. Before we skied?

The Jeep swerves as a gust catches it. Sure, says Liza. Just like you should have used your super-mother ESP to call Gwen that night, timing it just before she snuck out of her father's house. Even though she probably wouldn't have answered her phone. Even better, you never should have divorced that creep Des. Maybe she'd hate you just as much, but for different reasons.

I'm three or five breaths back. It's not that I haven't thought of everything in those sentences, but does Liza believe Gwen hates me? How quickly you lose the yogic certainty of the telemark turn. It wears off like heroin.

But you stopped at the top, I say, and no matter how good the conditions were, something made you ask about the pit. I'm wondering if Liza sensed the avalanche somehow. The night before Gwen ran away, I was up half the night, crying and writing in my journal, I was so worried for her. I knew her father wasn't paying attention, but there wasn't anything you could say to the courts about mother's intuition.

Just stop, Liza says. Stop with all the doubts. I'm sick of this shit.

You're right, I finally say. It's dark, but I can still see Liza's profile, her dark ponytail gone loose in the back and mashed down over her forehead from the helmet. The way she always holds her head so that her nose is tilted up, as if she's afraid to look at the ground. I realize I've been so wrapped up in my own disaster, it's been a long time since we've talked about her sons. Her loneliness is so frightening I wonder how I could have forgotten it.

Liza swings the Jeep around onto 14th Street, heading for where it crosses Pearl, a pedestrian mall at the heart of downtown Boulder. It's freezing outside, but the Goth, punk, and neo-hippie kids will be clustered in front of the courthouse, wearing nothing warm enough. I used to feel amused that the dropouts and rebels would hang in such an obvious place. You suck, they seem to say, don't take your eyes off us.

The gang sees us coming and most of the kids look away. They know who we are. I can tell right away Gwen's not there, and I don't see any of the people she used to hang around with, either. Except Liza's youngest son, Devi. Who probably heard the Jeep with whatever sixth sense teens have. He's already slouching off, half a block away. He reminds me of Squidward, Sponge-Bob's melancholic sidekick, his baseball cap on backwards, his huge torn sneakers flopping through the slush. Hard to imagine this kid joyfully leaping cornices, but only a year ago it was so.

He's probably as nauseated by the waves of nostalgia emanating from me as I am by the ennui coming from him. Yes, I'm beaming after him: remember how, when you were a preschooler, you would sleep over, and you always wanted hear that story I used to make up for Gwen? It wasn't really a story. Just this little mouse who crept into a summer cabin as the first snows were starting to fall. He found water dripping from a faucet. He found a smear of peanut butter in a cabinet. He found newspaper, which he used to make a nest near (but not too near) the pilot light in the stove. The list of mouse activities would get as long as it took to knock those kids out. A small creature making its way in the world, finding everything it needed.

Let him go, Liza says. We've smoked him out. Maybe he'll go home.

We don't want to go home ourselves. Hers will have that awful TV. Mine will be dark and cold. We too miss the shelter we were once able to create. We slip into a coffee shop where someone Liza knows is supposed to be playing. We should be too tired for this, but we're us. Able to work all week, cook up risotto and salmon, ski off cliffs, rescue men in distress, and like so many superheroes, fail spectacularly at family life.

There's not much to eat at the coffeehouse, just some slices of quiche and a few cookies, but we eat what we can find, slurping hot chocolate and watching people enjoy the music. The singer, a petite woman with long black hair, is performing wry songs about SUVs and high-end coffee-makers that she can't figure out how to work. The whisper deep in my head has built to a roar. Is she warm is she hungry is she murdered what can I do where I can I look who else can I ask. I see my chiropractor across the room, but I don't meet his eyes. He was against my decision to have my womb cauterized. He believes menstruation is cleansing and women are lucky to bleed. He says I'm denying the reality of my body to fit the male world.

In this room there are other people I know, women and couples I wave to across the noise. Maybe they had children in Gwen's Waldorf class or her Suzuki violin group, or maybe way, way back we were all in prenatal yoga together. Janet Hillman barges over, beaming. Have you found her?

No, I say, and her glance slides over my ski clothes. I hunch a little, feeling judged. Hell, I'm judging myself.

My phone rings. I yank it from my pocket, nearly dropping it. Liza spins toward me. It's not a number I recognize.

Hello? Hello?

It's only Pete with an update on Scott. Nothing new. Still unconscious, the injury to the spinal cord is quite serious, but the priority is the swelling on the brain. Pete's voice is hoarse and I can tell the emotion of the day has had time to settle.

The noise in my ears drains down through my throat and into my belly and pelvis. It feels like one of those blocks of ice in the debris field, except not cold. Heavy and angular, irregular. I want to leave, but where is there to go?

Thank you for calling me, I say. I'm disoriented by

the echoes of my own voice on the cell. I sound like myself in high school.

I wish I had better news, Pete says.

I know, I say, picturing Scott's red jacket emerging from the snow. I wish we could know for sure we saved him.

I pause.

You would have skied that face anyway, he says.

I think so, too, I say. I've skied it lots of times.

Seriously, Fay. They made the same call you did.

Thank you for phoning me, I say. I give Liza the news about Scott.

She reaches across the table and squeezes my hand. It was hangfire, that's all, she says. It's always hangfire, all the time, people just never think of it till they see an actual crown line.

The indicators should have been more clear, I say.

She says, I'll drop you at your car. I have to go home.

I stand up with her. I've realized I won't be able to go home. I'll get coffee and drive to Denver, cruise the mall down there, check the bus station. At 5 AM or so the clubs will let out and I'll search the debris, walking among the kids in their lingerie and fairy wings.

As we leave, the singer finishes a song. She's been going on about having supported her rock-star-wannabe husband for twenty years, waiting for him to make good on a promise that she'd be a mother someday. She looks as old as we are; it's probably too late for that dream. She's actually a little choked up with the emotion of her song.

Liza shakes her head at the singer. Fuck her, I say.

For planting her hopes on a guy. For thinking having kids was a good idea in the first place. For dithering on the edge of the cornice, and missing everything.

Hangfire previously appeared in Confrontation Magazine, in a slightly different form.

Moments of a Journey
Dean K. Miller

I've journeyed through life, noticing and forgetting, teaching and learning, breathing in and out. I am not lost; so, I cannot be found. A chapter in a just-finished book is titled "Chambered Nautilus." Two days after reading that chapter, I drove past a tree stump carved into an ocean scene, the curved and segmented form of a large, chambered nautilus shell most prominent street side. For me, tranquility always involves water, and often my thoughts return to the ocean.

Tonight's heavy rain will soon change into snow. Already I miss its random beat on my bedroom window. Soon the river will flow wildly, as snowmelt and spring run-off churn through the Big Thompson Canyon. Until the river calms, Leaky Boat Lake is my fishing haven and I return to catching largemouth bass. When I am alone on that small lake, the water seeping through a pin-hole in the boat's bow, I am taken back to when I fished with my youngest daughter in that same leaky boat. She held each fish she caught by its lower lip while I captured the memory on camera. Releasing the fish, she'd laugh when it would flip its tail, splashing cold water on her face. Further back in my memory, I sit with my brother and his son in their boat on a river in Washington.

I watch the interaction of father and son, noticing only subtle differences compared to mine with my three daughters. Our parents taught us well. Still deeper in my memory, I am racing upriver with my father as he deftly guides the wooden craft around logs and gravel bars. We stop to fish, and more often than not, find success. He is a master at the art of fishing and I wonder if I'll ever possess that much knowledge about anything. Beyond that recollection a younger me, wading with my brothers while we fished the small, icy cold rivers fed by the snow fields of Mt. Hood in Oregon. We knew a freedom without bounds—a freedom like one that allows a rock to skip endlessly across a pond.

This evening's moisture began its journey in the Gulf of Mexico. It gave birth to the clouds over the mountains and now cleanses the air, the land, and my thoughts. Should not the rain have the taste of salt, since it was brought from the sea? In the sea and along its shores, I have journeyed far: Hawaii, Oregon, California, Mexico, Florida, New Jersey, Canada, Washington, St. Thomas, St. Lucia. The water was always salty, sometimes calm, sometimes violent, yet always calling to my soul. Riding its waves I have experienced joy as unbinding as is possible, and faced my fears over and over again. Now the river and a small pond hold my humanity in loving care. Their waters will someday reach the sea; in their journey, they will transport a piece of me.

I am alive, and so my passage on this planet is not complete. My wistful memories typed out on keyboard and computer brings "back to now" the moments gone before. They are happening with each step I take.

In an email a friend asked of my memories after sharing one of his own. This is what I'll send to him: "I am lying in the sun amidst a field of green and gold, dreaming of the ocean, knowing I am home . . . and I am smiling."

Rawlins
William Haywood Henderson

Dad shook me awake. "We're here," he said. The van
doors were open, the air bitter cold. Spring break. March
1985. He took my wrist, tugged me hard, and I slid out
of the van, caught my balance against him. He pulled me
across the icy ground. It was a long, low motel, sandstone
walls lit with bright white neon. The pool was a rectangle
of battered ice—no steaming blue.

In the morning, Dad had left before we woke up.
He was filling in at a pharmacy for the week. He'd driven
us—Mom, my brother, and me—west from Indianapolis to
Rawlins, Wyoming. He said we could reconnect with Wyo-
ming. We'd left Laramie years earlier when he finished
pharmacy school, and we'd kept on moving, state after
state. That year, the fifth grade, I was on my third school
so far.

I sat at the window with my bowl of cereal, waited
for the icy fog to lift. The van was gone. I heard trucks
pass on the highway, trains pull through town.

"What are we going to do?" I said.

My mother looked at me from her perch against
the headboard. "You have homework, don't you?"

I was supposed to read a biography of Agatha
Christie. Sure, maybe it would take me most of the week,
and there was cable TV. "What's Donnie going to do?" He
was trying to diaper his stuffed bear with a washcloth.

Mom dropped her magazine, tugged at her hair,
looked past me into the white vapor. "Donnie doesn't care
like you do. Not yet. So don't make him unhappy."

I read about Agatha, but I couldn't keep the facts
straight, and I didn't have paper and pencil. I took such
a long shower that the hot water drained to cold. Then I
stood in front of the radiant heater until my skin felt tight
enough to split. Donnie was playing in a pillow fort. Mom
was working a crossword.

I bundled up and went outside. Mom's voice cut off with the click of the door. She didn't follow. The sky was light blue now, the wind tearing at the surface of Rawlins. Dry hills. White gullies. Old stone buildings. A few people working behind glass.

Dad wasn't at the drug store. "Try the hospital," the pharmacist said. "West end of town."

I waited in the drug store for my feet to thaw, turned the rack of comic books, leafed through a few, started a pile on the counter. Aquaman and all that green water. I bought the comics, carried them west, found the tiny hospital. Our van wasn't in the parking lot. Dad wasn't inside.

"Your father isn't working here," the receptionist said. "Check the drug store."

"I did."

"You sure your daddy's working in Rawlins?"

Maybe I had misunderstood. I walked back into town, straight through the hard wind. It felt like my eyes were going to freeze shut. In the motel room it was just Mom and Donnie. Mom was making sandwiches. I placed my stack of comics on the table.

"You aren't reading those," Mom said. "You have school work."

"Where's Dad?" I said.

"Can we go see Dad?" Donnie said.

"He's at work, boys."

"Where's he working?"

"I don't know."

"He's not at the drug store or hospital."

"Well, I'm sure he knows where he is."

She served lunch, and we sat at the foot of the bed, watched a cartoon about battling magpies. Donnie couldn't stop laughing, his voice went higher and higher in the small room, and finally I said, "Shut up," and Mom said, "That's enough from both of you," and she turned off the television and closed the drapes. We sat in the dark for a long time. Night came. She turned on the lights and made sandwiches. We ate without the television this time.

"Where's Dad?" I said.

"Do your school work." She dragged the phone into the bathroom, made phone calls, didn't tell me who she'd talked to. She turned on the television, got Donnie cozy beside her on the bed.

I bundled up again, went outside, and she didn't say anything. It was a lot colder. The wind sucked my breath away. My father didn't appear, day after day. I didn't do my school work. I didn't read my comics. Mom kept us in sandwiches and cereal. I don't know what she was waiting for.

I learned Rawlins, Wyoming, that week. It was a small grid of streets. I might've walked a hundred miles. You could ask me now about the order of the intersections, the fringe where the sagebrush took over, the hills and creek and highway and railroad that corralled the houses, what windows were lit after dark, and I'd still know it all. I still walk Rawlins sometimes when I'm thinking of something else, and I come around a corner or down a hill, back to the motel, where Mom is washing dishes in the sink and Donnie is flipping through my comics. Sometimes Mom will say, "Let's warm you up," and she'll run a hot bath, put out my pajamas.

The sixth night it was foggy again. I came back to the motel. The neon made a white dome that didn't reach far. The van was parked at the curb. Dad was sitting on the frozen surface of the pool. I tested the ice, then sat beside him. He breathed steam down into his collar, held the sides of his head with his bare hands. He was shaking.

"I was wrong," he said. "There wasn't anything in Rawlins."

"Where were you?"

"I got it wrong," he said. "No job. What was I going to do? I went south. I went to L.A. Now I'm back. It's okay. We'll go home."

I sat with him until Mom found us. Beyond the fog, trains and trucks were passing. We were on the road within the hour.

Previously published in *Fast Forward*, Volume 2, edited by K. Scott Forman, Kona Morris, Nancy Stohlman, 2009

Stealing Flowers
Vicki Lindner

I note the real estate sign in front of the green Victorian.
Night wanders through on its path to the mountains,
hiding my trespass through the wrought iron gate. Yet I
watch my back as I strip the rosebush, spraying pink pet-
als like fireworks.

Pink roses are easier to rip off than thorny suede-
textured reds. Obstinate lilacs, too, grip their bush,
making me twist their skinny tough wrists. Sometimes I
hide kitchen shears in my purse, better for severing their
amethyst cones.

Prudently I wait until night, or the April storm
that banged down a screen of icy drops. In a late spring
freeze, I thought, I'd preserve the brief drama of ephem-
eral plumes with my Great Lilac Heist. Passersby ducked
their heads into wind-slanted streams. No one saw me
yank and clip a heavy feather of white florets, its radiance
wasted on a parking lot. I forgot my sopping wet shoes: a
strange cry of joy, a rampaging Visigoth's guttural howl,
rose in my throat.

I got the idea from Lalla, Michael Ondaatje's grand-
mother, who also stole flowers and died in a flood. When
Ondaatje returned to Colombo to collect material for a
family memoir, he learned that Lalla compulsively robbed
blooms from churches and parks; she even picked bou-
quets for dinner parties in her hostess's flower beds. In
the owner's presence, Ondaatje wrote, Lalla would pull a
prize rose up by the roots and after gazing at it for a plea-
surable moment, "swallowing its qualities whole," handed
it over. She ravaged the best gardens and was banned
from the parks. Like Lalla I wanted to get locked outside

picket fences, purloin the object of a ravenous gaze.

In real life I remained a dutiful university professor, who taught Ondaatje's lyrical book, *Running in the Family*, to her autobiographical writing classes. Yet in that high cold university town I first helped myself to neighbors' daffodils, gilding their leftover skin of snow. I snatched chilly tulips and mosque-shaped globes of ocher Iris, too.

Now living in a city that I hope to love I maintain some scruples: I don't cross occupied property lines or steal flowers proudly cultivated for impressive variety. Unlike Lalla, I'd never pluck a Black Baccara in the Botanical Gardens. In well-tended beds I only take time to sniff the roses—how I learned that award-winning beauties don't smell like raspberries and licorice as the catalogues said. The white ones are as odorless as sterilized cotton. Fiery orange and magenta divas are likely to evoke stale thyme, or Chanel No. 5 in a bottle unopened since 1925. But the rampant pink clusters, my favorite marks, spill into alleyways, perfumed like the bathwater of silent film stars.

Although my mother smuggled European seeds into the country in order to plant them, she would have thought ravaging another's garden for fun was akin to eating the apple in Eden. She earned beauty with labor, crouching in dirt, collecting fungus beneath her nails. She crow-barred gray stones, split by fire, into ledges that cradled waxy day lilies. She could coax rare yellow primroses from the Jersey soil. Her opaque Iris, like those I would steal, survived hungry deer beneath wire netting. Only after weeding, fertilizing, protecting, and pruning did she let herself reap the blooms, secure their magnificence in crystal vases with metal-pronged frogs.

When Mom emerged from the fatal coma I tried to bring her back to herself by placing an African Violet on her chest. Her thickened fingers, guided by a vestigial nurturing instinct, like hair that keeps growing after death, mechanically trimmed away a crisp brown leaf; but instead of the velvety magenta flower, her dimming eyes saw her father and brother, both long dead. I then understood the persistent power of her creative energy, my inheritance.

After she died I regretted my grumpy forbearance when she dragged me through her flower beds, calling her horticultural triumphs by their Latin names. "One day you won't have a mother," she'd sigh, kneeling before quilts of russet chrysanthemums. For years I associated gardening with the push and pull of our disparate ways. I forbade hopeful suitors to bring me bouquets.

Now witness the compromise inherent in personal change: captured wet lilacs, dripping on their reflection in the table's grey glass. And behold these tattered pink roses, saved from darkness, triumphantly jammed in a black deco vase!

Dock
Paula Dawn Lietz

On Letting Oneself be Taken Care of
Adrienne Pine

As the eldest in a large family, I grew up taking care of others. Watching my younger siblings, I learned to develop a sixth sense; I reserved a part of my attention to wander on that periphery where something might flare up among any one of them, at any time.

This ability turned out to be useful during the decade in my young adulthood when I was a teacher. All children share a yearning and striving after something too unformed and unknown to put into words. A great teacher is someone who takes a student's poor question and, without any embarrassment to the student, transforms it into a profound inquiry with reverberant answers that ripple through the consciousness of the class like circles of water spreading outward in a pond. I wasn't a great teacher, but on my better days, I was a good teacher who got my students excited about learning and served as their guide.

All of my life, I have identified with being competent, dependable, responsible. My parents were strict with me and punished me for infractions. I absorbed their lessons and was hard on myself. I didn't allow myself to make mistakes, and when I made them, I suffered agonies. Self-torture was the price I paid for error. I missed opportunities where others might have helped me, because I wouldn't let them.

There were times when I wanted help, and I didn't get it. For a long time I was frustrated and unhappy. It took a paid professional—my therapist—to tell me that I didn't get the help I wanted because I never appeared as though I needed it. His observation stunned me. I thought others could tell when I felt needy and vulnerable. Apparently not. I had learned to conceal my feelings. I thought neediness ugly and repellent, and I was afraid of being vulnerable. Being vulnerable meant letting my defenses down, leaving myself open for attack.

It's often said that to be loved, one must be a lovable person, someone who knows how to love. It's the same with receiving help. To an extent, it's knowing how to ask. That was hard for me, because I always thought I had to be in charge. From my parents I had learned that any help they gave was in exchange for something else; they expected a return, often one I wasn't willing to give. The help they gave wasn't really help at all; it was barter.

I knew that not everyone was like them, but my fear of this transaction infected my interactions with others. When I needed help, I couldn't bring myself to ask for it until I was desperate, and when I did, it was with the expectation that the price would be too great, or else I would be turned down. The cycle fed on itself: my defeatist attitude ensured that I would be defeated.

And sometimes I was guilty of the same behavior that I deplored in my parents. I asked for help as if I were extracting a promise, and when I met with resentment in return, I had only myself to blame. That was another of my misperceptions.

In time I have come to see that the best help of all is that which arrives like a gift when we are in need, without our having asked for it. I think it is more available than we realize, but we are not always able to know it for what it is and benefit from it. It might come from a humbler source than we care to acknowledge. Or it might seem so obvious as to invite dismissal. It might not be what we had thought we needed at all, and yet it turns out to be exactly right.

How can we recognize this help when it is offered, and how can we profit from it? I think it comes from cultivating an outer alertness and inner attention that clarifies our perceptions and sharpens our sensibilities. In order to receive help, we must be prepared to accept it and learn from it.

One day at the height of summer when I was sixty

years old, I was in distress, and my mind was poisoned by evil thoughts. I was still in shock from having been laid off three weeks previously after seventeen-and-a-half years at the same job. After so long and successful a tenure, I thought I had proved myself valuable, if not indispensable. It is true that I was valuable to many people. But not to the people who made the decisions. At least not valuable enough.

And so one Friday morning at the end of June, I came into work, and no sooner had I gotten myself settled at my desk, turned on my computer, checked my email and listened to my messages than I got a call from the Executive Director to come to his office. As I knocked on his closed door, I gave his Administrative Secretary a quizzical look, and she averted her glance. And so I walked into the trap that had been prepared for me.

I have written about that experience elsewhere ("Selected for Separation"). Afterwards, people commiserated, "When one door closes, another opens." I believed this to be true, but I also knew that I hadn't quite closed that door, even if it had been closed on me.

That day in mid-July, the loss of my job was a constant source of distress in the background of my thoughts, but there was something more immediate that was causing me misery. The previous weekend all the contents of my parents' house—all that my sisters and I had not taken, and that was most of it—were sold at an estate sale that had been arranged by my two sisters, Mimi and Stacey, who were the executors under the terms of my father's will. The sale took place in our parents' house in Alabama, and none of us were there. However, on the second day of the sale, I received a text message from a distant relative by marriage, who had gone to the sale with her husband Gordon:

> "Just left the estate sale. While we were there, a guest found 3 envelopes of cash money. He returned it to Ron May. Gordon overheard Ron tell him that this has been happening all day....Thinks he said 2500$ and a box of silver dollars. This was

not including what Gordon saw the man returning, I'm guessing. Just fyi. We thought you should know. (Sale ends in 15 mins.) Love you, Hayley."

I called Hayley, and she turned the phone over to Gordon, who told me his story. He saw a man with a box of household items in one hand and three envelopes in the other come up to Ron May, whom my sisters had hired to run the sale. Gordon noticed the man because his attitude was secretive and excited. "He said to Ron, 'Look, I want to show you something,' and he pulled out the envelopes, and there was a wad of cash," Gordon reported to me. "It was all very hush-hush. I pretended to look around so they wouldn't notice me staring at them, but I was eavesdropping." Then he repeated what Hayley had texted: "Ron said that this had been happening all day, and he mentioned 2500$ and something about a box of silver dollars. The man asked, 'What can you do for me?' and Gordon peeled off a fifty and gave it to him, 'That's your finder's fee,' he said, 'and you can have what's in that box you're holding for free.'"

I asked Gordon what the man's name was, but he hadn't caught it. He repeated what he had said, as if for emphasis, and then handed the phone to his wife. She said to me, "I think you ought to let Ron May know what you know. Because my guess is, he won't tell you."

"No?"

"No. He looks like a slick operator to me, and Gordon thinks so, too."

I thanked her and hung up, pondering what they had said. Was it like my father to keep so much cash in the house? When my father died, he was 89 years old, with advanced Parkinson's disease. He couldn't drive any more, and he might have wanted to keep cash in the house in case of an emergency. His disease had affected his mind and his judgment, as well as his body. I thought it entirely possible that he might have stashed cash in envelopes in different places and then forgotten about them. Perhaps in that way he had accumulated $2,500. As for the silver dollars, I remembered him showing me some that he had when I was a child. I had owned silver dollars, too, given to me by my grandparents as gifts, that I kept in a sterling silver piggy bank that was one of my baby presents. I didn't know what had happened to Dad's silver dollars, nor did I know what had happened to mine. When I had gone off to college, I had left the silver piggy bank on a shelf in my closet, and one day when I was home on vacation, I noticed that it was missing. I had my suspicions, but I never learned what had happened to it or its contents.

As for my father, he was nothing if not tenacious, and he had not gone off and left his silver dollars unattended, as I had. I thought it entirely possible that he had them hidden away in a box somewhere, and that my sisters and I had overlooked them, as well as his paper money. We had had very little time to go through the house in preparation for the sale, and there had been a lot to go through.

I had never met Ron May or spoken to him, but I took his contact information off his website and called him. An answering machine picked up, and I left a message, identifying myself. I suspected he would not call me back. Then I called my sister Mimi and told her what Hayley and Gordon had said. She expressed skepticism. She reminded me that Ron May was recommended by our father's attorney. I replied that I did not know what to believe, but I didn't see what motive the Moores would have for fabricating their story. "I think you should contact Ron May," I told her. "You and Stacey are the ones who hired him, and he has the relationship with you. I also think you should hear what Gordon has to say."

A little while later, Mimi called me back. She said she had spoken to Ron May. He told her that there was $500 in the three envelopes the man had brought him. When Mimi told him what Gordon had said, he insisted that he had been talking about other estate sales. He claimed he had said, "This happens all the time," instead of "This has been happening all day." Mimi also reported, "He did admit to giving a finder's fee of $50 to the man, as well as all the stuff he was carrying for free. He takes a 25 percent cut, and he says he's entitled to 25 percent of the cash that was found. I don't really agree," Mimi admitted, "but I don't see what we can do about it."

It wasn't truly necessary for me to inform Stacey as well as Mimi. I could count on Mimi to tell Stacey about my phone call. Yet I wanted to speak to Stacey. The Moores' story had disturbed me. I didn't want to believe what they said, but I felt I had to take them seriously. I was better acquainted with them than my sisters were, because I had entertained them the previous autumn during their trip to New York. I knew them to be honest, well-meaning people who had been deeply attached to our father.

I was surprised by how unsettled I felt during the weekend of the estate sale. Even before Hayley texted me, I had continually thought of it taking place far away in Alabama. I had not expected to react this way. Along with my sisters, I had selected what was important to me of our parents' belongings. There was a lot left, including all of the furniture, because it wasn't valuable enough to justify the shipping expenses to our distant homes. None of us had claimed our mother's wedding china or our grandmother's. We already had our own sets of dishes and no space for extra storage. My father had not touched any of my mother's clothes after she died, and so there were all of her clothes and my father's, too, which did not fit us or our husbands. None of it I cared deeply about, but still I was surprised by how upset I was at the thought of our parents' lives being dismantled in this way. Except for the more valuable items, I had wanted to donate our parents' clothes, housewares, and furniture to a local charity— Community Furniture Bank, Home for the Homeless, or Goodwill Industries. I had researched these possibilities and sent my sisters emails about them. They ignored me. They were determined to sell everything they could, and what was left over after the estate sale, they had decided to place on consignment.

I felt bad at the thought that Ron May might be stealing from our family. Superstitiously I wondered if it were bad karma for having sold what would have been better to have given away. I kept this thought to myself, knowing that everyone but I would think it preposterous. However, I still wanted to speak to Stacey, but she didn't return my call.

Instead, she sent a group email:

"The sale was a success. Ron estimates that 1,100 people came through over the weekend. Almost all items were sold. The sale brought in $10,348.50. Ron's commission is $2,587. He'll be sending us a check made out to the estate for $7,761. He does not provide an itemized accounting, but will include a letter summarizing the sale along with the check. Mimi will scan the letter and post on our Google drive. Ron is taking care of removing the items that are left and cleaning the house.

Thanks,
Stacey"

I emailed her back, "Hi Stacey, there is something I need to talk to you about. I left you a message yesterday. I'll call you tonight."

When I called again, I got sent straight to her voice mail. The next day I received an email from her: "Hi Adrienne. Mimi and I talked and she filled me in. She has followed up with Ron."

Clearly, Stacey was avoiding me. I can be as tenacious as my father, and I wasn't ready to give up. I wrote back, "Hi Stacey, I've been trying to reach you but am without success."

No response.

I felt frustrated. By now, I was more upset by the fact that Stacey refused to speak to me than by what the Moores had said. Clearly, Stacey didn't want to talk to me, and she thought that she didn't have to. My feelings plummeted, exacerbated by memories of my previous conversation with Stacey.

After I was laid off, I had called her, seeking sympathy. She was familiar with my work, which was fundraising for a not-for-profit agency providing social services.

After years in local government, Stacey also worked for a not-for-profit in Berkeley, California, as Director of Operations. I had thought that she would commiserate with me.

But she didn't come across as sympathetic—or sympathetic enough. She said she was sorry, and then she declared, "They must have wanted to get rid of you." She proceeded to tell me about someone at her job "they" had wanted "to get rid of" and how they had done it—"not like you," she said, but then I wondered why she was telling me about it.

She was showing me her cold, managerial side. She clearly identified with the ones who "had gotten rid of" me. That was her job. She saw it from their point of view, not mine.

And then came the part of our conversation that I regretted the most—about money. I had never asked Stacey how much money she made, and she had never asked me. I knew she probably made more money than I did, and I knew that her husband made more money than my husband. But we never discussed it. I thought that she thought that I probably made more money than I did, and I wanted to keep it that way.

But then, in the midst of our conversation, she asked me how much money I made, and I told her. And immediately wished I hadn't.

She didn't tell me how much money she made, and I didn't ask her. Part of me wanted to ask her, but I was afraid that if I knew, I would be more upset, because it might be so much more money than I made, and yet she complained about the cut she had taken when she moved from city government to a not-for-profit. I thought she had sounded arrogant when she said, " But I'm going to take care of that when I negotiate my next contract. I told them I'm leaving, but I'll continue as a consultant. Now they'll have to pay me what I'm worth."

It seemed to me then that Stacey was rubbing salt in my wound by reminding me that she was negotiating more money for her work, whereas I was jobless. In my blacker moments, I believed that Stacey thought that she was better than I. By not returning my calls, she was sending me a message: she didn't have to call me back. Her time was valuable, and mine was not. She didn't have time for me, and she didn't want to hear what I had to say.

She was forcing me to correspond the way she wanted, by group emails. Emails are useful—I send as many of them as the next person—but this was one of those times that I wanted to talk first. I didn't want to involve our sister Lois until I had discussed the Moores' allegations with Stacey as well as Mimi. Lois was a loose cannon. We'd all been affected by her explosions in the past.

I felt the way I used to feel as a child when I had tried and failed to get a response from one or the other of our parents. It seemed that no one wanted to hear what I had to say—not at my former job, not my own sister.

> Stacey sent another group email:
> "Dear Sisters,
>
> Mimi and I have spoken at length about what happened. Mimi has spoken with Ron several times as well as with Gordon. Gordon told Mimi that he overheard portions of a conversation that Ron was having. Ron said that Gordon took incomplete comments out of context. Ron said the customer found envelopes with $500 in them. He said he made a few statements to the customer about finding money at other sales, silver coins, stocks and bonds, etc. Mimi and I feel comfortable that Ron is being truthful with us. He is operating a 30-year old family business and conducts estate sales almost weekly. I don't intend to pursue this any further."

Stacey didn't sign the email and I could hear her annoyance between the lines. I thought to myself, She is willing to talk to everyone but me. By now, my hurt had deepened; it wasn't about the sale or the money or who was telling the truth, Gordon or Ron. It was about us—Stacey and me. Even though I knew that this kind of thinking would only bring me damage, I couldn't stop myself. I was on a downward spiral of depression.

It was in this state of mind that I went berry picking at a U-Pic-Em place in Connecticut. It was a hot, sunny day—a beautiful day—but my spirits were low as I drove the scenic country roads, lined with farms and fields, old homes, green lawns, and flourishing trees. Normally I love being on my own, on an expedition, but that day I couldn't seem to shake the gloom that settled over me.

A sign for the berry farm led me off the road down a makeshift drive formed by two ruts across a field. There was a parking area next to an open wooden structure in the midst of rows and rows of berry bushes. I pulled in—there was only one other car. The wooden structure consisted of three walls, a roof, and a high, open counter behind which sat a pretty young woman in a green-and-yellow sundress and a boy about ten or eleven years old.

In response to my query, she told me the prices by weight, and she handed me a plastic gallon jug with the top cut off. "For the blueberries," she said.

"I want to pick raspberries first," I told her. "I'll pick blueberries afterwards, if I have time."

"You'll have to look for the raspberries," she said. "There are only four rows, and they've been picked through."

"I came for raspberries," I said. "I already have some, but I need more to make jam."

"You'll find some," she assured me, "look low down." She handed me two pint cardboard boxes. "Are these enough?"

"They should be."

The buzzing of insects rose and fell in crescendos. The sun blazed on the rows of ripening fruit. In addition to the berry bushes were apple, peach, and apricot trees. Yet the woman in the sundress had said there would be no peaches this year. On the way to the raspberries, I passed the peach trees, with their dark, glossy leaves, and I wondered why they weren't fruiting. I hadn't asked her.

At this farm they pruned their raspberry bushes to chest height. I squatted low to the ground, looking under the crepey, bright green, serrated leaves for the globed berries, red and soft and ripe enough to slip off their stems into my hand and then into the box. Gradually, the box began to fill up. I needn't have worried; there would be enough berries.

Sweat trickled down my back, but I didn't mind: I am a child of Alabama, and the heat rarely bothers me. Normally, berry picking is a relaxing, meditative activity for me, but today I couldn't seem to escape my miseries. I thought about my lost job. I remembered my father's comments to me that were not complimentary. I pondered Stacey's feelings of superiority over me, recalling that, several weeks ago, Mimi had called me to complain about Stacey. I had refused to take sides, and Mimi had been furious with me. Now, I thought, I know how Mimi felt. Despondently, I considered my family and our losses and how sad it all was.

I filled one box with raspberries and started another, and yet I couldn't seem to calm down the way I usually did. Like a cat chasing its tail, my agitated thoughts circled one another, going nowhere.

I sat down on the ground in the paint-spattered jeans I was wearing because I didn't care if they got berry stains and watched as an orange-and-black butterfly alighted on a leaf and folded and unfolded its wings. Like a dancer, it slowly lifted one threadlike leg and set it down. A dragonfly hovered in the air, and sunlight reflected off its translucent wings, revealing their delicate pattern of scales. Why can't I be happy? I wondered. The world is so beautiful, and now I don't have a job, I have time to enjoy it, at least for the summer.

But the dark thoughts whirred and buzzed in my mind, like insect wings. Gnats flew at my eyes, and I shooed them away. I had filled the second box of raspberries, and I brought both boxes to be weighed.

"So you didn't have trouble finding any," the woman in the sundress commented.

"No, and there's plenty more if anyone else comes," I said, gazing around the parking area. The other car had left, and there was only mine. "You're right; you just have to look down lower on the bushes, under the leaves."

She weighed my berries and asked me about packing them. I said that I planned to store them in the cooler I had in the trunk of my car, while I picked blueberries. I said plastic bags would be fine.

"You have to be careful about the berries smashing when you put them in the cooler," she warned me.

"It doesn't matter. I'm going to make jam when I get home."

"Oh, I love to cook!" she exclaimed with real enthusiasm. She turned to the boy, who was drawing something on a piece of paper. "We should make some jam, what do you say?"

"Is he your son?" I asked, though she looked too young to be his mother.

"No, he's my fiancé's cousin. They own this farm. I'm helping out, and he's keeping me company. He's my best friend. Aren't you, Bobby?" she turned to him, smiling. He put down his crayons and grinned back at her. "I don't know what I'd do without him. It would be really lonely here all day."

"I usually like being alone," I admitted. "I came here to be by myself and relax, but I can't seem to. I'm too upset."

I'm not sure what inspired me to confide in her. It was an impulse. She had an open, friendly face, and I warmed to her smile.

"You'd be surprised how many people come here when they're unhappy," she said. "I see it a lot."

"I've had a rough time. I lost my job after seventeen-and-a-half years."

"I lost my job, too," she said. "I know what that's like."

"How did you get through it?"

She shook her head. "I was a personal trainer in Philadelphia. The gyms there—well, they take advantage of you. I didn't like it, so they let me go." She sighed. "I hit rock-bottom. My bank account was less than zero. It's a long story. I was weak. But I'm much better now. I have faith, and that changed me. I don't know how you feel about that."

She looked at me as if she expected I might argue

with her. I noticed that she was wearing a cross around her neck.

"I believe in God," I said. "I try to, anyway. And I recognize the power that faith can have. I have seen it too many times not to believe it."

She nodded. Obeying the urge to confide, I went on, "It's not only my job. My father died at the end of February, nearly two years after my mother. I have a lot of sisters, and we're going through this emotional stuff getting ready to sell the house. It's not easy. I feel that my youngest sister thinks she's better than I am, because she has a job, and I don't, and she makes more money than I did at my job. She can't be bothered to return my phone calls." And I told her about the estate sale, and what had happened, and about my termination, and what Stacey had said.

She listened carefully. "A lot of people feel that way," she said. "They think they're better if they make more money. But it's not true. Everyone is equal. It doesn't matter how much money you make. It doesn't make you a better person. I have sisters, too," she went on. "I know it can get very complicated. After I lost my job, I was driving past my sister's house. I hadn't seen her for years, and I drove past, and then I changed my mind. I went back to see her. I was standing at the screen door, and she was on the other side, and she wouldn't let me in."

"Why not?"

"I told you, I was weak. I was crying, and she didn't want to know about it."

"Did she think you wanted to stay with her?"

The woman shook her head. "No, she knew I didn't. My mother said, 'Why did you go see her?'"

"Why not?" I interjected. "She *is* your sister."

"I don't get along with my mother," she admitted. "Like I told you, I was weak, and I let people take advantage of me. And my mother doesn't understand what I'm doing. Like now. She doesn't understand why I'm working here and not getting paid. But it's my fiancé's family's business, and when we get married, it will be my business, too, and I want to help out. She doesn't get it. But I'm much stronger now, and I don't care."

"You'll be all right," she declared. "It doesn't matter what your sister said, or what she thinks. It doesn't matter about your job. You have to believe in yourself and be strong."

"I know you're right," I replied. "Thank you for telling me. I need to hear it." And simple as her message was, I realized that I felt better for the first time in days.

"I'm hot," I said. "Is there a place around here to go swimming—a lake with public access?"

"There's a pond on the property. It's really beautiful. You could go swimming there."

"Really?" I was astounded. "Have you swum there?"

"No, but I've thought about it. It's hard to get to. There are grasses growing all around it, no beach or anything. You'll have to find a way in."

"Where is it? I think I might be able to do it. And I have a bathing suit in the car."

"See those trees?" She pointed at a row of poplars marking the edge of the lower field. "If you walk around them, you'll see the pond. Have you gone swimming there?" she turned to ask the boy, who had been listening to our conversation.

"I have," he said, "but you have to be careful. There are snakes and snapping turtles."

"Oh, boy," I said. "Do you think I'll be okay?"

He shrugged. "Probably. But maybe you shouldn't go."

"Let me think about it," I said. "I'll pick the blueberries first."

The blueberries were as abundant as the raspberries were picked through. On tall bushes with sage-green leaves, they grew in clumps, the berries turning from green to purply blue, and came off in my hand easily. It did not take me long to fill the gallon jug with ripe fruit. I felt like a different person, picking the blueberries. I had stopped obsessing about my sister and my job. Was it really so simple?

"I'm just going to go look at the pond," I said, when I brought my blueberries to be weighed.

"You probably shouldn't go swimming there," the

boy said again.

"You're probably right," I agreed.

I walked on the edge of the field, down the line of trees, and then doubled back to look at the pond, which the trees hid from view. Fringed by tall grasses, it was larger than I expected and lay cool and inviting, shimmering like a mirror in the late afternoon summer light. Sadly, I said goodbye to it. Despite the woman's impulsive invitation, there were too many reasons I could think of why I shouldn't accept it.

"I guess I better get going," I said, when I returned. I wrote a check for the berries and put down my phone number. If she ever wanted to, she would know how to get in touch with me. "Thanks for talking to me. I feel a lot better. I really mean that."

"You'll get better and better," she said. "I know you will."

As I was driving, I saw a sign for a local Audubon refuge and on the spur of the moment decided to visit. There was a map in the parking lot depicting a bog trail, a duck blind, a raptors aviary, and other features. I headed towards the bog trail, which was a boardwalk through wetlands. The flies and mosquitoes and gnats were fierce, and after awhile I left the bog for the duck blind.

I watched two mallards swim lazily in a pond in a haze of golden light, and then I came to the raptors aviary. It consisted of a dozen cages holding raptors of all descriptions arranged in two rows back to back. A sign proclaimed that all of the birds had suffered permanent damage inflicted by humans that would prevent them from surviving in the wild, and they were being maintained in the aviary for study purposes.

There was a red-tailed hawk, a crow, a raven, and a huge, ugly turkey buzzard, its bare pink head and neck wattled and wrinkled. There was a little screech owl and a large barred owl with golden irises rimming dark pupils. There was a Cooper's hawk, a bald eagle, and a small peregrine falcon with feathers like black-and-white bars. I walked slowly in an oval around the cages, and some of the birds looked back at me, and others ignored me. The raptors aviary awoke in me a complicated response, and I knew I wouldn't forget it.

That night I started to make my jam—raspberry first, and blueberry the next morning. I sterilized the jars in the oven, boiled water for pressure canning, measured the berries and crushed them with a potato masher, and measured the sugar. Into a heavy pot went the crushed berries, a package of pectin, and a teaspoon of butter. I turned up the heat and stirred the mixture until it was liquid and bright scarlet, studded with seeds. When it began to boil, I added the sugar all at once. This was my favorite part of the process: watching the mixture turn from scarlet to crimson, as the melting sugar added depth and substance, shine and darkness. Rapturously, I breathed in deeply the sweet, hot, fruity fragrance of the jam cooking, and when it came to a boil again, I stirred it vigorously until I couldn't stir down the boil any longer, and I turned off the heat and skimmed off the layer of scum that had risen to the top. Then I poured the jam into the clean sterilized jars, wiped the rims, and sealed them—some with pressurized lids and others with melted paraffin wax. The jars with pressurized lids I boiled under water for twenty minutes and fished out carefully with sturdy tongs, careful not to splash myself with boiling water. For the other jars I cut curlicues of string, laid them on the hardened wax, and poured another melted layer over them, leaving one end of the string free for easy removal. While I was making the jam, I felt engaged, too busy to think about anything else.

Days later I succeeded in having a conversation with Stacey. It was not a success. Before we spoke, we were already angry with each other—I with her for avoiding me, and she with me for demanding that she speak with me. She made excuses for herself—how she was busy at her job, how her daughter was unhappy at *her* job, how occupied she was with the renovation of her house.

"I'm not interested in hearing about all that," I said coldly. Usually I would have been sympathetic, but that day I wasn't going to let her get away with it. "I asked you to call me back, and you avoided me."

"I didn't need to talk to you. Mimi is handling the house and its contents.

And I didn't like what you said about Ron May."

"I don't know him. I never met him. I don't have any opinions about him. But Gordon is family, at least by marriage, and he made a serious allegation that I felt I had to respond to it seriously. That's why I wanted to speak to you."

"I emailed you instead."

"I wanted to talk to you."

"I prefer emails."

"And I'm sick and tired of the emails."

"So what are you saying? You're not going to read my emails?"

"I'm not saying that. I'm saying I'm tired of being managed like someone who works for you. I'm not your employee. I'm your sister."

As I said, it was not a successful conversation. After I hung up, I thought about the woman at the berry farm and her advice. The good feeling she had engendered in me had lingered for a while, but it had not lasted. I knew I could be a better person, and I felt bad about what I had said to Stacey.

She sent another group email.

"Dear Sisters,

As you know, I will be in Alabama next week overseeing the installation of the carpets and painting before the house is put up for sale. Please remind me if you left anything at the house that needs to be taken care of when I am there.

I know there is a box of letters that needs to be mailed to our cousin in Australia, but I can't remember what else was left.

Thanks,
Stacey"

I wrote back to her, titling the email "Apology" in the subject line:

"Dear Stacey,

I'm sorry I got upset with you. It's been a hard

time for me and I hope we can move on, and that
your trip is a success.

You asked about 'stuff.' There is a box of thou-
sands of color slides that I packed from Dad's carou-
sels in May. At that time, you said you would ship the
box to me when you were next in Alabama.

It would be a terrible shame if all that history
were thrown in the trash. I only had time to examine
a few of the slides. I was packing them the morning
of the day I left, and I was in a big hurry.

Love,

Adrienne"

I was still a little angry with Stacey; I could feel it
when I wrote the email, and it accounted for the stiffness
of my language. I *was* sorry for what I had said, and I
could feel that my anger had dissipated, but I still didn't
trust myself entirely.

Stacey wrote back:

"Adrienne—it is ok. Thanks for your email. I
know it has been a hard time for you. I try to be as
responsive as possible, but lately I have felt like I am
just trying to get through each day without dropping
too many balls.

I will definitely ship the color slide box to you.

I will try to call you from Alabama. Now, I am
off to pack. Will be glad when the week is over.

xo Stacey"

Friends you can choose, sisters are forever. Since our
parents' deaths, we have interests in common, which are
being separated. When the house is sold, and the assets
are divided, there will be nothing material yoking us any
longer. We will continue to be connected by blood, by up-
bringing, by shared memories. Our parents left us a com-
plicated legacy. They paid lip service to unity and sowed
division. They didn't care about fairness, and they weren't
fair. My father had a limited imagination, and my mother
perhaps had too much, susceptible as she was to paranoia.

When it came to siblings, they were novices. Neither had sisters. My father was an only child, and my mother had only one brother from whom she was estranged. In this, as in so many other things, they were not the best guides for us.

We have laid them to rest with their flaws and their fears, the love that they needed and didn't get, the love they got and didn't value, or didn't value enough. In looking forward, I also look back. I remember a conversation I had more than thirty years ago with my great-aunt Helen, my mother's brother's sister, who lived in North Hollywood, California. My husband and I were in our young adulthood, and we were traveling. So much lay ahead of us, including the decision to have a child.

Aunt Helen did not understand what had happened to my family. She knew that Mimi was troubled, because Mimi had stayed with her on several occasions when she was at business school at UCLA, and she had observed Mimi's eating disorders that compelled her to starve herself during the day and raid the refrigerator in secret.

"We left her in our apartment when we went away for the weekend," Aunt Helen told me, "and when we came back the freezer was half-empty, but still she wouldn't eat with us. Your mother says she's allergic, but I don't think your parents know what's going on. Mimi pulled the wool over their eyes."

Even then I knew that Mimi's food problems had their source with our parents and their obsession with weight and appearance, their desire that we remain like little girls, instead of develop into women. I opened up to Aunt Helen that day. I told her about Mimi's problems, about Lois's problems. I described the conflicts that had fractured our family and broken us apart.

Aunt Helen had only one son, a conscientious objector who had dodged the draft during the Vietnam War by fleeing to Canada. She and had supported him, and she would have given anything to have been close to him, but he had turned his back on her and his father. Aunt Helen listened attentively to the catalogue of my family's woes. "Your mother threw her children away," she commented, and there was a well of sadness in her voice. I had never thought of it in quite that way, but I realized that she was right.

When Aunt Helen died a widow, she made her son her executor. If he were to predecease her, her second choice was my mother. In addition, she left all of us small legacies.

My mother was taken by surprise. "Imagine that!" she exclaimed. She said she had no idea that Aunt Helen had valued her so highly. In her voice I discerned a note of fear or dread that somehow she didn't measure up to Aunt Helen's estimation of her. It took me aback. My mother was usually so well defended that I had never glimpsed so clearly her deep reservoir of inadequacy. It occurred to me that her attacks on us were motivated by this lack, as well as by her dissatisfaction with our father, and this realization complicated my resentment of her by arousing my pity for her.

Looking back, I am able to understand better how in taking care of others, I was cared for as well. Now the tables have turned, and my younger sisters, Mimi and Stacey, as executors of our father's estate, are taking care of things *for* me, and thus are taking care *of* me as well. It might not be my way, but that is their prerogative. And though at times I might grow "sick and tired" of group emails, I recognize that my sisters are seeking to discharge their obligations in a spirit of cooperation that is new in our family. One of my yoga teachers once said, "Happiness cannot be owned, earned, worn, or consumed. It's the act of living every single day with love, grace, and gratitude for what you already have." I am grateful for my sisters, and I am grateful for people like the woman at the berry farm who appear in my life like angels to remind me that I can create my own strength, my own peace:

> There never was a war that was
>   not inward; I must
> fight till I have conquered in myself what
>   causes war...[1]

---

1 Marianne Moore, "In Distrust of Merits."

Three Poems
Jordi Alonso

The Meteorologist in the Morning

Clouds puffed, turning heavy as dark rain swelled them;
floating water fluttered like early eyelids
barely woken taking the trudging trail to
                    morning and tea time.

Jeong (Korean)[1] 정

for Mara Vulgamore

Let everyone long for love––
I have no need
of sweet-flowered hibiscuses,
bursting for a day:

Junipers bloom even in winter.

---

1 Noun: a feeling stronger than romantic love, linking two
people, often through adversity.

Jordi Alonso

Mistimanchachi (Quichua)[2]

for Phoebe Carter

Why would I need an umbrella?
Your hands are warm enough
to forget the rain.

---

2 Noun: a light rain. Lit: "something that scares Spanish-
speaking urbanites"

You Must Love the Children

You draw their bright follicles on large sheets
of cheap paper taped to the wall. A dutiful
copier, you're quick to capture the profile,
but some chins are defensive. Some faces hardly
enter the plane of the paper. Each silhouette
looks like a question if you stand far enough
back. But you've promised these 11-year olds
you'll help them pour stories into their faces
in that pasty morning light. So this is it,
what you do: hold each shadow immobile
so next week they can fill it with decoration
and sport, whatever they love, with their *dichos*.
The room is cacophony. You land a smile
on the lazy, and consider the dubious kid
in the corner stuck in the energy of his wrinkled
magazine pages, his night hair, the watchful
slope of his eyes. Rather than let the privileged
take up your time, you crouch beside Domingo
or Evelin or Mia, or he whose name you cannot
pronounce, to patriot a story in whispers
and colors. You're unprepared for these battles,
but the way it turns out, tracing kids at this age
means a new way of listening, means you're
entering their customs and habits, your palm
cupped, but sideways, to grasp what you can.

Lauren Camp

What is Perfect

We held our glasses and the teapot
and the knives from dinner. We held all
the hundreds of details and names
from our lives, and our grazings
and warnings moved gently
away. There was hardly noise, just
cottonwood flutter, those strong trees
in their untidy orbit. Winter was about to bloom,
and we noticed the fragrance as a reverie
in our hands. We were escaping the calendar
that kept repeating all it had spoken before.
We sat by the arc of the window *this close*
to understanding the foundation
of sumac, and we wanted to keep going
though the week's words tried to pry us away,
words we heard while we stood and peeled
onions, or on the road, the words of drones
and low hopes, of the blind dark
and its display of strange colors. Before long,
the words began eating up the mountain.
How jagged and mortal. I chose to look straight
despite the wind —rigorous, sharp—
into chokecherry, wild corn, angles of gold.
You followed my eyes, remaining quiet.
We took a chance, sort of pleading with
our vulnerable selves to ignore the swatches
of newsprint. Everywhere you turn: hello fist,
goodbye train. How can we listen? Every hour
our hearts actually sleep while the news
keeps repeating its many diaries
left open. The universe undresses to the length
of a sentence, or every curve of the day, and our ears
work to postpone the repercussion
of excess, the conversation we never wanted.
We ask to be left alone to neglect other questions
about desperate time that cannot be emptied.
To be uncertain, hopeful, about later,
and how we will get there.

Summer Drifting in Shy Talk

I thought to walk by pine and sage
to a river bed (all dry, of course).

Thankful for a breeze in leaves,
I sat beside a yarrow crop. I sat

as ants rushed back and forth,
and sometimes talked. I walked

and walked along the rocks
around the back to grass and past

the aspen, past the house,
past the first of early clouds

already turning mauve. The hush
that came was mine, inside.

I heard the wind and honks,
and folks off to the east. I heard

the dark descend by notes,
and then an anxious bird. I stood

until another bird crossed by
to claim the first. I heard them

chitter, heard one soothe.
The psalms of night revolved.

The Boy Who Loved Too Much
William Cass

I know a boy who loved too much. He's my cousin, Ben. I first noticed when he was seven, two summers ago when his dad went off to fight the big fires along the Canadian border.

We'd come up to their place from Grangeville for the summer after my junior year in high school. We stayed in a little silver tag-along trailer they had at the back of their small farm, my mom and me. My mom was there to help her sister get her new beauty shop ready to open in town, and I came along to help my uncle on the farm. We didn't have any other commitments at home; my mom wasn't able to find much in the way of regular work at the time and neither was I.

We heard about the fires on the radio throughout August. But Ben's dad didn't leave until the day after all the hay was in and we could see smoke in several places just north of the Selkirk Range. Helicopters and planes dangling big water buckets had been flying over regularly for the past week. So, Ben's dad finally went off with another couple of fellows from the volunteer fire department in Priest River one evening in an old red pick-up truck.

Before he left, we all had a big supper: cold chicken, new corn, fresh beets. Then Ben and his dad played catch like they always did afterwards out next to the vegetable garden. Evening was just starting to fall. Ben's dad already had his duffel bag under the maple tree. When the other men drove up, his dad squatted down on the grass and Ben ran to him with that tangle of brown hair and those big eyes. They hugged one another for a long time. When his father climbed into the truck with the other men, Ben stood with his head tucked into one shoulder. He didn't watch them as they drove out the long gravel road to the north.

The next morning, Ben came into the barn while I was milking the cows. He shuffled around next to an empty pen scratching a stick in the sawdust.

After a while, I asked, "You miss your dad?"

He tucked his head down towards his shoulder again like he'd done the night before and nodded.

"You worried about him?"

He shrugged. I tried to bend down to look into his face, but he tucked his head lower and turned away.

"He'll be okay," I said.

He blew out his breath, but didn't look up. He went back to scratching with the stick, and I returned to milking. When I looked up next, he was gone.

Later that day, I saw him in the backyard playing tug-a-war with their old Sheltie, Jake. They were using a ragged towel tied in knots. They were both growling, but Jake's tail was wagging happily.

Jake pulled the towel loose and they both sat down hard and suddenly on the grass. Jake dropped the towel and jumped on Ben. Ben turned his head away down into his shoulder, which was natural enough given the way Jake was licking at this face. But, then Jake settled his head onto Ben's lap and as he scratched Jake behind the ears, Ben kept his head turned away. I found that odd.

I went up the road after supper to bring the horses in from the little five-acre field the neighbor let them graze in while it went fallow for a year. It was still hot, though the sun had already gone down and the wide sky was darkening towards ink except for the dusty canopy over the mountains were the fires were. I could smell the smoke for the first time.

When I came back in through the screen door to the kitchen, my mom and aunt were taking peanut butter cookies out of the oven. Ben was sitting at the linoleum table cradling his baby sister. He held an empty bottle of formula in one hand and was tickling the bottoms of her feet with the other. Her mouth was open with laughter, though no sound came out because of whatever it was that was wrong with her speaking and hearing.

She squirmed with delight, but his head was tucked away again into his shoulder.

It was hotter still the next day. The morning news, though, said that they'd contained the biggest blazes, which were scattered along the north-easternmost corner of Bonner County.

After lunch, the neighbor with the fallow field, a man named Hank, came by pulling the hay wagon he'd borrowed from my uncle. His two sons rode up on the back with him: towheaded boys a year or two older than Ben. They asked him if he wanted to come over to swim in their irrigation ditch. He said sure, and they went along. I spent the afternoon in the barn, where it was a little cooler, repairing machinery.

I heard my mom and her sister arrive back home several hours later, and shortly afterward, Hank walked Ben home. My aunt came out to meet them, wiping her hands on her apron. I watched them from the barn. Ben hugged her around the hips, then she sent him in to wash up for supper.

She thanked Hank and asked him if Ben had minded his manners.

"And then some," Hank said. He took his cap off and scratched his head. "Curious thing happened, point of fact. Boys had fun swimming and such. I had a couple of errands to run up to town afterwards, so I took them in for an ice cream, it being so hot. I got them their cones, then left them on that bench in front of the hardware store while I went inside for some carriage bolts. Soon as I come out, I seen a big plop of ice cream – vanilla, so I knowed it was my older boy's – melting on the sidewalk.

Him, he was setting there with an empty cone in one hand and eating Ben's rainbow sherbet with the other."

A helicopter went by then, not too high, and they both looked up at it. They watched it go towards the three big plumes of smoke that had come up that afternoon above Chimney Rock. hen they looked at each other again.

Hank cleared his throat and said, "Course, I asked my older boy about it, and he just said it slid off, so then Ben give him his. I tried to make Ben take it back or let me buy him a new one, but he wouldn't do neither. Curious thing was he just sort of sat tucking his head under his arm-like. Acted kind of like I seen hurt birds do when they're spooked."

My aunt waved her hand at him. "Don't think nothing of it. He's just a little off since his dad left."

Hank nodded slowly. "All right," he said. "You hear anything from Will?"

My aunt told him that she hadn't, and they talked for a while about the fires and weather and the harvest. After a few minutes, she thanked him again and he turned up the road. My aunt shook out her apron and went back into the kitchen, the screen door swinging slowly shut behind her.

That night, my mom and I did the dishes while Ben's mom sat with him on the sofa reading stories. He kept his head tucked into her side as she read. I know my mom could see them, too – we were both standing next to each other at the sink.

Afterwards, we all sat on the front step and sang some songs, the few I could manage on my harmonica. Ben sat against one of the porch pillars with his head tucked down. I sat against the other. My mom and aunt sat on the glider, and the baby lay asleep between them. Crickets joined us.

The more we sang, it seemed, the more Ben tucked his head down. I watched my mom and aunt exchange glances as he did. He was a small boy for his age, I realized, waifish. Looking at him quickly, you might think he was no older than four or five.

When we got back to the trailer, I decided to ask my mom about Ben. She didn't seem surprised. She sat down on the narrow bed and sighed.

"Well, it is hard to figure, but Ann says he's just a little boy who loves too much. She says he gets all full up with it and doesn't know what to do. She says he's embarrassed, can't look at you, confused I guess. After all, he's only just seven. Ann says he's usually all right when his dad's around. I'm sure he's anxious about his dad, poor little guy."

I asked, "Is he always like that?"

"Well, he's always been pretty sensitive about things. A couple of years ago when they came to visit, you remember, I found him in the stairwell with his hand on our dad's picture and his head tucked down like he does. He'd only seen his grandpa that once in the rest home. Another time, I found him in the same way fingering a little bouquet of wildflowers on the coffee table Ann says he hears a gospel choir on the radio, he's got to leave the room, he gets so beside himself."

I said, "Gee," or something like that.

"She told me they went into Spokane one time and saw a homeless man by the railroad depot. Ben gave the man his candy bar. Apparently, he had trouble both looking up and sleeping for several days afterwards."

I said, "I didn't know any of that. Or, at least, I never noticed."

"Until now, though I'm glad you have." She smiled. "You been pretty full up with your own affairs."

It was still and hot in that trailer. My mom pushed a stray strand of damp hair behind her ear, then slid the tiny window open above her bunk as far as it would go.

I heard Ben go by in the gravel as I was milking the last cow the next morning. I listened to the gate to the first field unlatch, then shut again. After I'd finished, I followed him out there. He was sitting on a little berm against some discarded hay bales. I sat down next to him. His head was already tucked down and he was whimpering a little.

I looked across the fields towards the mountains. The pink of the sunrise under the brown hue seemed otherworldly. I could smell the smoke more heavily than before.

"I missed my dad when he left," I said as quietly as I could. "Only yours'll come back. I know he will."

It was completely still, except for his quiet crying. It wasn't hot yet. For as far as I could see, there were cleanly harvested, low, brown fields, and beyond them, gray-green mountains and sky.

I tousled his hair and said, "Bet your mom's got breakfast on."

He didn't say anything. I chewed on a piece of straw and watched the pale sky lighten to blue above the haze. Some birds rose in a far field, crows I think, and lifted towards the road. After a moment, I stood up and followed them back towards the house.

Things stayed about the same for the next few days. Then one night, late, a rumble woke me up. I thought at first that it was a plane going by up high until I tasted the cool on my tongue. I sat up. A big clap of thunder rolled down from the mountains and the first splat of rain plinked on the aluminum roof.

My mom sat up, too, and looked at me with eyes that were wide but full of sleep. It took her a moment to smile.

The rain fell through the rest of the night. While I was taking my boots off on the back step before breakfast, I heard my aunt tell my mom that the radio reported no new fires because of lightning. She said that already the rain had put out a good portion of the worst blazes.

It continued on and off the following day and the morning after, as well. Ben's dad came home when we were finishing supper that next evening. He came in through the kitchen door, soot-stained and smelling like crushed ash, while we were finishing our pie. Ben was first across to hug him. We all took turns after, then my mom and I excused ourselves so they could be alone. I went out to the barn to finish the evening milking.

Ben and his dad came outside carrying their mitts and ball an hour later. From my stool in the barn, I could see that my uncle had taken a bath; his hair was combed wet and he had on clean khakis and a short-sleeved plaid shirt. They stood out next to the vegetable garden with their mitts on, my uncle a few feet away holding the softball, Ben with his head tucked down. I stopped milking.

In a voice I could barely hear, my uncle said, "Come on, son." He walked over and knelt down in front of Ben. "Let me see that handsome face I missed so much." He gently turned Ben's face until they were looking at each other. My uncle kissed Ben on the forehead then, and Ben smiled.

I said, "Gee," or something like that. It was like having a rainbow appear inside of me to watch Ben grinning like that as he and his father tossed the ball back and forth.

We headed back to Grangeville a few days later. The beauty shop was all fixed up, and it was about time for me to start school again.

My mom found temporary work after Halloween as a filing clerk for the outfit that was building the new chain motel out the highway. That lasted through the first part of the next spring, and she did well enough that she was asked to come back to Des Moines where they were based to work fulltime when the project was finished.

So, we did. That's where I finished school. I started working for the same outfit in their tool room right after I graduated.

My mom and her sister write back and forth pretty regularly. The beauty shop has worked all right, though they haven't been able to do much for the little girl's ears. They leased another forty acres and planted it in rye. Jake got hit this past winter by a truck on the county road when it was slick with black ice, and limps now in one of his hind legs.

Then a short while ago, another letter came, a worse one that told us that Ben had gone into a deep sleep. My aunt wrote that it was due to complications associated with the pneumonia he'd gotten running after Jake the night he got hit. They weren't calling it a coma yet because he roused every now and again, but it was something along those lines, she said, something pretty close to that.

She'd waited to let us know, hoping that he might come around, but several weeks had passed, and he'd been moved up to a bigger hospital in Spokane. She said they were hoping for the best. So do I. Ben's nine, about the age I was when my dad left for the last time.

My boss gave me some time off, and I've bought a bus ticket to Spokane. I'm packed and ready to leave in the morning. I'm not sure what I'll do when I get there. Sit by his bed, read to him, hold his hand, talk to him, say some prayers, whatever it takes. Maybe, if I'm there when he wakes up, I can say something, do something, to help him stay awake. I don't know. I'll stay as long as I need to.

They say that when something like this happens to someone you care about, there's a hole left where they've been. They say that such a hole gradually closes, that time heals, but I don't actually believe that in Ben's case. I don't actually believe that a place can be refilled for a boy like that.

They say that what happened to Ben was caused by an illness that just got out of hand, but I'm not so sure it wasn't, at least partly, from a broken heart. It might have been Jake's accident, it might have been the trouble with his sister's ears, it might have been the wonder of snow falling quietly one night or the cry of newborn calf. For a boy who loves too much, some things become both more of a joy and more of a burden than they do for you and me.

Peace at the Center
Adapted from *Sweetwater*,
a narrative nonfiction work-in-progress
Page Lambert

Chickasaw author Linda Hogan writes, "Nature is now too often defined by people who are fragmented from the land. Such a world is seldom one that carries and creates the human spirit." She goes on to say, "Soul Loss is what happens as the world around us disappears."[1]

When I made the hard decision to leave the ranch in the Black Hills, where I had reared my children and lived with my husband of twenty-five years, I feared that I would experience this loss of soul—part of me forever left behind. Torn from the sagebrush prairies and red-slashed draws, from coyote dens and redtail hawks, I feared that I would be *less* than I had been while rooted to the land. This concept of "Soul Loss" that Linda Hogan writes about cut as deeply as any axe.

A month in seclusion at a remote cabin in the Big-horn Mountains after I left the ranch reinforced what two trips on the Colorado River in the Grand Canyon, and two trips on the wild Babine River in remote British Columbia, had taught me – that no affiliation with technology "gives back soul" in the same way that a handful of earth sifting through one's fingers does.

I filled four journals with nearly 400 pages of writing while alone at the cabin, which had no electricity, no running water, no phone, no fax, no computer. I brought along a mandala coloring book given me by a young Canadian woman with terminal cancer, and a box of 64 crayons with names like cadet blue, burnt orange and magenta.

---

1 *Parabola, Magazine of Myth and Tradition: Nature*; Volume 24 No. 1, 1999 "The Great Without." P.22.

Few of us experience journ
and peace as heroic as Siddhart
his youth, exploring the externa
through the inner eye of the hea
Nature cannot touch us, cannot
there to be touched by it. The s
after a rain cannot find its way i
not there, standing among the damp trees, rooted to our
own private awareness, rooted to *that* spot in *that* forest
on *that* mountain. No one else can experience *for us* the
sound of a cow elk mewing to her calf, the sight of a doe
dipping her head, a bird lifting its wings. It is the outside
of Nature leads us to the inside of Soul.

David Abrams writes in his book *The Spell of the
Sensuous*[2] that "to touch the course skin of a tree is to...
feel oneself touched by the tree...we might as well say that
we are organs of this world...flesh of its flesh, and that
the world is perceiving itself through us...if we dwell in
the forest for many months, or years, then our experience
may shift yet again – we may come to feel that we are a
part of this forest, consanguineous with it, and that our
experience of the forest is nothing other than the for-
est experiencing itself....our sentient bodies are entirely
continuous with the vast body of the land, that the pres-
ence of the world is precisely the presence of its flesh to
my flesh."

Susan Griffin, author of *Woman and Nature: The
Roaring Inside Her* describes this reciprocity of percep-
tion in her own way: "Hand and breast know each one to
the other. Wood in the table knows clay in the bowl. Air
knows grass knows water knows mud knows beetle knows
frost knows sunlight knows the shape of the earth knows
death knows not dying. And all this knowledge is in the
souls of everything, behind naming, before speaking,
beneath words...."[3]

---

2 *The Spell of the Sensuous*, Vintage Books, Random House,
New York, 1996. P.68.
3 *Woman and Nature: The Roaring Inside Her*; Sierra Club
Books, San Francisco, 1978. P. 192-193.

ph Campbell tells us that there are fateful blun-
at catapult us through the doorway of our own des-
s. There were times at the cabin when I had hoped
awaken, as if from a badly blundered dream, when I
wondered how I could leave the marriage, the ranch, the
animals, the hills that had cradled me.

Blunders are not the merest chance, Campbell tells
us, but the result of suppressed desires and conflicts,
ripples on the surface of life produced by deep-fed unsus-
pected springs. "The blunder may amount to the opening
of a destiny...the call rings up the curtain, always, on a
mystery of transfiguration – a rite, or moment, of spiritual
passage, which, when complete, amounts to a dying and a
birth.... The familiar life horizon has been outgrown; the
old concepts, ideals, and emotional patterns no longer fit;
the time for the passing of a threshold is at hand. Typi-
cal of the circumstances of the call are the dark forest, the
great tree, the babbling spring, and the loathly, underesti-
mated appearance of the carrier of the powers of destiny." [4]

On Day 16 at the cabin, a cold drizzly day, I lit the
cook stove and journaled into the late afternoon. We all
search, I realized, for waters large enough to contain our
souls, oceans without shores that would allow us to ex-
plore the breadth and depth of knowing and being.

Most heroes' journeys are fraught with obstacles that
test the hero's will, physical dangers and dark demons
who thwart the hero's journey. But my time at the cabin
was no trial, no grueling trek across the wildness com-
plete with ogres and tempests. It was a slice of heaven,
a month's reprieve from stress and emotional angst.
Where, then, was the initiation, unless it was the Call to
move deep into the dark thickets of self.

On Day 18, I began coloring the mandala. Man-
dala in Sanskrit means "the holy circle, the sum total of
life contained in its perimeter, the contain-ness of life,
and the Buddha sits in the center of it." I spread out all
64 crayons on the table, found the black one, and started
with the center circle. *For the shadow that holds our*

4 *The Hero with a Thousand Faces*; MJF Books, NY, 1949.
P.49-51.

loneliest moments. As an exercise in letting go of control, I closed my eyes and picked the next color, and the next, and the next. I used every color in the box, chosen at random, and attaching an emotion to each color. *Raw Umber: the color of deep wounds. Sepia: the broken vessel. Plum: the tension between wild and domestic. Salmon: the desire to return to the womb.* I started at the inside of my life, and worked my way outward.

One morning, I brought back from my hike a sprig of western red currant, the red stem of a willow, the hip joints of a fawn, the feathers from a sapsucker, and the dark shadow of sadness. It clung to me every step of the way. In the afternoon, I read the essay "Burnished Gold" by Christopher Banford. "This undercurrent of sadness is not uncommon," he writes. "We find it wherever and whenever our heart turns toward the world...to guide our deeper listening....a subtle, barely audible otherworldy call inviting us into the unknown. Perhaps," he ponders, "it is the language of the birds."

He goes on to say that "if we hold it like a seed within our inner darkness, nurturing it patiently with silence, the sad mood that takes us in such moments can germinate in profoundly knowing and transformative ways."[5] If Sadness lives in the shadows of life as Banford suggests, in the nuances that deny the absolutes, in the dusk that drives away the glaring light of day, then it is this burnished sadness that gives patina to our souls.

I decided to observe the shadows in the forest that afternoon—the dark mirrored stretch of pine upon the mulched ground, the caped entrance to a rock chuck's den, the flitting shadows of dragonflies, the mountain silhouetted against the aspen canyon as the sun lowered itself over the horizon.

In the middle of the night, I awoke and went outside in search of the moon. The canyon, alive with nocturnal creatures, urged me to join them, to go deeper into the darkness. In the morning, I heard an elk cow calling to her calf and found their empty bed—a trodden circle of

5 *Parabola, Magazine of Myth and Tradition: The Shadow*; Volume 22, No. 2, 1997. P. 26-32.

grass where they had lain during the night. Their scent wafted up from the earth. I knelt, breathing in the muskiness of their curled bodies, longing to tuck my own children into the folds of my arms. Yet the Buddhist purpose of mediation on nature is not to establish an emotional relationship with it, but to see *uncontrived* nature as it is, and to recognize that nature in ourselves. I ought not try to make the cow like me, but instead, ought to try and feel her animal nature within my humanness.

Coloring the mandala that night, I pondered the Buddha sitting at the center. From this holy circle arose the pure Wind of the Mind, and above this wind, arose the Mandala of the Wind, or Air, primal element that permeated everything. Finally the mandalas of Fire, Water and Earth arose—the Universe as container of all.

As I hiked, I meditated—exploring the interweaving of emotion and wildness. I plucked a blade of grass, a twist of sedge, a twig, a leaf, a fluff of fur, downy thistle, seeds floating in the breeze, blue grouse breast feathers. I brought this bit of nature to the cabin, to the nest weaving itself within my mind. Each day, I slid deeper into the spirit of the woods, let go more harsh edges, more rigid angles. Each day I grew more fluid, felt myself slip into the unknown. I saw my skeleton like a downed tree, my branches deadfall on the path. Even the grouse no longer feared me. Timid rabbits quenched their thirst with my dew, beaded like raindrops on the leaves of wild lilies. The wind gathered my breath and carried it across the divide. Eagles snatched my bones to build their nests. Weightless, I evaporated into the night as the moon called me home.

On my last evening at the cabin, only a few crayons remained from which to choose. The coloring of the mandala was almost complete. I closed my eyes and reached out my fingers until they closed around a crayon. I opened my eyes. *Bittersweet.*

Leaving the mountain cabin would be both sad and beautiful. Visiting the ranch had become a bittersweet thing. Yet I knew that peace lay within the ability to love—every fiber, every thought, every animal who walked this journey with me, all the friends who waited on the far side of yesterday, my son, my daughter, even—*especially*—the husband who no longer was. This canyon. This mountain. The rain that was falling. The wood that was burning. The muted sound of my footsteps on the sodden earth. These things I could love.

I looked at the black circle in the middle of the mandala. The Unknown. The Emptiness that was All. Here was where I had always longed to be—at the center of a life that radiated outward into the world, spiraling toward that Holy Center.

Mountains
Chrystal Berche

Deity
Ariella Carmell

he with the brine-soaked ears
we spend the day molding mountaintops
considering the trembling menagerie below
with keen eyes, god-slathering hands
drunk on the dew of olympus

swift, he grabs stars into fists
cocks a grin my way
iotas seeping from finger-crevices
like garden snakes

I watch him play, deft
with what he possesses
the sky turns a shade of dread
deep as a pit of fruit
as the cavern in my gut

the clouds closing in, folding
unto themselves like flowers
blooming in reverse. The world
is at his design, every wisp of fancy
a tremor through the earth
slicing the core in half

my split blood & I
clutch at what we have
strew clods of soil
at our prone knees

I Shouldn't Be Doing This
Kevin Houchin

Unearth
Laura Pritchett

Claire spends too much time at the abandoned cemetery, and yes, she knows she ought to limit the time she spends there because, yes, there's only so much that can be gained from the past. But it's hard to resist the half-buried, lichen-encrusted tombstones. The heart wants what it wants, after all, and at this stage in her life, she's learned to give her heart a little more of what it asks for.

Today she has gone too far. She knows it. She's working on her excuse if any passersby see her from the distant county roads, and yes, that's possible since the old cemetery rests on the south side of the ranch, the side nearest the new subdivision that is nestled, with her, in these foothills of the Rocky Mountains. It's entirely likely that someone might notice a middle-aged woman in jeans and a white tank-top and ponytailed gray hair standing near the largest tombstone with a shovel in her hand. Surely they would wonder, but she hopes any curiosity remains submerged. She simply doesn't want to explain why she's digging up moist earth in search of a lost soul.

Claire has forgotten how much pain a body can hold – she hasn't felt this much hurt since the birth of her son decades ago. Really, what the body can bear in this regard is outstanding. Her arm muscles ache, her hands are covered with blisters, her torso throbs from lifting the shovel. She wipes the sweat from the side of her face with her forearm and as she does so, feels the skin stretch on her bare shoulders, tight with sunburn. She's put a pebble in her mouth to ward off thirst, and she rolls it around on her tongue and meanwhile coaxes herself: *Think pioneers crossing plains, think French trappers lonely and tired, press on, press on.*

At least there's been the recent rain. It makes this easier. All the yucca and mountain mahogany plants seem clean and fresh, and there is a new scent to the air, of sweet sage and tangy wet soil, of life, and, although this seems crazy, there seems to be a hum of gratefulness coming from the earth itself. Also, this digging is only possible because the water has softened the earth, and has caused enough erosion on this slope to make her goal feasible. She's often thought how the ground offers a gift in return for water, in this case, in the form of compliance, a willingness to be moved. And there's also the earth's curious ability to spit up treasures after a rain: arrowheads, glass bottles, bits of crockery. Water falls and the earth offers up, and today she is counting on just that – the chance to witness an exchange.

The shovel thuds against wood. Fear and a bit of glee surge through her chest with such force that her body sways back from the impact, and she drops the shovel and walks away. She wants to hold on to this moment, to let the thrill take hold.

There is a small bench she has brought for visitors to the cemetery, and she eases herself down onto it and surveys the tumble of land before her. Here are the lives lost to stillbirths, scarlet fever, whooping cough, typhoid, suicide. One hundred and seven people are buried here, all the early settlers in the region. She has written a book, one that took years of research – a slow process of unearthing stories, piecing together information. The book is not a morbid necrology, she writes in her introduction, but a celebration of ordinary lives. Because of her, none of the dead are just initials or names any longer. The barely-visible, clumsily-engraved letters have new meaning. She likes to think that because of her, their lives have been somewhat resurrected.

She looks at the stones of these people she's been laboring for. When her own time comes to join them, she knows there won't be much time to peruse the possibilities for the best last thoughts. She is prepared. She ticks off the list of things to say to herself in that last moment of life: First, it will be "Oh!" – or some sort of yelp of surprise – and then, "Damn!" – because of course she'll be furious – and then, "I'm scared." The next part she says to herself over and over as she examines the land in front of her. "Shhh, shhh, don't worry. Think of mountains. Think of the spiral in mountain mahogany. Think of how the heart feels on a hot summer day," she whispers, and then, "Goodbye to the soul of Claire."

Probably it is ridiculous, this rehearsal. But she has learned about the importance of a proper goodbye, and she wants to give herself what she can of a comforting farewell.

Since Claire first discovered the grave of Alphonse Morrisette, she has been holding long conversations with him in her mind. His was the very first burial recorded in the county – 1878 – and she figures there's a lot of catching up to do. She has explained what cars are and how they run. She tells him what housing developments are and why they all look alike, about the world's current population and about new farm technologies and the current price of cattle. She tells him of the New West, how small landowners are getting forced out, how the pseudo-cowboys have moved in, how Subarus have replaced pickups and fleece has replaced wool. She tells him about his French trapper father and his Oglala Sioux mother and how, after Custer, they were forced to move to Pine Ridge. She acknowledges his surprise at things such as computers and planes – she explains how they work, when they came into being. He'd be surprised that she wears pants, that she has control over her life – women's rights, Claire thinks, are a true paradigm shift. She argues with Alphonse about the changes she perceives as good but which she imagines he has trouble digesting ("it was wrong of you to think that women were not your equal") and sympathizes with him regarding the changes that are clearly wrong ("yes, look at that foothill, covered with houses – doesn't it make your heart break?")

She supposes others have these conversations with people of the past. But she wonders if anyone is so dedicated to them as she. She has an insatiable curiosity about this man for reasons she can't quite pin down. Perhaps because he was the first settler of this land. Perhaps because her farmhouse is built on the remnants of his log cabin. Perhaps because she occasionally finds old glass bottles, nails, handmade tools that she knows were his. In any case, she knows that such a strong curiosity is some people's definition of love. If that's so, then she has loved Alphonse for quite some time.

She rolls the pebble around in her mouth and gazes at the hill of gray tombstones and the waves of blue mountains rising behind them. A stretch of meadow spreads out where her Herefords graze, a blue heron flies above the line of cottonwoods that border the river, the horses stand in the vee of a fence corner flipping their tails against the flies.

It's true: Alphonse Morrisette and she have, by whatever bit of fortune, found themselves on the most glorious place on earth. Though their present state is not one which either prefers – he being dead and she about to lose everything – she supposes that the sheer beauty of their current location should cause them to feel awed and at peace.

That's what they have in common, she and Alphonse. They have shared this bit of earth. He died in the process of defending it for his family. She, on the other hand, is going to let it go. But before she sells this ranch, she's going to tell this man goodbye, a moment she will not be cheated of again.

She's so thirsty, but she doesn't want to stop now – she's too close. All she needs to do is pry the boards loose. She's on her hands and knees, with the crowbar, and the timber is thicker and darker than she imagined it would be, and as she fights with the rotten wood, she pleads with herself: *Try not to be bitter. Try not to be sad.* She reminds herself that when she was young, she balked at the audacity of the old, who complained about their failing health, their forced relocations, their trials, their pain of having to lose what they loved most. How dare they complain, those who had been given the chance, the honor, the gift, of living an entire lifetime?

Mostly hogwash, she realizes now. The old must see things whittled away, and in certain deep ways, that is no honor or gift. The body, the memory, the land – diminishing. She imagines, even, the mountains are being eaten away. But still, she tells herself not to utter a word of sorrow tomorrow, when she signs the papers. Two million dollars for two hundred acres in these foothills of the Rocky Mountains.

A developer has drawn up plans for all but the cemetery, which will, he assures her, of course remain an important historical site. Claire has written her son, Mason, who wrote her a postcard: "Sounds good to me. You'll be rich!"

Her heart cracked a bit when she read it. She was hoping he'd argue, plead, get down on his knees and say, "Once this land is developed, it will never be the same. Cement sidewalks will take the place of the paths I took down to the river, fishing pole in one hand and a coffeecan of worms in the other. The gravel road, with its snake of grass in the middle, will be asphalt. Houses with those godawful garages eclipsing the entrance will sit where the ground has never been tilled since the first roots took hold there. Doesn't she understand the value of a place? How it is worth so much more than two million dollars?"

In her imagination, he tells her how he will come home, and how working together, they will save the ranch. He will have knowledge that her husband Daniel didn't – Daniel in his old, sweat-stained ballcap, squinting at a computer screen and tapping away at the keyboard with those beat-up hands of his, trying to figure out futures and options and a way to save the place. Daniel, who, like a fool, believed up until the end that they'd continue living in the old rambling farmhouse, continue checking on cows and selling fresh eggs and cutting hay. Maybe it would have worked, she thinks, if from nothing else, the sheer force of his will. It's just that on his way to check a pregnant heifer last March, his heart stopped too early. And he fell to the ground, and died, before she ever got to tell him goodbye.

In her imagination, her son comes back to pick up where Daniel left off. In her mind, such a thing is possible. Because in her daydreams, her son knows about the cows, that they must be fed, checked, doctored, birthed, weaned. He knows about the weeds that need to be killed, fields irrigated, trees watered, fences mended, about the garden needs tending and the apple trees pruned, that the pump needs to be fixed, about the meetings to attend, taxes to pay, books to balance, cattle to sell. He knows that this is too much for a single aging woman, and he will fiercely battle for her and for the place, and he knows that although it makes for a humble existence that the land is worth it because this place is a beautiful place, and it is a place to belong to. Even when she knows there's no chance of such a dream coming true, she likes to imagine the possibilities.

And anyway, why not let the land be developed? A few more people will enjoy the view; perhaps someone will even appreciate it as much as she does. These new homesteaders will have their own smaller parcels of glory.

Besides, she did what she could, didn't she? This past year, she searched high and low for a buyer who would ranch the land, or for someone who'd keep it intact and safe. In the end, there were too many taxes, not enough money, nobody interested. So she settled for eighty acres of open space around the cemetery. That's something, isn't it? Perhaps not enough, but God knows she tried.

She pushes her weight down on the crowbar. She's going to let it all go, with as much goodwill as she can muster.

Claire's face and breath contort with the effort of something at the cusp of her ability. She pauses to cuss at the crowbar and wood and sky and then starts again, and finally wood splinters and she is able, with more prying and pushing and gasping, to move a thick board to the side. The moment it shifts, the faint smell of wood mixed with something like wet wool rolls out at her, and although there is no movement, she imagines the newly-released air floating past her. She catches her breath because, for an instant, she is afraid of it entering her body. Then she exhales all her own pent up air, pushing it toward the skeleton that has just come into view. She shakes herself, trying to clear away the prickles in her neck and spine, and then shakes herself again, this time sending away the tears that press against her eyes.

What she sees is hair, black hair, coarse and wiry.

She sees it hanging from a skeleton face that's caved in on one side.

She sees a long lean body covered yet in leather.

She leans back, surprised. She's done it! Then she crouches forward again to pry off a second board. Now the full skeleton is in view. She feels as if she should pause, but she cannot wait to touch him. She leans in so she can reach him, and fingers the black hair, then moves her hand to the place above the right ear, where the skull is broken. Here it is, the wound that killed him. Tangible and real and glorious. She touches the very spot that caused the end of a young life, proving the microfiched newspaper accounts of it true, and therefore proving all her research true, her hobby and her fascination valid. But more than that: here is the *exact place* where life was taken, and perhaps in touching it her body will absorb his loss in a way that newspaper accounts and diaries will not allow her to do.

When she takes her hand away, she is startled to see what looks like a flake of dried blood on her finger. She looks at the dark, wispy fleck, this essence of Alphonse Morrisette. She wishes she could make it turn to liquid and flow again. There is so much she'd like to share with him. She would like to hear his voice speak whatever was last in his mind, and see his eyes drift across their land.

She reaches in the coffin and lifts out his skull. She only has to twist it a bit to free it from the spot where it has rested for so long. She holds it in front of her. Part of the cheekbone on one side is caved in, and the bone is cracked and dusty. But the jaw is intact. And all that hair – she can't get over how long it is – it's not what she imagined at all.

"I shouldn't be doing this," she says at last.

The sun pulses down bright light from its afternoon position, hanging above the mountains, and Claire turns a little so that the sun hits the side of her face instead of head-on. She does this so she can see, but it feels more like the movement of a person being accused, someone who turns her head slightly to deflect judgment. As she moves her own head, a shard from the skull's cheekbone falls to the ground. She watches it settle among the rocks and dirt.

"I suppose you'd like to know what hit you." Her

voice is just a whisper, so she clears her throat and starts again, louder. "First you were walking home on a cold March night, and the next thing you knew was darkness. Did you know you were dying? Did you have a chance to tell yourself goodbye?"

She looks past the skull to the rest of the body. This man was quite tall, just as she'd assumed. The legs are covered with leather pants, cut narrow, and fit like jeans. The leather is surprisingly soft and clean. There are no boots – this doesn't surprise her, since she knows shoes were so valuable they often weren't left on the body. Brown wool socks cover the feet, though, and through the material she can feel the crumbled bones of his toes. There's also a short leather jacket with wide lapels over his torso and arm bones.

She doesn't know what she expected, but she didn't expect this – to find him so intact, still clothed, after a hundred and twenty-seven years. How can it be that he's still so much in the form of a human body, so close to being able to sit up and laugh and hold a conversation?

It takes some time before she can speak again, but when she does, her words rush out in a torrent. "Let me tell you about your last night. I read your cousin Minnie's diary. She said you'd gotten in a fight, defending your mother's Indian blood, defending your family's right to stay on the property. The Custer thing had happened and all the French-Indian families left in 1878, first to Red Cloud and then to Pine Ridge, but your daddy refused to leave, refused to let White Owl leave, refused to sell the land. I bet the old timers didn't care, but maybe one of the new settlers did. You left a bar one night and before you got home, an ax had been plunged into your head. You'd been talking about the mountains, the good river bottomland, said you were going to plant an orchard, said you were going to be the richest fellow in town. Said you were going to protect this place from all the condos, forty-acre ranchettes, strip malls that were to come. Okay, well, you didn't say that. But apparently you said enough. Because on the way home, whoever you'd been bragging to – no one knows, because no one was ever charged – whacked you with an ax." After a moment, she mumbles: "I'm sorry. It's a terrible way to die, when you don't see what's coming." She pictures him falling, falling, his head ricocheting slightly off the ground. If only she could have been there to hold his head in her lap.

"I'm sorry your land is gone. It got parceled off and sold over the years. I own the last two hundred acres. Have you heard any of my conversations to you? I have to move away now, because at some point, a person just has to give in. I'm sorry to let you down about that, but it's complicated. There are taxes and debt and I just don't want to die, I guess, in the attempt to hold it together. Plus my son doesn't want to live here. This place meant sacrifice. My husband and I loved it for that, but my son hated it for the same reason, and all he remembers is the duct-tape on his shoes. I keep telling myself that sacrifice must be kept in check, or it becomes the ruin of souls. Isn't that right, Alphonse?"

She considers the skull, which she has put on the ground beside her. "You had some passion for this earth. We would have walked it together, across the deer trails," she says. "Or, no, probably we would have hated each other – because I can see where you might be a tough bastard, a hard man – but who knows, maybe we would have been happy. We're both a bit ornery, a bit odd, a bit dreamy, aren't we Alphonse, aren't we?"

His jawbone looks like it might be smiling. She wonders if he enjoys feeling the warm mountain air, which still has undercurrents of cool from the rain. "My husband and I used to walk the land together, too, looking for arrowheads and bits of junk you left behind. Bottles and tools. Perhaps you were the person who touched them last, before me. That makes us not so distant after all, doesn't it? It's funny in how certain ways time can be collapsed." She runs her finger across the leather above where his heart once beat.

She hears a rustle nearby, and jerks her head up to look, but it is only a meadowlark flying out from some foxtail grass. She looks down the valley at her white farmhouse and the cottonwoods clustered around it. There is the beat-up pickup, her peacock fanning his tail in the reflection of an old bathroom mirror she'd left out for him, chickens wandering around the yard.

She picks up the skull again and puts it back in the coffin and smoothes the coarse hair from the flat bone of the forehead. His skull tilts to one side a bit, and some of the black hairs rise up in the breeze. "So, your life. Now it's all a bland piece of history. My life will be the same, of course. All that drama and joy and pain ends up as a newspaper blurb. We all get reduced, smoothed over. I did what I could to keep that from happening, but I think it helped only a little." She feels the sting of tears rising, and wipes at her eyes with a forearm that smells of salty sweat and dirt. "This was my last cockamamie search for a lost soul, Alphonse. Goodbye."

She stands up, brushes the dirt from her jeans, and begins to replace the boards, stepping on them to press them tight. Then she picks up the shovel to move the dirt back in. Evening is on its way, full of deep blues, and she watches the color shift and darken across mountain and sky. As she works, the speech she used to give during her tours of the cemetery runs through her mind. She tries to stop it, but there it is anyway, circling: "There are certain things to be learned from what has come before, and this is what I believe to be true –

"One, the past happened.

"Two, it can't be recovered.

"Three, but archaeology can be done, and it can be done well. There will be gaps, of course there will be gaps, but really, there's no alternative. History and its archives, archaeology and its artifacts. It has to be enough."

She always ended with this list. Then she would add: "We can dig into the past, and discover the limitations, or we can not do it. I choose to do it." She repeated this last bit with an air of grand finality. Even now, in her mind and with no audience at all, she punctuates these last words.

Well, today she's accomplished what she set out to do, which is to verify that the limitations might be too damn great. That's all she needed to know. And so now she'll try to end her conversations with Alphonse Morrisette, and with Daniel too, and try to remember how much earth separates them all. When she forgets this, she will think of how alive the earth smells when dug up, how smooth it feels in her rough hand, how it cleaves when a shovel slices.

She gently spits the pebble onto one of the boards and stares at it—the small stone wet with saliva, wet with all the words her tongue wanted to form, drying, now, blending in with the others. She is about to fling a shovelful of dirt on it but instead steps right onto the small rock, onto the board, onto Alphonse. She cocks her ear and focuses, but there's no evidence of them going deeper, farther away. The wood does not crack, the ground does not give, but she can feel a shudder moving up her leg bones all the same, all her strength being received into the earth and the earth accepting it, and in turn, searching for the gift it will offer back.

Morning
Kevin Houchin

Sweetwater Cabin, Day 22, Big Horn Mountains, Wyoming
Page Lambert

I listen as a herd of wild elk makes its way down the slope of the mountain to the beaver pond only twenty yards from the cabin. The bulls bugle, the cows mew to the calves. Calves stumble over deadfall in their eagerness to get to the pond. I watch their brown bodies appear and disappear through the trees, watch the bulls ease their antlers through the low-hanging branches, listen to the sharp retort of sticks breaking beneath their hooves.

A large, six-point bull walks up the path in front of the cabin. I desperately want to join the herd, but dare not frighten them away. I hear calves splashing in the pond, hear long legs wading across the water, picture the dragonflies flitting around the sedge-thick edges.

Twenty minutes later, I hear more splashing as the elk cross to the far side of the pond. Then, except for the occasional sharp sound of a stick breaking, or the gentle entreaty of a cow calling her calf, it grows quiet as they gradually work their way up the aspen draw. From high on the far ridge, a lone bull bugles as the herd departs. Later, he makes his way down to the water. After they are all gone, I walk up to the pond.

I have stepped into a cathedral. The air is pregnant with their presence. Every fiber of my body resonates, as if I am a brass bell and they have struck an ancient chord. I wonder, standing in the stillness, where sound goes. Where is the liquid sound of their splashing now? The percussive explosion of their passage through the woods? The engorged bellows of the bulls? The maternal mewing of the cows?

And then I realize that not only does every fiber of

my being resonate with their presence, but every stone, every pinecone, every needle of every tree, every scrap of bark, every dragonfly, woodpecker and wren, every sapling and thistle, wild rose, aster and ant, even the mountain lions who claim the granite peaks, everything resonates with their passage...

*   *   *

Excerpted from the narrative nonfiction work-in-progress *Sweetwater: A Mountain Cabin.* Previously published in *Pilgrimage: Story. Spirit. Witness. Place,* "Atmosphere," Volume 35, Issue 2, Fall 2010, page 91-92. Editor and publisher Maria Melendez, P.O. Box 9110, Pueblo, CO 81008. Info@pilgrimagepress.org; www.pilgrimagepress.org.

Three Poems
Virginia Bach Folger

March Snow

She arrives in a clatter
of icy pebbles, shifts
to a hush of white feathers
floating to ground , smothering
the hope of spring.

She buries patchy brown grass
under her wizened shawl,
works with slipper-footed stealth,
not to wake the worms asleep
in their tunnels.

Her pale shadow blocks the sun.
Though the earth is bone cold,
she declares it too soon
for spring. No robins return
to sink slender feet into
her brittle crust.

Sparrow

Half hidden
in the grass
speckled feathers
mimicking
the interplay
of sun and shadow
lying on your side
almost overlooked
as we pass by.

Silent bird
whose song
unseen mixed
with the just
completed dawn
life drained away
beside this tiny
blooming violet
singing purple
into the nooning light

Virginia Bach Folger

Water Lilies

Those flowers that made old Claude famous
strewn across his vast canvas are alive
here, too, floating on a still pond, under
the summer sun of Stresa in a garden
on an island in a lake rimmed with mountains,
their pointed petals colored with the sky.
I could linger here a lifetime,
Breathing the lake air.

Lorraine Currelley

Billy Joel Heard Her Prayers

she aches for truth in laughter
sun kissed smiles
life seasoned passion
music making love to soul
silent comfort
and easy togetherness
Billy Joel heard her prayers
and she won't go changing
just to please
they'll have to love her
just the way she is

she discovered love is not
ordered movements
robotic smiles
empty words
masked in pleasantries
and sterile conversation
she discovered joy
and need buried within her sadness

she once existed twisted
never having known tender love
programmed to please
if you're good in the bedroom
a good cook in the kitchen
and a lady in the parlor
he'll leave his penis and heart at home

misogyny
threatening to kill her
she feigned passion and desire
on scary nights
hid bleeding tears and sad heart
his touch masturbation
no participation from her
nor evidence of feeling present
she finding kisses, gentle touch,

Lorraine Currelley

and laughter living only in dreams
with each empty stroke an assault

what does real love feel and taste like
is it sweet like honey lemon tea
mama's freshly baked buttered biscuits
cool summer nights
the feel of rain on thirsty wanting skin
is it lovers lips on breast
and passion loving skin to bone
is it sticky wetness
like sweet icing on warm cinnamon buns
is it tongue searching
and mouth welcoming
is it lovers secrets gently whispered
nature's cry
and smiles bathed in pleasure
is it heart longing for more of a lovers touch
please tell me
what does real love feel and taste like

Harlem No Longer Smiles

took the Bronx 19 bus
to 145 street and Amsterdam
neighbors laughing and talking
gentrification boarded the bus
blue eyed
long blond extensions
draped in African fabric
hatred owning her eyes
nose turned up in disdain
did my great grandmothers
experience thoughts and feelings
of impending danger and genocide
on the reservation
in her village
when ghost colored men arrived
on ships named enslavement

 Our Writing for Peace Advisors are artists and activists who have achieved a level of personal integrity in their work that inspires us to search for our own truth. This is our first DoveTales Adviser Feature, and we hope it will inspire you to consider new ways that your work can make a difference.

Featured Advisor
Lorraine Currelley

Advisor Lorraine Currelley is a poet and writer who founded The Currelley Literary Journal and Poets Network & Exchange, Inc., a supportive space for writers to develop their craft. Beyond her literary honors, Lorraine is a mental health counselor and human rights advocate who has been honored for her community efforts with the homeless. In this vein, she founded the L.C. Information and Resource Center to provide mental health and bereavement services, public education, and outreach to survivors of child abuse, domestic, elder, gender and sexual violence. She sets a high bar for all of us who hope to change the world with our work.

Lorraine Currelley shares some thoughts about her poetry and activism. Many thanks to Lorraine's friend and fellow poet, Iona Samuels, who interviews her here.

[I.S.] Do you think a poet has a significant role in shaping society?

Every human being, including poets, plays a significant role in shaping society. Our experiences are uniquely our own, meaning how we experience them psychologically, emotionally, physically and spiritually. Poets, and other artists, reflect and give voice to what is happening in society.

[I.S.] When did you know you wanted to be a poet and writer?

I started writing compositions, essays, and poems as a
child. I enjoyed writing and sharing my work, and I en-
joyed the responses and resulting feelings of accomplish-
ment. During my high school years I became involved in
social and political justice and racial equality movements.
In the 1960's and 1970's I attended poetry readings, hu-
man rights, civil rights and social justice gatherings and I
heard poets and writers challenging the status quo. I at-
tended readings featuring The Last Poets, Nikki Giovanni,
Sonia Sanchez and other poets, writers and prominent
figures during that era. The seed was planted and I started
to think of myself as a poet or writer of poetry. If memory
serves me, it was not until I was in my late twenties I said
it aloud with conviction and meant it. I learned activism
from my mother, family, elementary school principal and
socially and politically engaged community activists.

*[I.S.] Was there a major event in your life that played a
role?*

My love of reading and writing, and my mother and
brother were major catalysts. My mother loved reading
and writing and instilled the love of reading in us as chil-
dren. I remember attending plays produced by the Negro
Ensemble Company's playwright workshop in New York
City. I made a comment which resulted in my brother
Edward challenging me to write plays. I picked up my pen
and responded to the challenge. There
were so many factors which played a role.

[I.S.] Who are your major influences as a poet?

My major influence has been me, specifically my life ex-
periences. I love the masters both men and women of the
Harlem Renaissance! Langston Hughes is one of my first
loves. I was introduced to his work at home and school as
a young child. I try and read everyone! I've read many of
the popular poets and little known poets over the years,

including present company. Among many I enjoy reading and hearing are Anton Nimblett, Gary Johnston, Mercy L. Tullis Bukhari, Carmen Bardeguez Brown, Yadira De La Riva, Cathy Linh Che, and Patricia Smith. Recently I've been introduced to the voices of poets and writers through my Writing for Peace family, such as Sam Hamill, Wang Ping, Veronica Golos, Lyla June Johnston, Mary Carroll-Hackett, Djelloul Marbrook, David S. Pointer, Robert Kostuck, Vicki Lindner, Patricia Jabbeth Wesley, Melissa Hassard, Pilar Rodriguez Aranda, Paula Dawn Lietz, Andrea W. Doray, Richard Krawiec, Carmel Mawle, and so many more.

[I.S.] Why do you like to write?

I write because I have to.

[I.S.] What advice can you give to fellow poets and writers?

Write, then write some more. Attend writing workshops. Writing is more than just picking up a pen and placing words on paper. Writing requires study, and reading. Take the time to learn craft, whether formally or informally. I admit to attending specific venues for their level and quality of scholarship, and I appreciate constructive feedback that's craft based. If you don't already have a mentor or someone you respect to talk craft with and honesty, get someone!

If you can't afford to pay, seek out free workshops at libraries and look for literary organizations that offer inexpensive workshops. My organization Poets Network & Exchange, Inc. provides poetry readings, poetry and creative writing workshops, an open mic, panel discussions, and a scholar lecture series free of charge. Seek out these types of opportunities that challenge us not only as writers. Become active in issues affecting your community and this nation. Become a positive catalyst for change. For instance, we facilitated a panel discussion called "Black Women Creating and Building, A New Narrative" that provided a forum to discuss our needs as intelligent, articulate, creative women, capable of speaking for and defining ourselves, psychologically, emotionally, spiritually and physically. Together, we're replacing the old paradigm with a new narrative.

Poets Network & Exchange, Inc. is on the front lines helping to inform, educate, and act as a catalyst for change. As a poet, it's critical that I add my voice to those in the Black and diverse communities uniting around police brutality, the murders of Blacks and people of color and the poor, the #BlackLivesMatter and #BlackPoetsSpeakOut movements. I implemented panel discussions on Black women and girls and poor self esteem, colorism light versus dark skin, skin bleaching, hair straightening, stereotyping and the sexualizing of Black women and girls as well as the criminalization of the Black community, communities of color and the poor. Words are powerful and have the power to create movements and change.

I have dedicated my private funds and countless volunteer hours for the last four years to create and grow Poets Network & Exchange, Inc. We believe quality programming and instruction should be accessible to everyone. We expanded our programming in response to community needs by creating our Scholar Lecture Series. I utilize my training as a mental health counselor to address the needs of my community, and include professionals and laypersons in our programming who are doing political and social justice work in the community, organizing around food justice, obesity, hypertension (high blood pressure), and environmental issues, such as the dumping of waste in impoverished communities of color.

Generous grants from Poets & Writers, Inc. have made it possible to begin paying some of our featured guests, and we plan to apply for funding from foundations and private sources in order to grow our programming and provide needed staff and technologies. I recognize that educational and cultural organizations must respond to the needs of those we serve. Along with writing workshops, we must find ways in which to assist those in need of housing, clothing, food and affordable health care, or share the information needed to obtain these necessities. I've seen these programs change lives, and together we are changing the world. It's poetry in action.

[I.S.] Define the meaning of poetry?

The following is my definition of poetry and who I am as experienced through me. This poem was written in 1985.

I
be
an African
classical note
a woman
of hunger and thirst
nature's raw essence
a wanting tongue kiss
bursting from
Ms. Annie's sacred womb

[I.S.] What does being a poet mean to you?

It's feeling of being blessed to create and be a part of a craft I love.

Nature's Dance

splashes of color
nature and human entwined
in both dance and symphony
raw
earthy
wildly feminine
and free
kissing our spirits with magic
we smile
accepting hearts full.

Me vs. Myself
Elizabeth Hoyle

They've plastered my face all over the apartment, in spite
of my requests not to. I look around, revulsion settling
in my heart as bile rises to the back of my throat. Every
side of me is here, on these walls. Me as a mother. Me as
a geisha. Me as a professional volleyball player. Me as a
fine Victorian lady, parasol and all. A doctor, a lawyer, a
writer; an actress, a musician, an acrobat. You name it,
I've been it. All for other people, never for myself, you
understand. The only thing I've ever done expressly of my
own volition was sign a modeling contract when I was six-
teen. Little did I know then that I had signed my life away.

I step further into the apartment, pulling my luggage
behind me, knowing that a reporter doing a story about
my career will be here soon. I'm not ready to play twenty
questions about the romance novels my agent said would
be a good move to model for but there's nothing I can
do about it. There is champagne in an ice bucket and a
platter of figs on a coffee table. No doubt my agent made
sure they were placed especially for me. My old modeling
coach told me to eat figs before a shoot, to clean me out so
I'd look even thinner for the cameras. I used to eat them
religiously but as time has gone on, I've lost my taste for
them. I put my luggage in the bedroom and pour myself
some champagne and drink, not even hoping it will steady
my nerves, but that it will make me so drunk that they'll
never bother me again, not the reporters, not the photog-
raphers, not anybody. But like all my wishes, it's useless.
There's a knock at the door. I slowly count to three before
setting my glass down and answering.

"Hi, I'm Michael Cornmeyer and I'm here for the interview," he says in a rush, too young and eager to even be out of college, let alone interviewing me.

"Of course," I reply, flashing him my trademark smile. "Do come in." He enters timidly as if he's expecting to fall into a trap if he takes the wrong step.

"Champagne?" He nods and settles on the sofa, pulling out magazines from his messenger bag. I pour him a glass and set it before him.

"You might want to sit down, Ms. Avon, I have plenty of questions for you." Unwillingly I sit down on an overly plush armchair opposite him. I kick off my $900 stilettos and toss them aside like garbage. Michael piles at least twenty magazines on the coffee table, all with me on the front cover. I don't know whether to sneer or tear them up, so I finish my champagne instead.

"I've been doing a lot of research about you, Ms. Avon. I've read every interview you've given that I could find. You've shared a lot about yourself," he pauses to clear his throat and pushes a wayward black curl out of his blue eyes. "And yet there seems to be something missing, something you haven't shared with any reporter before."

I chuckle. "I don't know what you think I'm hiding, but ask your questions."

"Okay." He gets a notepad out. He's got to be one of the only reporters who still uses notepads, but for some reason this comforts me. "What is your real name?"

"Well that's one thing you've unearthed," I say as I reach for the champagne bottle. "No one else has guessed that Shelby Avon is just a pseudonym the modeling agency and I thought sounded better than Michelle Lavonivitz." He scribbles my name down. Clearly this is not going to be any ordinary interview.

"How did you get into modeling?"

"As I'm sure you're aware, I won Mississippi's Little Miss contest when I was four and was in and out of beauty pageants until I signed my first modeling contract when I was sixteen."

"That must have been an interesting way to grow up," Michael remarks. "How did that interfere with your education?" The memories of the looks the guys at my tiny high school gave me when word got around still make my skin crawl.

"I did leave high school, yes, but I made sure to keep learning through cyber schooling. That's how I got my high school diploma, then I got my Bachelor's at the University of Texas."

"You modeled to help pay the bills, correct?"

"Yes." *Those and the psychiatrist*, I nearly blurt out, but fortunately he moves on to the next question.

"There's barely any designer you haven't modeled for, plus you're an active philanthropist. Whenever anyone in the fashion world thinks of the word 'beautiful', it is your face they see. How do you feel about all the attention you get?"

"I think if you read that issue of *Vogue*, third from the top, you'll find my answer to that question," I reply, nodding to the coffee table. Michael fixes me with a keen look.

"I'd like to know what you *really* think."

"I'm not supposed to say what I really think, Mr. Cornmeyer." I can still hear my old modeling coach hammering that advice into by skull, back in the early days when I thought people truly cared about me.

"Try me."

"Why? So you can bag the story of a lifetime? 'World's best model Shelby Avon tells all on page 6'? No, thank you." He fidgets, clearly too inexperienced to know when to give up.

"You must have some fascinating insights about life, Ms. Avon. I'm asking you to share only those you'd feel comfortable revealing to the public." My champagne glass shatters, I've been gripping it so firmly. The alcohol dribbles down my designer jeans and soils the immaculate armchair. My hand is bleeding, but I don't care.

"Okay, but you write specifically what I say, no revisions." He nods, looking a little frightened. It's only going to get worse from here.

"Most models are suckers," I begin. "Designers and agencies flatter us, they tell us we're beautiful and make promises of a better life. And we believe them. No one warns you of the personal cost that comes with it. We're just billboards to them, billboards with faces, breasts, bellies, butts, arms, and legs that are to be dressed to every advantage to sell whatever it is. Whether it's mommy-porn romance novels or the spring collection of some unheard of fashion prodigy, all they care about is that you look perfect for the camera so they can make money." I pause to catch my breath and let him finish his notes.

"But surely," he asks slowly as he writes, "the disadvantages of your career have also had many benefits. What about your work in Africa?"

"Those idiots who run the charities couldn't solve a problem if the solution was right under their noses. While it's true, they're a great help in many areas, they're only ensuring that certain problems continue on. They're handing out condoms in areas riddled with sexual violence and abuse instead of stopping the violence and providing proper sexual education. They're just propagating the problem instead of solving it."

"There are some problems that will never be solved-"

I cut him off. "Yes, but that doesn't mean they have to make them worse." I close my eyes and hear the bed creaking after he'd gotten up to get a fresh condom, coming back for me like a tiger going in for the final kill.

"How do you feel about your career?" Michael prompts. "What do you see when you see your picture?" I take one look at the gallery of me on the walls around us then turn away before I throw up.

"How do you think I feel when everyone assumes I'm perfect yet doesn't know me at all? How do you think it feels to know that men and women see nothing of you but your body? What do you think it feels like when you know it's your pictures boys are looking at when they masturbate? Because it's awful. I can tell you. I see nothing when I look at a picture of myself that anyone but my mama took. I don't see myself, I see only a version of me that people have made in order to make it seem like I'm an otherworldly angel, but I'm not. I'll let you in on a few secrets, Mr. Cornmeyer." I stop to pick a few shards of glass out of my still bleeding hand. He's looking really scared now.

"I think of ways to destroy the cameras during the endless photo shoots; I've gotten really creative over the years. I'm on my way to earning a Master's degree just to prove that anyone who models isn't stupid. I've purposefully gained weight despite my agent's pleading. I haven't been home since I left. I've thought of several ways to kill myself and others. And here's the one big secret I've held back, the one you haven't sniffed out: I was raped when I was nine."

Michael stops writing. "You never told anyone that?"

"No, not even my high school psychologist, who was the best of all of them." It's taking all I have to remain calm. "My neighbor, who used to take care of me after school when both my parents were still at work, found he couldn't control himself around me. He made me aware of this fact, again and again and again."

"You never told your parents?"

"I didn't have to. His wife walked in on him, took me home, told my parents, then filed for divorce. I wouldn't talk about it and after a while, they assumed I was okay. But I wasn't."

"Then why model?"

"I thought I was unlovable. My own parents couldn't be bothered to ensure I was alright after what had happened to me. These people told me I was beautiful, that they loved me and wanted to share me with the world. What I thought would be me salvation became my damnation. But to everyone else, I'm one of the luckiest people alive." I brush a tear away; I had thought myself beyond crying.

"Empathy really needs to come back in style," I say. "If people used their brains and honestly thought about others for even just the tiniest moment, the world would be a much better place, you know?"

"I know," he answers. There are tears in his eyes and he's stopped writing. I stand and go to the kitchen to look for something to wrap around my hand. A minute later, I return to the living room, my hand cleaned and bandaged in a dish towel.

Michael runs a hand though his curls. "Ms. Avon, I—"

"I don't want pity, Mr. Cornmeyer. You've managed to get my secrets out of me, now go splash them across the pages of your magazine."

"I just wanted to say that none of this interview ever happened. I'll call my editor and tell him I couldn't reach you." He gets up, packs his belongings and slings his bag over his shoulder.

"Tell them I'm done with modeling. Make that your story. Tell them I'm done." He nods.

"Why are you doing this?" I can't help but ask.

He looks me straight in the eye. "The world has had enough of you. Everyone deserves at least a few secrets."

We shake hands and he departs. I'm feeling ravaged, like a tornado has been raging inside of me yet I'm lighter than I remember being in years, if ever. I take a look at the walls of me, pick up the platter of sweet-smelling figs, throw, and hit myself square between the eyes. The bottle of champagne shatters musically against the walls and just as I'm leaving, I see the perfected images of me peeling away, revealing the true reality beneath.

Doldrums
Smriti Verma

i. Depression
noun de·pres·sion \di-'pre-shən, dē-\
(a) a disease whether the mind is not one's own, where it
wanders, unlike the daughter you did not love

The wintery nights seem to woefully percolate from the
little gaps in the windows into our homes – like little
leeching insects, they discreetly occupy the spaces be-
tween our toes, between the finger-like waves of your
discoloured hair, between the pits of our red eyes, be-
tween doors sick of being slammed shut and between
syllables that swirl in the atmosphere and dance around
until absorbed and applauded for recognition. What is left
behind is the deafening silence of the car-horns outside
that becomes us when silence seems too heavy a word to
throw around – I dive into this noise, embrace it with a
body half-crumbling and half-crumbled. Papa tells me to
stay away from the woman that is you, the body that is
you, the mummy that is you – he tells me to go and find
solace in the dead yellow grasses of the proverbial park
out front, in the raindrops that seem full of little angry
gods whenever they land on my scalp, in the eerie glow
of the monochromatic night moon that scares me with
its simplicity, with the light flooding from the starry skies
caught in the glint of each little object. But solace comes
only at intervals, and I hear it when I see you preparing
the dinner meals. I hear it when I see you up and about, a
gown creating ruffles in the air wherever you walk. I hear
it, low at times, when your arms nestle me in an embrace,
squishing my hands into a mess of bones, my cartilage

315

ears bending under your fingernails – bending, but never breaking. I hear it in your dialogues, and I hear it in mine. But it only comes at intervals – it goes when you retire in the bedroom where you spend three-fourths of your day, it goes when the suspended syllables in the air, brimming with the ferocity, land on my young skin and put me under. So, I agree with father and tell him I'll find solace wherever it finds me.

ii. Depression (n)
(b) a state of being

A state of being, I repeat the phrase to myself like a prayer which never turns to fruition, *a state of being*. I soak it in the messy quilts on our thirty year old mattresses, I soak it in the empty medicine bottles on the cabinet which I now use for keeping U-pins in, I soak it in my bones that seem to turn heavier each day until they start feeling brittle and break. You have turned thinner, full of water, a seasick wave, a body standing for the sake of standing and papa says it is your nature but it will go away when the pills you have been taking finally make you better instead of making you thinner, when they turn your skin the same smooth white like an expanse of lush grasses instead of colouring it a tone between blue and purple whose name I know but can't quite put my finger on. But I drown my days in printed books full of knowledge which makes more sense to me than your behaviour, and I do well at school, I do very well, I do too well that the teachers begin asking like a couple of irritating mosquitoes that buzz about your hair even after you've walked away. You open the door when I come home today and even before my right foot has stepped on the Aquinas marble beneath, a phantom limb of yours reaches out and a slap wrings on my left cheek, a very loyal and generous imprint of your hand on it. I brush it off, like everything else you ever did or do or will do. Papa finally sits me down on our couch ridden with dust bunnies, and says it is in the nature of your condition to behave this way, to have frequent bouts of anger and a need to tear the curtains that look ill all the

time, a need to overturn chairs whose rusted wood makes
you gag and a need to slap the daughter whose black
circles and stillness and mouth that is perpetually turned
downward makes you scream and cry and wrench the
flesh off your thighs until all that remains is a bandaged
human, a walking dead. But whatever papa says, I know it
your nature but not the nature of people.

iii. Depression (n)
(c) perpetual abandonment
I roam the halls of our two-bedroom termite-infested flat,
my childhood home now stripped of everything – stripped
of you and empty medicine bottles and slaps that turned
to dust in the sliver of a second and suspended syllables
that vanished when you went away. I roam the halls with
ghosts supporting me if I fall, I roam the halls dream-
ing of the doldrums that occupied each fibre of my infant
body, of my teenage body, and now signifies about half
a part of me. I roam the halls asking for deliverance, like
the prayers we all have and all our eyelash wishes that are
never fulfilled. But no liberation resides for me here and I
resign myself to my nightmares of you, muffling my long
withheld screams into new, ready-made and clean pillows.

Mercy4-7r
Fred Tarr

;1/14: •7 U 'ₛeeeyei i have this
peculia; r calling, an instinct, maybe,
likestopping to get out of my truck to keep my
bladder from exploding

finding my dick, like grabbi g clothespins to put in my
mouth, biting down..eyeitig the empty spot d'ere! on the
wash line, a rubber chicken out of a play boxpassing
water, something as NATmina tural as after-visions
from the cinema:

Whenever-I see a man beating his dog, a chill goes
through me like a spring windin' my body, and if Fm
driving, I stop the car, get out, and as the chill winds
like a spring tightly 'in the back of my head, I Ao over
and say, "Hey, stop beating   10Tur dog!" Ifs gotten me
in a lot of trouble over the years. If I see a man beating his
wife;., or beati g his child, the exact same thing happens:
the chill deep inside and winding in
me

likeaspringuntil it buzz buzze in the
crown ?fray head, the compulsion to
get out, go over to the person and ay,
Hey, stop beating your wife,   stop
beating your kid. It's a dangerous
thing. F24 instance, check out my
318

nose here. I got that in Peoria one day
when I had the urge, the need to stop
the car and say to a man, Hey, stop
beating your dog.

Since I've had to live with it,
I've looked at it from all angles.
In order to survive my calling,
I've developed a system. In Los
Angeles, in Reno,PA. Now when I
see a man beating his victim, I
stop the car, walk over slowly and

pretend I've just discovered

a patch of wild

mountainflowersblooming lusciously

around the victim. I make myself

blind and then proceed. Smiling
my biggest and best,
arms outstretched, looking
at my riotous color of flowers
everywhere, I say, Oh! My!
Look! You're beating your dog!
(wife)(child!), all the time
picturing infinite Beauty. I watch
him, carefully. He catches it

right away. Yeah ...he says,

straightening up,

scratching his head, club in hand
..the sonata bitch, or, wipeing
his nose, he's gonna oooo gonna get it.....
sonoooo—faaaa bitccch HUH!

Again, (whaaa) looking toward
me, appreciating my interest...
yeah.. god damn whore. I say, Yes!
Exactly! I know wh#$6,t you mean!
Looking at the **righteous bloom
around** the victim, I continue'
...with this particular breed
though, you may have forgotten
something. Me,? he says. Yeah,
You, I say. Oh, he says. Look
here, I say, bending over as if
to pick the flowers of Eternal
Grace;
slowly, slowly he bends with
me. Suddenly, we are bent over
almost nose to nose.

I straigh.t :1 up and say, Where do you live? He tells me.
I say, 'know where I'm from? I tell him. What do you
do for a living? He tells me....then I say, yATwanna know what I
do for

a living? I tell him. Then I show him my hand, —   a scar I got

in the sixth grade. (look) **He looks at me**; Y look at him. bEy now his victim

(dog, child, woman) has moved away to a safe distance. In front of me a crouched

Figure

, club at half mast, sweat pouring, eyes fixed, hands, arms on kneeld bony knee

at rest from **starting** again,. Thinking where, starting ^again, **hard work** to hit someone, they yell, move around, piss their pants,cry, dodge, RUN, runs, talks to hold, freeZE/ me coming WAITe **there in the** midst

of flowers he

isn't.

JUST

how well does my system work? Well, the first time

I did it, the dog gettin' beaten thought I wasn't taking its plight seriously

enough SO **it bit me.** It was the line o f least resistance. And once when a woman was receiving a public bbee---)hating of a certain severity:

standing near her with my best smile, breaking into the. skin of it,

Fred Tarr

I looked at my flowers growing around her. Watching my
arms

seeing me wink, she felt doubly doomed & calling upon several
cent-errries

of feminine rancor; sun-Limning
all the strength of the Holy Triad
whereupon sheeeey recovered
from fainting, set upon the

assailant and me, routing us
over the hill with a rain of
furious

'blowwoos

   But most of the time it works, —the chill leaves the crown

 of my skull, the wind starts

bbhoughneeen thaeruh da trees

again, the literal scene capriciously

washed in burnt sienna,

 the meritriciousness of a

Fragonard

, and when I leave in my car, I see in my mind's eye,

a man talking it over with his dog, a woman talkin to   the
sky,

standing where I stood, arms outstretched. Yes. I have that in
my   m^nd's $2ye.

Z /0)* d'\a

fanbuloso5

I get in and drive away. I ask my alter ego bennie, who isn't get out, I look over, would jewwww' did that, huh saved that one' eh? Wuld jew hav?

No answer. He looks straight ahead, I drive he is replaying the eiger sanction in his mind, his trench coat is in tatters,

*&ll__%@ yu

I say in mortal disgust, (the state of, I suppose) " I will never ask u for another cigarette again." He turns and laughs, h'e er outfoxx-ed me once agga'ine. He culd uv' added ...don't ask me to plant flowers every again and all over da earth as well, fool.

Three Poems
Samantha Terrell

At What Cost

once upon a sordid time
the rooster crowed,
announcing the morn
which woke the hen with a start
who, feeling badgered,
and with a saddened heart,
rose to do her daily grind
despite feeling out of sorts

until one morning
unlike the rest
she didn't rise
to meet that cock's requests,
deciding instead
to take a nobler stance
against the bullying
ways of arrogance

but while basking in a moment's peace,
her once fearful heart
finally at ease,
she realized the victimizing
she had unwittingly done
while in the clutches of dread,
wasting opportunities
to commune with the rising sun

Enough is Enough

an herb is no better
than a shrub,
a turnip no less lovely
than a tulip, but while
nature provides beauty in
abundance and variety,
humanity insanely seeks
plentitude through sameness,
challenging creation, its
creatures walk in ignorance
working stubbornly
against the greater good,
as though inherently better
rather than accepting,
Enough, trumps Much

Samantha Terrell

Seasons

child, as you yearn,
the adolescent strains,
adults strive, and
elders wane

how I would spare you
hurt and pain, but
to do so would spoil,
and rob you of life's toil

which teaches all,
regardless of age or race;
so with each season,
know the burden is simple:

accept, and embrace

Jari Thymian

Laughing Forward

     -- After *tres mujeres,* gouache, colored pencil, and
pen on paper, by Lili Basulto, 2008

These three women are the source of the outbreak.

Their sides split like ripe plums. Their heads thrown
back to guffaw at the incongruity of gods and hate.

Partiers move closer together, then roll in the aisles
with the sourpuss neighbor from across the hall

who leaves the party, a trail of chortle
like pheromones wandering down the road.

Later, the sunrise feels the clouds giggle into thunder and rain.
A continent away, a rainbow of burkas shimmers like aurora

borealis. Clean hands, medicines and money will not stop the spread
of endorphins to war zones and hate groups. Countries drop

their differences, their fears. Defenses dissolve like ice in hot tea,
expose millions of inner selves, vulnerable and sweet to cross

the shortest distance to peace in our nature—laughing at
ourselves.

Jari Thymian

I Am Acquainted with Terrorism

I have bitten my brother's arm black and blue,
kicked a hungry dog, and cursed a help desk
man in India. I have outraged and coerced
my ex-husband, spewing insults to the sky
and his specific body part, in scorching hope
of adding a bloody morsel of his ego
to mine, a gleeful hostile take-over.

I have screamed shards of rightness
at my mother, adding *I hate you, I hate you*
to defile my nine months in her womb.
I know dark nights consumed with re-living
some supposed discourtesy or insult.
Let me remember how lonely, how final,
to strap dynamite over my heart daily.

Broken Crayons
  --after *The War Photo No One Would Publish*, The
  Atlantic, 2014, by Torre Rose DeGhett

The wide angle of war
is thousands of miles away, doesn't
interfere with your coffee or fresh fruit,
doesn't put your comfort or home at risk.

A scrapyard of rusted, mangled trucks, detonated
mine holes along a deserted road. No dead bodies,
just a heap of melted metal with distant GPS coordinates,
a desert road called the Highway of Death.

A brilliant sunset, a tank and a camel in silhouette
like clearly defined, romantic lines of right, wrong,
believers, non-believers, cultural and country
borders. This photo, like your bathroom, is sanitized.

The telephoto image of war wears a face—
a man, his hand holding the windshield frame
as he tries to escape while his skin crackles in fire,
turns his flesh to charred muscle held together

by a web of bones. Muscle striations like an anatomy
drawing in charcoal and ash. His gleaming white teeth
clenched, lipless. The brutal reality of power looks you
in the eye. Near the truck, even the searing sand is scorched

by flames. More bodies. Weapons and body parts,
a snapshot of a smiling child's birthday party.
Broken crayons melted in desert sand draw
the true lines between innocent and accomplice.

Three Poems
Roseville Nidea

Stigma

Indeed, indeed, indeed,
Beauty is a creature in bordered wild
Exoticism is diffused in color
Here Brown, there White, there Black,
There is even Ivory.

Indeed, indeed, indeed,
Every country changes its shape and shade
Complementing bounded sight
Like that of the proud Eagle in the Occident
Like that of the earthy Ox in the Orient.

Come. Come, to realize
Beauty is a creature in the wild
Varying, still, you must know and see
Depending on what the individual portrays
Depending on how one self-declares.

Rising Above Two Poles

I watched how the sun rose from the layered clouds
I have seen men rise up to the noise of their clocks.
Heaven and Earth breathe both in silence and in sighs;
I wonder how many sounds I've already heard
I ponder the silences I've never shared.

I watched how the stars mated with the night sky
I watched how lovers burned their flames in their cries.
Heaven and Earth deliver an outright taste of desire
A bitter-sweet treat, tendered on a chain of fire
Delight and pain clasp each other. Neither can fight.

I watched how the rain ploughed into the soft loam
I watched how it pressed every flower that blooms.
The Earth beams, gleams in a heaven's heavy tears;
I muse on how many thorns a bud needs to be a just rose
I muse on the sower whose lust it is to smell its blossom.

I have never doubted, that I, too, am a swimmer
I am moving through the water of two opposite shores:
 I have to dive, gently, into the depths to breathe
To touch the light, I ought to float, resolute, on the surface.
The many wars in my heart, I submit to my mind.
The unsettled doubts in my mind, I surrender to my heart.

Roseville Nidea

Larentiine

Can you stop the sun
from coming after dark,
the moon from shining in the sky
to illuminate the ground at night?

Can you stop the hands from changing
the world with their palms,
 the liberated eyes from seeing
the old a confinement?

In acceptance, many thought themselves
how to bend like water :
 ice in the winter
free-flowing during the summer,
others how to be like a pliant bamboo
that stoops to every kind of wind that blows.

And I?
I remain, not in resistance
or I lack the ability of full flexibility.

Do you think I have the freedom like the others if
 I was designed
with the moon, the stars as the only lights that can
sustain my linear flight in the night
in search of essential.

If you see me beating
my powdery wings against
the lamp on your porch, or
fluttering around your candle flame,
it is not because I fancy
or am pleased by their radiance

I am lost

and that I am doomed to be --
 burned.

Previously appeared on *The Apple Tree*, Screechowl.com

melancholy

i. prelude
I am not existing so readily. I am not existing so readily. I
am not existing so readily.

ii. melancholy#1
you have melancholy eyes slanted to hold
in numeric universes inside, scrolling in
scrolling your tight miniature ocean syntax speech, tidbits
of news stripped of vapidity, what it lacked was satire- the
thin lip of your boot slicked, but oh
thunder in your hair that you tuft and lightning but never
gets out, your lonely body merely debris after-rain so pale,
window curtain sadness
because you know the moon is crying even when it is
waxed, you know
you're alone in the dark night always but you know you are
the dark night always.

iii. melancholy#2
you are made of milk and buried tributaries,
a lost thing. maybe you are a displaced city, all atmosphere in your hair
and the bare simplicity of human bones.
deconstruct all of me and we can watch the sun set in a
kind of afterlife eternity.
i'm sorry always for taking you to staircases
and driving me crazy
pretending as if the moon could dream,
its pale liquidity dripping along the tenement front and freezing
me in a summer night eternity on this porch (here is another
empty house glimmering
with substantial not-life)
so it's autumn, so its freight barreling into the front of my
face, rusted vestiges
of civilization trembling my vertebrate
in manufactured calamities, yet again
here is a thing more powerful in itself
than ever man intended (your
lost dark eyes and features so carefully
alpine, the mouth railed in displacement
lines, the feathered periphery
of motion in and out
of rooms, whatever). i'll always.

Elena Botts

**we are aliens looking at the stars trying to get back
home**
as if we could hold butterflies in our hands unknowingly,
as if movement were a dream we hadn't yet.
on the ride away from you,
the mountains were filled with glowing fog and the pas-
sengers
were dark silhouettes all coming to a common point be-
fore riding
on again.
this is for your eyes only please don't do that to your brain
here are flowers
flowers
flowers
flowers
flowers
flowers
do you understand me? i left unpunctuated bodies
i am here
now whether i like it or not.

(and jump out)
once i open the window (and jump out), i am a real body
and nothing
more or less, the stars summoning darkness
and folding it gradually between them
i must have abandoned love to the ocean (there was
no other option), mailed my
soul to the wrong address, regardless
the sun outlines the sky in terrible
light before bowing to its pale shadow,
that brother, moon. i imagine you
in the alien hours of your life, humming
with inaudible dreams, reams and reams
of silence gracing your bones but
coming undone somewhere around those
wild rosy eyes, like unlit mountainous skies.
it's strange to think of you like after
forest fires, waning and crippled, the shivering
as though an endless all-consuming
ghost of fire embraced birches, you
held me long past my lifetime, as though
we were becoming, oh
i don't know.

Elena Botts

vows

this is for you , for better or for the sleepy blue shenan-
doah in smokey fog
for richer (all of you, complete and unreal, and you) for
small veined creatures under the chasm of sky (by the
sea), in wilting flowers after rainstorm and in basking
wide-eyed and far-flung cumulus scattered and lovely
dove-eyed flying, to

oh that thing i cannot define for it makes   meaning for
all other words, carries our little boats far into the deadly
atlantic
and to cherish; hold your psalm palms so solid, innately
delicate (neither of us exist)

from this hour, the freight onward marching into a fiery
sunset until the sweet hand of the universe makes us
only real bodies under the sleeping earth do us part (but
still exhalingly being)

the strange skeletal human beings running wild under the
blue-skied sun. let's just us get lost in an infinity beyond
this one.

it is raining because you are not here
yet again.
tuck the ghosts in,
the sun ever so sound-
ly sleeping, the moon fitfully
dreaming, your speaking brain
in a cornfield dilapidated, its sunfilled boards and the nar-
row art of nails
into the blank stream and sweeping pasture,
ghosts hourly moving through the sunlit veins
of eternal and unspeakable afternoon.
yellow finch birds everywhere, in the
restless grasses, the melting shingle,
the that of this place which steeps your
mind so thick in convincing nonexist-
ence, a roaring fog over the trees and an
inextricable breeze pulling your
weeping synapses, the rusted neurons,
your singing deadness from river body
out to sea, yellow finch birds gathered
ceaselessly omnipresent.

Elena Botts

sundial
like god misconstrued time, swept
the sky clean (where are you, dear heart, lingering in the
aftermath
of a senseless storm, traipsing comatose
through the restless cumulonimbus?)
of the strange pale hours, like cirrus clouds
billowing into the distance, i wish
you knew me like this under the sun beating
bloodless and brilliant. you took the moon
under your sleeve, and so sweetly
ushered away the months, the days, in a ceaseless trance
of reckless circumstance, the minutes so carefully
ascending, ruinously within me, returning my formless
form to the steadfast nothingness,
committing my slipstream veins, blue
skeleton to the irrevocable ocean.
and then swim. and then swim.

Brush Fire
  after *Where the Golden Apples Grow,* artist Osnat Tzadok

The field flamed as result of anonymous
disregard. A callous toss of embering butt
triggered full-fledged consumption of blade
and bark. In the center, lone apple tree waits
for embrace of rising pyre. Joan of Arc,
unjustly sentenced to burn. We watched
from a distance, helpless, as she too began to spark,
filling the air with the strangely inappropriate
scent of pie.

A.J. Huffman

The Fallen Log

rode the river like a kayak. Twin
leaves as drivers, or maybe just passengers,
perched on squirrel's ex apartment door.
I watched it flow with the current, gaining
speed as it approached a small rocky rapid.
The catastrophe was inevitable. Without life
preservers, the passengers could not overcome
the roll. Capsized, it beached itself
after the initial rush. The leaves never resurfaced.

Atmospheric Ambiguity

Florida's winter weather is bipolar, changes
extremes in a matter of minutes. Forty to eighty-five degrees
inside the course of one day is not unfeasible or even
unusual. I moved to the alleged Sunshine State
for continuity of climate, never expected I would need
the wool sweaters and parkas I abandoned
with my Northeast address. Apparently, it is an ongoing joke
for locals. They laugh and quip "if you don't like the weather,
just wait five minutes." I do not
laugh, just hibernate, barricade
myself under blankets, my down
fortress against the unwelcome
winds and rain, wait
for whatever temperature tantrum mother nature throws my way.

In February 5, 2011 the American southwest and northern Mexico was gripped by a cold wave with temperatures dipping to lows not seen in over 60 years. Widespread power outages affected most of the region. This is the story of when bad things happen to good animals.

Un Espiritu Libre
Jane Hertenstein

The macaw had never been this cold. Fluttering back and forth for warmth, the bird finally alighted on a perch; her reptile-like talons gripped the wood, somehow more solid this evening. She shook her blue and teal-tipped wings and drew them in tightly as if wrapping a coat around herself and peered down into the crocodile cage, or rather cement basin. The crocodile and its mate had not moved from beside their small heated pool for a very long time.

"Is anyone out there?"

In the dry, crackling air, stray noises seemed to boom, the sound traveling further than usual like the echoing ping of a beak pecking against metal bars.

A monkey poked his head out of a hillock of straw. Splintered stars above pulsed and the frosty air stung his pink nose. A circle of black fur on top of his head gave the appearance of a monk's skullcap. Cream-colored fur draped his neck and shoulders like a cowl. The capuchin blinked rapidly as if trying to clear his mind.

"Is anyone out there?" the parrot cawed again.

"Is he coming?" the monkey answered with his own question, a note of urgency behind his high-pitched chirrup.

"How should I know?"

"I simply thought—"

"Climb up here and have a look yourself."

The monkey sprung up and grabbed a low-lying limb and then swung up to an upper branch. From this height he could observe the spectacled bears burrowing deeper into their plastic rock grotto. The bruin pair was from the south and had never learned to hibernate.

Where is he? The capuchin-monkey wondered. Water in his bowl had formed a clear, firm coating. When he dropped the butt-end of a carrot from the treetop the water broke, shattering into pieces.

"Do you think he'll come?" the monkey posited the question again. He slapped his thick hands against his chest for a minute of slim warmth. Along the city skyline very few lights glowed.

"No, and I doubt he will," the macaw cawed in return.

"Why do you say that?" It was hard to remember a night as dark as this one. Stars were everywhere.

"Why should he care about us? If I were him I would stay at home under a mound of hay. Perhaps his zookeeper is looking out for him." The tufted plumage on the crest of her head was blood red.

"He has never been anything but kind to us, bringing us gifts—"

"*¡Monito eres tremendamente maricón!*"

The monkey did not understand.

"Of course he feeds us, it is his job. It doesn't mean he likes us."

For some reason the fur on the back of the monkey's neck rankled. He passed his hand over his face and head, a nervous habit of sorts.

"Never mind. I'm sure we can figure something out." The bird's breath came out in smoke-like puffs.

It seemed to the monkey that there was nothing to figure out. He was beginning to shiver.

The bird continued to fly circles around her chain-link domed cage. "I know he's not coming."

"How can you be so sure?"

For as long as he'd lived at the Chihuahua Zoo, the man with a strip of fur under his nose had always taken care of him, bringing him bananas in the afternoon, the peelings of which lay at that moment below him in a hardened pile. "I believe he is."

The macaw landed not far from the monkey on a hollow outcropping. "Would you care to bet?"

The monkey looked around his rubbish-strewn cage. If he had anything to bet he would. On the other hand, what did it matter? *Why not?* He thought.

"Sure," he answered.

"All right," said the macaw, lifting her tail, suddenly excited. At least talking took her mind off the feather-snapping cold. She wasn't willing to sit there and do nothing.

"What will I win?" asked the monkey.

"Well, now, if you are right, señor, we will both be rescued."

It hurt to breathe. Surely they would be rescued, for if not . . . . "And if you are right?" the monkey queried the bird.

"You are a slow one. Of course, if he doesn't come soon we'll all die."

That wasn't any kind of prize. Yet, even in his numbed state, the monkey knew it was the truth. They relied on the zookeeper; without him there was no food, no water, no swishing out their cages of the accumulated muck. Unless . . . The thought was unimaginable. "Well, then, I pray he does come."

The macaw screeched and flapped her wings. After a second she settled back down, smoothing her ruffled feathers.

"Why not just have faith?" suggested the capuchin.

"Faith!" she squawked. "What does faith have to do with anything?"

He was suddenly confused, not sure how to answer. He wanted to go bury his head in the straw.

"Does faith come and make the box over there blow warm air?"

It was true. In the past whenever it had gotten cold, the zookeeper had made sure their cages stayed warm at night. A box forced air in noisy wisps throughout their cages. Most of the time, though, they were fine, once the sun rose and the shadows ran away.

"*¡Anda!*" boasted the macaw. "You know I'm right. I saw you shiver."

"It cannot be denied, madam."

"Senorita," she corrected him.

"My apologies."

"I have never mated." She paused, "And you?"

"I have remained celibate." He tossed some straw, in an attempt to make a new bed. "It would be easy for me to say there was never the opportunity, but there were other reasons. Let's just leave it at this—one cannot perform under so much scrutiny."

"Ay! Ay!" she called out to no one in particular. "Our stories are much the same," she now said, addressing the monkey.

"Before I became a showpiece," she went on, "I used to skim the treetops. I lived each day as it came. Food was bountiful. I can still remember . . ." She shifted from talon to talon, as if in a hurry to get away. "Soaring. The feel of the rushing wind, the sky holding me up."

She made the sound again. "Ay! Ay!" Rising up on taloned-toes, she resettled, for a second withdrawing into herself. "Sorry, that last part, the bit about the sky, was something I overheard. My last owner kept the telenovelas on during the day when he was out so that I would learn to mimic."

The capuchin watched her with glistening eyes. "Don't be sorry, it was beautiful." He sat back on his haunches, melancholy and reminiscent. "When I look up at the heavens, somehow I am able to forget, forget that I am enclosed."

"How long have you been imprisoned?"

The capuchin scratched his ear and then smelled his fingers. He'd never thought of the zoo as a prison. True he couldn't leave, but he'd never considered it a loss. He'd observed the rushing cars and motorcycles over the wall. They reminded him of the hyenas pacing restlessly two cages over. This night they were unusually quiet. They had a routine once the zookeeper left of bullying him, trying to scare him with their exaggerated barking sound, as if they were hacking up a fur-ball, which never ceased to startle and consequently embarrass him. Out there, outside of his cage people made funny faces, jumped around, imping him—much like the hyenas. No, he was much happier where he was, or if not happier at least content. And if not content, then safe.

"Never mind," the macaw interrupted the monkey's mental meandering. "He's not coming."

"I'm poor and uneducated," the capuchin confessed. "I was taken from the jungle at a young age and brought here, in a round about way."

"Brought here against your will," calculated the macaw. "I know that story. I was passed around from owner to owner. The last one was better than others. At least he left me alone during the day with the TV on." She craned her neck away from the monkey.

"I'm sorry." And he sincerely felt something for the parrot.

"You don't need to look at me like that," she snapped.

The capuchin ducked his head and cast a watery eye in her direction.

"I love your colors," he said, changing the subject. "They brighten up this bleary night."

"Thank you. What is that?"

"Señorita?"

"This stuff. What do you call it?" she indicated with her frosted beak the white powder sticking to her steel bars.

"I'm not sure—"

"The sky is falling!"

The monkey scurried to the back of his cage.

"Hahaha," she croaked, and the hyenas stirred, lifting their freckled faces before recurling into a ball, burrowing their heads into their sides, under their tails.

"Made you look, *pendejo*," she ridiculed him.

The capuchin ambled out on all fours. "I see. A type of game. Good one!" He played along. Fear was not helpful. "Go on. You were saying?"

"Saying? Oh, yeah, about how I got here. A common story. One day I was netted and sold. And resold." She took on a weary tone. "Traded and re-traded. The worse was the drugs. The injections. The mishandling." She shuddered to think about it. A scarlet feather floated to the cage floor.

"What about you?" she asked. "Don't you miss home?"

"Well now, there is a question I haven't thought

about for a while. I suppose I do. To be honest it's been so long, I'm not sure I could tell you where home is."

"Not me," she piped. "It is mapped on my brain. If given half a chance I'd escape, rise above the walls, cross rivers and mountains, and return to where I came from."

Listening to her made the monkey's heart race, warming him. "Of course."

Encouraged she went on, "Across the rust-colored sands, above the stones and dry bones, arroyos and hundred-year cactus."

"My girl! How you have a way with words!"

"Cross an ocean of seas and seas of oceans."

He closed his eyes. Yes!

The darkness and cold pressed in around them. He leaned back, resting against the tree trunk pressed out of plywood. He recalled a time when he was much younger, high up in the mountains, of being carried by his mother, of being held close to her. Up in the treetops, hidden by leaves the size of those rushing cars, clinging to her he would suck, drink until drowsy. He remembered waking up and seeing her there. Even as a youngster he understood the bond between them, that he belonged to her, that he was special. It is this memory that carries him still—especially when the humans stand before his cage mocking him. He tells himself he is here for a reason.

The macaw screeched a sneeze.

"God bless you!"

She fluttered, losing more feathers. "I am freezing."

He wished he could hold the poor bird, but his digits were finding it hard to grasp. "I remember the forested mountains, where I grew up, yet it never got this cold."

"We're all going to die!"

"My dear, my dear," he tried to coo like her. "Try to remember."

"¿Que?" She pounced on his words.

"Because," he stopped for a faltering heartbeat, "because it is much easier to believe than not to. It saves so much energy, energy that can be better spent staying warm, staying alive."

"Survival of the fittest, you mean."

"Is that your creed?" he asked.

"I suppose," she sniffed.

"So you are a believer after all," and he curled his lips revealing his teeth and gums—his way of smiling.

"Whatever," she dismissed him. "I believe we get what we deserve."

"So this is our fate?" He looked out through the bars, to the wall facing them, and the darkness surrounding them.

Together they would trek through thick jungles, he at first only a babe holding on tight, then later toddling behind her only to tire and climb onto her back. Before bed his mother would sit him down in front of her and with her long fingers groom him, picking through his scalp. He'd lean back into her, feeling her gently lift his hair; she knew every bit of him. Even now he could still recall her touch, the way she picked around and in his ears for the squirmy, itchy bugs, the sound she made eating them, chewing with her lips open, the way she smelled like ripe bananas—his favorite. How she spoke endearments to him as the noisy jungle settled into an insect hum, the sun sinking, disappearing into the treetops.

"He has forgotten us," she declared.

"Who?" he asked, confused.

When he woke up, she wasn't there. For days he swung from tree to tree looking for his mother, his clan, for anyone he knew or might know him, being ever on the look-out for snakes—especially the kind that slither through the thick leaves and creep up unawares.

"The zookeeper!" she spewed as if spitting out seeds.

And that is where the dream ends. Always he awakes just as the viper lunges, its mouth stretched and fangs extended. Always the nightmare ends with him jumping and going berserk.

The frightened parrot fled, flying the perimeter of her cage, landing on a bough. "*¿¡Cómo!?*"

Startling even himself with the far-reaching sound coming from deep inside him, the monkey admitted, "I'm afraid."

Ha! "I knew it. So you have given up?"

"Excuse me?"

"Waiting for the zookeeper."

The capuchin shook his head back and forth, though it could have been the tremors taking over his body.

"I just want to know," she continued to ask, "do you still believe."

He could hardly feel his fingertips when he rubbed his thumb along them. "I believe—"

"*¡Idiota!*" she squawked.

"And disbelieve."

"Both? At the same time? Impossible!"

The cold was muddling his thoughts. He attempted to explain. "Is it not true that the sea is the color of the sky?"

"Si. The bluest blue," she replied.

"One is down." With one arm the monkey swung down a notch.

The parrot followed him with her piercing onyx eye.

"And the other is up." He slipped and slid onto the lowest branch.

"What are you getting at?"

"Both of these are true. Yet they are opposites, as far away as one can get from one another."

The monkey was starting to annoy her. "The crocodile has not blinked even once." Nights usually found the croc on the mud flats next to the eaves of his manicured pool. He appeared as rigid as the fake log propped up in his cage.

"Let's stay with the subject, please," the monkey tried to gently guide her.

"What were we talking about? The cold has affected me. I am a bird brain."

"Survival, my dear." He appreciated her sense of humor.

"What do you think our chances are?" she pondered out loud.

"I'm not sure how they are calculated. Fifty-fifty," he guessed.

"Now you sound like a realist." She hopped closer.

"I can be both a realist and a believer. One does not cancel the other out."

"Yes, but the odds are against us," she stated.

He didn't know if the bird was ridiculing or agreeing with him. She was right about one thing, though. Never prone to a flurry of activity, the crocodile had been resting for a *very* long time. "Where is the sun?" he asked.

"I have no idea. All I know is my claws feel like they've been cut off."

For a minute the capuchin was silent. Thinking again of home, he said, "Somewhere in the world it is hot."

Wild wind rattled the bars of her cage, sweeping the white dust into corners. The macaw sighed. "To think, there is a place."

He went on, "While we are in darkness somewhere the sun is shining."

The very notion caused the parrot to shake her feathers. "I think I see over there, above the hills, a faint light."

The monkey climbed higher, level with the bird. "We must cling to hope."

He was captured and dropped into a sack and brought down off the mountain and into a market. From inside the sack he heard many sounds, ones he later came to recognize as the shuffling of sandaled-feet over hardened ground, the waspy hiss motorbikes make, the chatter of humans much like monkeys—which made him homesick. He was wild to see his mother.

"There is a river that cuts through the jungle, whose yellow waters bend and twist like the body of a serpent."

The capuchin squirmed. He did not like the direction the conversation was going.

"I have been to the mouth of this snake. I have seen the tail. Its colors shimmering in its wet oiliness, especially as it winds its way to the delta and salt flats."

"Can we talk of something else?"

She cocked her head. "I thought you told me to think warm thoughts?"

When he didn't answer, she tilted her head back again, observing him with one eye surrounded by a patch of white tattooed with red squiggles. The monkey had picked up his tail and was chewing on the end of it.

For days—how long?—he didn't know, but finally he

was saved. It was the zookeeper who lifted him up, who brought him to this, his new home. Now every day he comes to see him, always with a banana. The capuchin sighed in hungry contemplation.

The parrot broke in. "Why should he care for you or me? A macaw and a monkey?"

"Because we're valuable," the monkey said, stating what he thought was obvious.

"Okay, *sabelotodo*, you seem to have all the answers."

Now she *was* mocking him. Was she a mockingbird, after all? He was thinking about how to phrase the joke when she accused him. "You think you're such a big shot."

"You must be thinking of the gorilla."

She continued, "Maybe the zookeeper likes you because you are so popular. The people flock around your cage."

"Again you are confusing me with the baboons that pick their asses and fling their poo."

She parted the mandibles of her bill in a smile and swayed.

"Ay! Hang on!" he called out.

She righted herself. "Stop yelling."

"Sorry, my little chickadee," he said lovingly.

"One, I am not a chickadee. And two, how can you be so sure?"

"Remember last summer all I wanted to do was lay around."

"Good for nothing," she teased.

"I curled up on the floor of my cage covered in straw and shit. I refused to eat. Even when the zookeeper brought me a banana."

"What was the matter?"

The capuchin shrugged. "I felt that if I had to live one more day in a zoo I'd go crazy. Beserk!"

"There once was a chimp—"

"Yes, yes. I've heard the same story. It was a long slog, but I willed myself to live one more day with these walls and bars."

"We all have our moments, I guess." She shivered.

"The things of this world had left me cold."

"I'm with you now . . . sort of."

"Life has to be more than this," the capuchin philosophized.

"There is! A whole world, right over that fence."

"Right, but I had forgotten."

"Not a day goes by where I don't think about escaping."

"So you know what I'm talking about?" he asked with some doubt in his voice. "About hope."

"Sure." She'd give him that. "So you think hope is going to get us out of here? Out of this mess we're in?" she asked, scoffing.

He wouldn't allow himself to be made fun of. "No I don't."

"Cha!!!" The bird fanned her tail. "I win!"

"Is this still about the bet?"

She didn't bother answering; she was busy chipping away at a pumpkin popsicle still covered with seeds.

"At least it is better to hope we are going to make it than to doubt we will not."

"Which may very well be the case."

"You mean the bit about hope?"

"No, the bit that we might not make it out of here." She continued to jab at the brick of frozen squash using her beak like a jackhammer.

The white dust fell around them, sweeping the empty sidewalks and gathering in near the zoo wall. The zoo had grown almost too quiet. Not a creature was stirring, not even the pesky rat that squeezed through the bars and scavenged from the bottom of the monkey's cage. Even he needed the zookeeper just as much as the monkey. They all depended on him.

She let the delicacy fall with a dull thud. "So we're back to the beginning."

"Huh?"

"It's up to us to figure something out because he isn't coming."

"He will come," the capuchin insisted.

"Geez." She clicked her tongue. "Will you just quit."

"I can't. I know it deep down in my bones—"

"Well, my bones are fucking cold!"

Together they were silent for a minute. The parrot slid

to the end of her perch. She already knew the crocodile was dead. She thought about moving to another perch. "I am so tired."

"The sky is softening."

"Perhaps," she whispered, closing her eyes.

"Take care!" cried the capuchin.

She fell, but caught herself just in time, softly gliding onto a landing.

"Tell me," he began, climbing down to her, "which is best. Fur or feathers?"

"Is this another one of your stupid questions?"

"No," he deferred. "I am not as clever as you. I am curious—what is the difference between instinct and habit?"

"Huh?"

"Earlier, you said something about knowing the way home."

"That's right," she said woozily. "I believe I can remember . . . ." It was as if her eight slender claws had turned into pumice stone. Everything was getting harder and harder. Becoming all the same.

"Try!" he called out to her. "Try to remember, please, parrot bird."

"I am flying. The sun warms my back. Orchids grow in the treetops. It is like soaring over a rainbow.

"It is getting lighter over there."

"It is fig, fig," she stuttered, her whole feathered frame shaking. "A figment of your imagination. It is the city."

For as long as he lived he would never forget his mother leaning into him, her warm mouth next to his ear while nit picking. Whispering in her mother tongue, I am here. I am here.

"I'm afraid," the parrot rasped meekly.

She didn't abandon him. She was with him now.

"Ssshh," the capuchin hushed her. "I'm here. I'm here."

Three Poems
Jeremy Nathan Marks

Burns at every step

-for Alice Keys

All of this blue ball

grokked like an egg or seed

We bury one of ours today

but in the interring a pigeon

landed on stone; an ancient stand

Felled to make the bier;

these histories fill a gaze, one

complete turn of all raised in that

Half globe of the mule's watching.

Cart to lawn and shoulder to ground,

this seeing burns at every step.

Myrrh

When the pulp on the block
was at last bled out
I looked past
the privy and shamble fence

To the clapboard church
and dog, chained yard patched in
burrs he having swallowed
the creek bank shard
and bones

When that pulp turned hollow
I saw the flint spark
of dry January nights red
eye dust on the sill
those stars counting four footed
spectres

So I chased the chain loose
from my porch and what stole
beyond the barrel bled
out in myrrh.

Jeremy Nathan Marks

Turtles

Turtles –without cities on their backs-
swim much of their year in a botanical pond
willowed in shadow, leading the life of monks

Like good gardeners they farm their
plots with praise and smack their gums while
they eat, a sound that ripples off the Kingfisher's feet

At dawn the first turtle leads the sun
through an elaborate charade of having slept
all night in a cocoon of dark preparation counting stars

He is waiting on Venus as they flicker
out. A dragonfly lands on his snout.

Elk
Chrystal Berche

Trading Places
Barry W. North

I'm sitting in the doctor's office,
glancing at a hunting magazine.
I flip through the pages
and see three hunters,
all in camouflage,
like soldiers returned from a war,
kneeling behind a row of Canadian geese,
laid out on the hard ground,
like executed enemy lieutenants,
identically dressed,
awaiting burial.

The birds are stunning,
even in repose -
shades of brown
along the back and side,
gradually tapering to
the worsted, snow-white breast
beneath a long and elegant
pure black collar,
with a touch of white,
like a bow-tie,
at the chin.

If I could,
I would trade places
with the oldest one,
the one in the middle.
That way I could apprehend
the thrill I could never fathom
of watching the approaching long necks,

oblivious, not only
to their own grace and beauty,
but also to the imminent danger they are in,
as I, with consummate skill,
alter their path
across the flyway,
by calling them in
and calling them in,
slowly,
slowly,
waiting,
for the exact moment
at which, I know,
there is no escape from my dominion.

And he,
in my place,
could sit here and wonder,
for just a moment, if,
in a divine touch of poetic justice,
we too,
at a level far beyond our ability to comprehend,
like a skein of geese trying to understand
the deadly mechanics of a twelve-gauge shotgun,
are nothing but sport
to our own well concealed gods,
wherever they might be.

Animals in Heat
Nicholas Alexander Roos

Our story begins with two girls in junior high. They
sit side by side in homeroom and never speak to each
other. Meghan is eager, but Brooke has no jaw, just flaccid
skin and a hole in her neck to help her breathe. She will
never speak. She spends the period coughing on saliva
and snot and getting wiped clean by her nurse/helper,
who often sits through too many gag/coughs for Meghan's
taste.

Brooke dies during high school, and Meg thinks
about her even now--14 years later--especially near the
bear exhibit. She works security at the Lincoln Park Zoo,
where she operates with a kind of wounded swagger that
makes her colleague Columbus feel the urge to be impres-
sive. Conversation comes easily between them. Even their
silences are comfortable. They watch the people. They
watch the animals. They think about various lives every-
thing could be living.

Especially the animals.

Most would be hunters given the chance. Killers.

Ask your average wild animal: When did you last kill
something?

Today, is the answer for most.

Would you ever hesitate to kill? Never.

Now ask your average human. Answers vary.

Guards have to think about these things during night
shifts, walking by the big cats or Komodo dragons: the
convicted killers.

Columbus voices his meditations. "Could these
dragons eat us, you think? Like right now, if we let 'em go,
who'd kill who?"

"You mean without weapons?" Meg can tell who he thinks would win.

"Sure, they don't have weapons."

"They have venom. Some kind of paralyzing goo."

"We got thumbs."

"Which are great, for using weapons."

"Or for choking fools out." Columbus flexes into a submission hold. "I'd choke a dragon out, if I had to."

A crazed roar rumbles nearby then echoes through the grounds. The big cats are awake and aware their hunting days are done. Both guards shudder-flinch in secret and reach for their flashlights.

"Fuckin' lions . . . king o' my ass."

"Think you could strangle one of them? With your thumbs?"

"Maybe. What's he gonna do when I'm on his back, arms wrapped around his neck?"

"Eat you?"

"Nah, you're slower than me, so they'd probably eat you while I found high ground.Strike from above when they're full and digesting." Columbus flexes again--multiple poses this time--and the guards laugh together.

A week later, working a day shift, Meghan pauses to watch some kids pointing and laughing and throwing things at the jawless bear, Sunny. This kind of thing happens all the time. Sunny's bottom lip is gone. Her long tongue hangs straight down, raining a steady stream of saliva from the tip. She loses so much water in the Chicago summers just breathing and drooling that her keepers have to tranquilize her and hook up an IV on the hottest days.

Columbus sees Meg watching the bear and says "We should spring that poor bastard, huh?"

"Spring her?"

"Bust him outta here. Get him away from all these assholes." Columbus nods toward the group of children now sticking their tongues out at the bear, taking turns to find out who can best mimic Sunny's malady.

"Those kids are like ten."

"*Assholes!*"

"Okay, so what're you gonna do with a jawless bear?"

"Move him in at my place. Get him out of this humidity."

"You know Sunny's a girl bear, right?"

"Who gives a shit? It's handicapped! I can't stand it, watching her drool and sweat and pass out all day!"

Thus begins the planning. The operation takes shape over the next week, the two of them studying Sunny's caretakers and finding out how they can purchase and prepare the liquid mash the bear eats by curling her tongue and sort of spooning it up little by little. They even spend a couple nights watching documentaries on Netflix after dinner and drinks.

When the big night arrives, fate intervenes. Three high school kids break in and start picking at locks and cracking open cages with bolt cutters. By the time the guards know anything has gone awry, they stand face-to-face with two Komodo dragons—Columbus carrying the just-tranquilized bear over his shoulder.

"Don't move," he says. "We're way bigger than them. They'll back away."

"I still have a dart loaded. I could put one down."

"Yeah well I don't, so we're still dead if you hit."

"So drop the bear and load another!"

The dragons start circling the humans, going opposite directions to pen them in.

"It takes a second to load! They're too close!"

"They get any closer I'm shooting! Better odds with one down."

The dragon circling left makes its move, sprinting at them with its mouth open. The size of the thing up close horrifies Meg, who does not fire but does manage to jump out of the way. Columbus attempts the same but trips and drops Sunny as he falls. The bear bounces and rolls on the pavement then wakes and tries to stand before wobbling back down to the ground. The second dragon runs toward her.

Meghan jumps into its path and kicks at the creature, which veers and snaps but misses. They square off, the dragon showing its side and back to look as big as possible. Meg takes aim and fires. Her dart strikes and stays in its neck. The beast does not react.

Columbus sinks his just-loaded dart into the same dragon's hindquarters. It staggers, shaking its head in wild spurts before collapsing.

The other dragon charges again from behind. The humans don't see it coming. The dragon, however, sees an easy meal—cannibalism being common among monitor lizards—and sprints right past them to begin tearing at the creature they'd just tranquilized. Meghan sees her window. "Let's bounce! Now!"

But Columbus is already headed toward the massacre, flashlight waving in his hand. "Hey!" He kicks the dragon. It pulls up from its meal and strikes, snapping at air as Columbus jukes away.

Meghan has her last dart ready and shoots it into the lizard's leg. It roars and staggers but recovers and charges in a rage. The dragon is too fast for her. It pounces at her thigh.

But Sunny is there, T-boning the dragon like an intersection car wreck and pouncing again before it can recover, slashing and slicing at its head and back.

When the lizard emerges, it takes off running. Sunny lies down again after a moment and settles into a kind of sleep mode. She's awake and responsive but allows the guards to load her into a golf cart and then into the car, where she falls asleep for the next several hours.

The bleeding Komodo survives his wounds.

Nobody suspects foul play with regard to Sunny, who lives the too-hot days sleeping in Columbus' basement and the nicer ones playing with a young Golden Retriever in the backyard. On Meg's days off, she comes to visit, circling the dates in smiley faces on her wall calendar when the schedule comes out.

Most people think the escaped dragon is long dead by now, but the truth is different. True Chicagoans know the city is built on a top of its past self, cannibalizing whatever it can. The dragon thrives in that underworld, slumming around the sewers, staying near the hotspots: hunting for warm meals.

Three Poems
Cheryl Pearson

Bat (A Sonnet)

The thin wing-spokes turned inside out
like a flimsy umbrella in high wind.
Just last night I saw, flickering about,
three, four, hitching star to star with bounced sound,

casting ripples around the moon, sound-stones
deftly skipped. Now there's this: stiff in the grass;
alien. Look at the fine fan of bones.
Fox-ears, fur. Look at its fixed, curdled face,

see your own occur in it. Palmed, it's dry
and cool as leather. Little sky-mouse.
Moth-mouthed predator. A vacant space high
in the roof, a tenant less in the house -

say a prayer for its small life. Say a spell.
Incant its names: Grey. Vampire. Pipistrelle.

Fox

The fox stops dead on the dark ice.
Equally frozen. Both ears pricked. Her eyes
Blaze on like lights, go dim again as she snaps

Her narrow head to cast a black look
At some imagined noise. The roast duck
Gleams in her sights, a lucky

Prize she'll sneak back, mother-mouth mere vise
Clamped down on our oily scraps - six cubs
Mewling for a skinflint meal will feast

Tonight! Off she takes at a level trot.
Quicker now, light as rain on her quick feet.
The sealed pond is printless, complicit.

Tomorrow, only a hint of grease will last.
And a faint animal hint the dogs will browse,
Thrilled, flared-nostrilled, quivering in the grass.

Cheryl Pearson

Woods

First light, and no-one's about.
And at first, silence
until our ears
adjust
to the sounds of a wood
being absolutely and utterly
a wood -

a hoot, desolate, gathers momentum
a rain patters roundly on the ground-leaves.
Underneath, the almost inaudible
arrival of new mice,
new bluebells.

We enter as much as the woods allow
while keeping their otherness, and us separate.
Like walking in someone's memory of a wood

both real and removed,
the way a pond

remembers the silent
boom of circles a stone made before it settled,
and landed,
and became pond.

The world is in the twig tips.
The stitch of birds from leaf to leaf
and moth to moon
and back.

How small our humanness in this dripping green.
How brief the moment

the woods breathe in to accommodate our footfall,
how easily they breathe us out again.

December
Christopher Woods

Lust
Sarina Bosco

My boyfriend thought he was doing me a favor. He was rarely this excited, walking me to the passenger side of the car and smirking the smirk that had made me look up from my books in high school. I should have been excited, too (his attention was so fleeting those days) but I couldn't find it in me – instead I was afraid of the great oak that stretched over his parents' house, of the way the branches were cracking overhead – the sound of them ricocheting through the air.

It was December 2009.

I could remember a childhood of white Christmases, but my teenage years and these exhausting twenties were full of black ice and the kind of wind that makes your bones feel hollow. An oddly dry month.

You'll love this, he said, or something like it, my memory glosses over the moment in a way that says more about us than anything else ever has or ever will.

Six miles down the back roads, two stop signs and one right turn, to a farm that I'd always remembered as empty. No lights on in the house, no cars in the drive, only cattle occasionally and even then only five of them at the most. Lowing to themselves in the field closest to the road. Standing, never moving.

My uncle's house, the sound of the car doors empty-ing out around us. *He has a horse.*

But something was wrong. The doors of the barn were open and the cattle were in the back field. The wind was picking up, branches were falling out of trees back behind the house, the bodies of rusted trucks all faced us across the yard.

His palm – rough, the base of a square hand and

368

thick fingers that I would look for in others years and years after this – held open the tall door as I turned my body sideways, unwilling to touch the splintered wood. With my nose just inches from the edge I could see frost nested there between the knots and ridges.

The dark inside was overwhelming. Next to me, he was also dark, a darkness that I was used to. I saw it often at night when he got up from the bed and left the room. He was always sinking, blending into the surrounding shadows and I could never hold him there with me under the window with the shade cocked sideways.

Somehow the shrunken boards of the place kept the wind out. The dirt that served as a floor was as cold and hard as the ground outside, as unforgiving on the balls of my feet. He moved beside me and I could feel his grin there. With his hand just hovering over the small of my back he led us to the north side of the barn, further into the dark and the stalls. The cattle were rubbing their hides against the panels. I could hear them lowing and slowed.

His breath was hot on my neck as he took my forearm and led me to the right, where a narrow hall of stalls was separated from the rest by bales. I heard it there in the dark – long before I saw it – the solid thud of hooves on packed earth, the wet of breath through nostrils and I swear it the hush of lashes coming down.

He thought he was doing me a favor.

Not *horses,* I realized then. I could feel on the surface of my skin that there was nothing else alive in the barn with us except the heat in the stall before us.

Just one.

He put me before the gate and it thundered out of the dark at me, reared up against the iron and he laughed when I jerked back.

The horse was white and stunted. Far smaller than a male his age should be. He had the bent back of an old man, the ribs barely holding flesh up over the organs and his eyes were milky. The lightest blue ringing huge staring pupils. From my days spent at the trick farm, learning to stand on the swell of their rumps and clean the soft parts of their hooves, my lips began to form the word *pony.* But that was wrong.

I asked why it was here and who put it here and didn't it ever go outside?

He said no – put a hand through the bars to flick the horse on the nose, it shuddered and protested – told me that it tried to kill things, other animals, the cows, the men who jumped the fence to bring hay into the field. His uncle had a scar of puckered skin on his right thigh. It was vicious and would attack any breathing thing.

Even you, he said, that smirk dissipating as he turned to jar the old harnesses hanging, flaking away on the wall.

I moved closer. The horse lowered its head, blew air through his nose twice as though he was tired. His eyes met mine and he ambled toward the far wall where I nearly lost him in the dark if it hadn't been for that white coat. His hooves were grown too long, curling at the edges.

The tail twitched and he leaned heavy against the boards that groaned under his weight, that were worn under his shoulder and hip. He swayed there.

The cattle outside moaned and the ground vibrated briefly as they moved away from the barn, away from what it contained.

I listened to him breathing there in the dark, alone. The iron was cold in the folds of my palms and when behind me he threw open the two huge doors again, I turned to see the snow beginning – falling slow through the emptiness, burying itself in the hollows and mounds of frozen mud.

He thought he was doing me a favor.

They'll kill him someday soon, he said, turning to look at me over his shoulder. *Before he can kill them.*

That smirk – what was it about that smirk that had drawn my gaze?

On the other side of the barn the cows lowed, their voices lost in the wind. We walked out across the gravel and the doors *boomed* behind us. When the air was still again it was easy to hear the harnesses rattling against the nails inside. The sound turned effortlessly into that of a branch hurtling through the maples, shivering on its way down to crash just inches from where he stood at the driver's side door.

With my fingertips frosting to the handle I stared at his expression and thought of the horse, the creature. The white skin draped over bones. His mad dash toward the fence. His eyes rolling. His hooves ripping up the earth.

I swayed there. Overhead another branch cracked, and he shouted something at me, lost in the sudden wind. Under my coat my ribs pushed against the thick layers as I inhaled. Over all of it, all of the sound and texture, I could hear the rhythmic thudding coming from the stall in the north corner of the barn.

He thought he was doing me a favor.

Three Poems
Frederick Glaysher

Tohoku Earthquake

As I watched the news reports on 3/11 about the earth-
quake and tsunami in Japan, I found myself thinking of
my former students who had friends and family in To-
hoku, the northeast prefectures, pouring my heart into
haiku.

"I was filled with a great sadness which stayed with me
and was made all the deeper by the sound of a temple
bell we heard that evening on Shiogama shore." —From
Basho's Oku-no-Hosomichi, "Journey to the Far North."

Tohoku earthquake.
Let there be a bell left on
Shiogama shore.

***

Like Murasaki,
wipe tears with our sleeves.
Shining Genji gone.

***

A ten foot square hut.
The flowing water of this life.
Some foam swirling by.

***

In Omi towered
the mighty royal palace,
now passing ruins.

The Golden Tripod

The oracles of the Pythian priestess,
wafting up from the chasm, a breath below,
that man might know the Olympian god,
Apollo, returns, reigns again at Delphi.

Frederick Glaysher

At My Funeral

Say, he has returned to the Moon,
that far height, out of reach for us,
until we, too, like all fragile things,
meet on that plane, high above the Earth.

Seated Figure
Sam Hamill

It is a long way from there to here.
It is longer than all the old roads of exile,
longer even than the silence of the heron.
The landscapes changed. Someone
numbered the dead, someone mapped the pain.

Once, they say, the animals came to us,
and licked our palms for the salt,
and looked at us with huge, knowing eyes,
then turned and left
alone. And entered Paradise.

Previously published in *Habitation*, by LOST HORSE PRESS, 2014

Chair
Christopher Woods

Contributors

Jordi Alonso graduated with an AB in English with an emphasis in Creative Writing from Kenyon College in the spring of 2014, where he studied poetry and literary translation. He currently is a Turner Fellow in Poetry at SUNY Stony Brook Southampton and has been published or has work forthcoming in *The Southampton Review, Edible, The Colorado Review, Graze,* and other journals. His first book, a collection of erotic poems inspired by Sappho entitled *Honeyvoiced* was published by XOXOX Press in November of 2014.

Pilar Rodríguez Aranda is a poet, video-maker, and translator. She lives in Malinalco, Estado de Mexico. She has received grants and awards as a video artist in Mexico and the US and has works published in magazines and anthologies in America and Europe. Her first book of poetry, *Asunto de mujeres* appeared in 2012, and in 2014 she published *Verdes Lazos*, a poetry placket. In 2013, she received a prize for her poem *Nuestras Luchitas* at the San Miguel Writers' Conference. She considers herself an "ARTivist" and is a founding member of *Colectiva Poéticas*, coordinator of *100 Thousand Poets for Change*, Mexico chapter, and a *Writing for Peace* Adviser. For more info: http://pilarpoeta.blogspot.com.

Jasmine V. Bailey's poems have appeared in many journals, her chapbook, *Sleep and What Precedes It*, is available from Longleaf Press, and her book-length collection, *Alexandria*, is available from Carnegie Mellon University Press.

Pratima Annapurna Balabhadrapathruni is a writer-poet-artist, with an Advanced Seminar in Non-Fiction, from IWP Univ. of Iowa. She won third place in the Poetry Sans Frontieres Hemingway contest this year. Her blog is at wordsatnine.com.

Danny P. Barbare resides in the Upstate of the Carolinas.

Zeina Hashem Beck is a Lebanese poet with a BA and an MA in English Literature from the American University of Beirut. Her first poetry collection, *To Live in Autumn* (The Backwaters Press, 2014), won the 2013 Backwaters Prize, judged by Lola Haskins, was a runner up for the Julie Suk Award, and has been included on *Split This Rock*'s list of recommended poetry books for 2014. Nominated for two Pushcart prizes, her poems have been published in literary magazines in the U.S. and the U.K., including *Ploughshares, Nimrod, Poetry Northwest, The Common, Mizna, The Midwest Quarterly, Mslexia,* and *Magma*. She lives in Dubai, where she hosts PUNCH, a poetry and open mic collective. She will read at the 2015 Emirates Airlines Festival of Literature. Her website is www.zeinahashembeck.com.

Sarina Bosco is a New Englander, full-time student, and exhausted homeowner. When not writing she hikes the trails in the area, spoils her pitbull, or reads good poetry. She is also constantly repainting and washing dishes.

Elena Botts lives in Northern Virginia. She's been published in over twenty literary magazines, and is the winner of four poetry contests, including Word Works Young Poets'. Her poetry has been exhibited at the Greater Reston Art Center. You can find her poetry book, *a little luminescence*, at allbook-books.com, and her award-winning visual art at o-mourning-dove.tumblr.com.

Bredt Bredthauer is a poet, bicyclist, and English teacher. He earned a BA from the University of Texas, an MA from the University of North Texas, and an MFA from the University of Florida. After completing his MFA in 2012, Bredthauer gave away everything he owned and spent the next two years riding his rusty steel bicycle around the world. Currently, he is living and working in Saudi Arabia.

Lauren Camp is the author of two collections, most recently *The Dailiness*, winner of the National Federation of Press Women 2014 Poetry Book Prize and a World Literature Today "Editor's Pick." Her third book, *One Hundred Hungers*, selected by David Wojahn for the Dorset Prize, is forthcoming from Tupelo Press. Her poems have appeared

378

in *Tinderbox Poetry Journal, Beloit Poetry Journal, The Boiler Journal, Memorious, Nimrod* and other journals. She hosts "Audio Saucepan," a global music/poetry program on Santa Fe Public Radio. www.laurencamp.com.

Hélène Cardona is a poet and actress, author of *Dreaming My Animal Selves* (Salmon Poetry, 2013), winner of the Pinnacle Book Award and 2014 Readers' Favorite Award, *The Astonished Universe* (Red Hen Press, 2006), *Life in Suspension* (Salmon Poetry, 2016), *Ce que nous portons* (Éditions du Cygne, 2014), her translation of *What We Carry* by Dorianne Laux, and *Beyond Elsewhere*, her translation of Gabriel Arnou-Laujeac. She holds a Master's in American Literature from the Sorbonne, taught at Hamilton College and Loyola Marymount University, and received the Poiesis Award of Honor and fellowships from the Goethe-Institut and Universidad Internacional de Andalucía. She is Chief Executive Editor of *Dublin Poetry Review* and *Levure Littéraire*, and Managing Editor of *Fulcrum*. Publications include *Washington Square, World Literature Today, Poetry International, The Warwick Review, Irish Literary Times*, & many more.

Ariella Carmell lives in California and is a senior at Marlborough School. Recognized by the Poetry Society of the United Kingdom and the Scholastic Art & Writing Awards, her writing has appeared or is forthcoming in *Cadaverine, Crack the Spine, Eunoia Review*, and *Canvas Literary Journal*, among others.

Mary Carroll-Hackett holds an MFA from Bennington College. Her work has appeared in many journals including *Carolina Quarterly, Superstition Review*, and *The Prose-Poem Project*. She is the author of *The Real Politics of Lipstick*, winner of Slipstream's 2010 poetry competition, *Animal Soul, If We Could Know Our Bones*, and most recently, *The Night I Heard Everything* from FutureCycle Press. She teaches at Longwood University and as low-residency MFA faculty at West Virginia Wesleyan College. Mary is working on a memoir.

William Cass has had a little over seventy-five short stories accepted for publication in a variety of literary magazines and anthologies. He lives and works as an educator in San Diego, California.

Yuan Changming, 8-time Pushcart nominee and author of 4 chapbooks (including *Mindscaping* [2014]), is the most widely published poetry author who speaks Mandarin but writes English. Growing up in a remote village, Yuan began to learn the English alphabet at 19 and published several monographs on English-Chinese translation before leaving China. With a PhD in English, Yuan currently tutors and co-edits *Poetry Pacific* with Allen Qing Yuan in Vancouver. Since mid-2005, Changming has had poetry appearing in 989 literary publications across 31 countries, including *Best Canadian Poetry (2009,12,14), BestNewPoemsOnline, Cincinnati Review* and *Threepenny Review*.

Jennifer Clark lives in Kalamazoo, Michigan. Her first book of poems, *Necessary Clearings*, was recently published by Shabda Press. Her work has been published in *Failbetter, Fiction Fix, Windhover, Concho River Review, Structo, poemeleon,* and *The Midwest Quarterly*.

Edward D. Currelley is an author and artist. He was awarded honorable status in 2008 by Writer's Digest for Stage Playwriting. His children's book *I'm Not Lost, I'm with You* will be published in 2015. He is the president of Pen to Mind Book & Child Development Concepts, Inc. He resides in New York City.

Lorraine Currelley, poet, writer, mental health counselor, human rights and mental health advocate, founded and directs Poets Network & Exchange, Inc. to produce poetry readings, workshops, open mics and a lecture series. She is widely anthologized in literary publications, and served as president of The Harlem Arts Fund. Lorraine holds a Masters in mental health counseling, a Certificate in Thanatology (grief and bereavement), and is the recipient of many community service awards for her work with the homeless and on behalf of poets and writers. Most recently she is the recipient of the 2015 New York Public

Library Arts for a Lifetime Award. Lorraine is the founder of The Currelley Literary Journal and the LC Information and Resource Center, a blog which provides links to nationwide resources and addressing domestic and sexual violence, mental health, and gerontology.

Darlene P. Campos is an MFA candidate at the University of Texas at El Paso's Creative Writing Program. In 2013, she won the Glass Mountain magazine contest for prose and was awarded the Sylvan N. Karchmer Fiction Prize. Her work appears in *Prism Review, Cleaver, Red Fez, Bartleby Snopes, Elohi Gadugi, The Writing Disorder, Connotation Press, Word Riot, Plain China,* and many others. She is from Guayaquil, Ecuador but has lived in Houston all her life. Her website is www.darlenepcampos.com.

Maija Rhee Devine (이매자) is a Korean-born writer, Korean War survivor, and the author of an award-winning autobiographical novel/love story, *The Voices of Heaven* set during the Korean War, and a poetry chapbook, *Long Walks on Short Days.* Her BA is from Sogang Jesuit University in Seoul, her MA from St. Louis University. Her works have appeared in literary journals including *The Kenyon Review.* Honors include an NEA grant, finalist in William Faulkner Creative Writing Competition, Emily Dickinson Poetry Award, and nominations to the Pushcart Prize and O. Henry Awards. In her TEDx Talk (http://youtu.be/GFD-6JFLF5A), she discusses how the Korean War era stories told in *The Voices of Heaven* uncovers realities about today's S. Korean society. Her testimonies-based novel, *Journals of Comfort Women,* tells the stories of Korean and other Asian countries' comfort women, and the Japanese soldiers who used their services during WWII.

Virginia Bach Folger lives in Schenectady, New York and has a BA from Montclair State University and an MA from Seton Hall University. Ginny has worked as a gas station attendant, paralegal, switchboard operator, claims adjuster and corporate learning and development manager. She has previously published in *Horticulture, Constellations: A Journal of Poetry and Fiction, Adanna* and *Muddy River Poetry Review.*

Stuart Friebert, with the help of colleagues, founded and for some twenty years directed Oberlin's Writing Program before retiring in 1997. He's published 13 books of poems (4 early on in German), among them *Funeral Pie*, co-winner of the Four Way Book Award; 10 volumes of translations; co-edited several anthologies; and in 2015 *The Language of the Enemy*: stories & memoir pieces, will appear from Black Mountain Press.

Eve Gaal received a typewriter at age four, and began writing stories, poems, newsletters, advertising copy, articles and essays. When high school friend commissioned a poem, her destiny was written in stone. Her writing can be found at http://evegaal.com and in *Fiction Noir-13 Stories, God Makes Lemonade, My Funny Valentine* and *Goose River Anthologies*, among others.

Kelle Grace Gaddis received her MFA in Creative Writing & Poetics from the University of Washington. She hosted UWave Radio's Arts, Literature and Music Hour. Her poems and short stories have appeared in *Clamor Literary Journal, Knot Literary & Arts Magazine* and in *Blackmail Presses, Edition 37*. She is a 2015 4Culture "Poetry On Buses" winner, with work appearing on Seattle buses beginning March of 2015. Kelle was a winner in Poetry.org's 2004 National Poetry contest and is a finalist in the Omnidawn national chapbook contest. An AmeriCorps Alum, Kelle advocates for earth and social justice. Her book *Polishing a Gem on the Surface of the Sea* (University of Washington Press) is being revised for republication.

Frederick Glaysher is an epic poet, rhapsode, poet-critic, and the author or editor of a dozen books, including his epic poem The Parliament of Poets (2012), and the collection *The Myth of the Enlightenment: Essays* (2014). He holds two degrees from the University of Michigan and has lived, taught, or traveled in Japan, China, Hong Kong, Taiwan, England, and much of the United States, including the Colorado River Indian Tribes Reservation in Arizona. A recipient of a Fulbright-Hays (China) and an NEH scholarship (India), he is the Literary Executor of the Robert Hayden Estate and resides in Rochester, Michigan. Find Glaysher' at fglaysher.com.

Sharon Goodier is a poet in Toronto, Ontario, a member of the League of Canadian Poets and of Renaissance Revival poets' workshop. she is working on a collection of poems about the physical and emotional effects of PTSD from poverty, war and planetary abuse from our failure to address global warming. These poems are from that collection which is entitled *Waking Up the Dragon*.

Ben Gunsberg is an English professor at Utah State University. His poetry appears or is forthcoming in *CutBank, Chattahoochee Review, The South Carolina Review* and other journals. His poetry manuscript, *Cut Time*, won the University of Michigan's Hopwood Award for Poetry Writing. He lives in Logan, Utah, at the foot of the Bear River Mountains.

Sam Hamill was born in 1943 and grew up on a Utah farm. He is Founding Editor of Copper Canyon Press and served as Editor there for thirty-two years. He taught in artist-in-residency programs in schools and prisons and worked with Domestic Violence programs. He directed the Port Townsend Writers Conference for nine years, and in 2003, founded Poets Against the War. He is the author of more than forty books, including celebrated translations from ancient Chinese, Japanese, Greek and Latin.

William Haywood Henderson is the author of three novels: *Native, The Rest of the Earth*, and *Augusta Locke*. He teaches at Lighthouse Writers Workshop in Denver and in the MFA program at Ashland University.

Jane Hertenstein is the author of over 30 published stories, a combination of fiction, creative non-fiction, and blurred micro and macro genre, has published a YA novel, *Beyond Paradise* and a non-fiction project, *Orphan Girl: The Memoir of a Chicago Bag Lady*, which garnered national reviews, and has received a grant from the Illinois Arts Council. Her work has appeared or is forthcoming in: *Hunger Mountain, Rosebud, Word Riot, Flashquake, Fiction Fix, Frostwriting, Tonopah Review*, and others. Find Jane at http//memoirouswrite.blogspot.com.

Don Hogle is a poet, travel blogger, and brand and communications strategist living in New York. His poetry has appeared or is forthcoming in *Minetta Review*, the inaugural print issue of *Mud Season Review*, *The Gambler* (House Wins Issue) and the inaugural issue of *Shooter in the UK*.

Qumyka Rasheeda Howell is an award winning philanthropist, educator, speaker, poet and writer, with a MA from Stone Brook University. She facilitates empowerment groups for survivors of sexual and domestic violence in New York City and across the country, leads art and healing retreats for survivors, and works with organizations focusing on social change and the elimination of the sexual violence culture. She founded and directs Innocence Stolen Innocent Still (I.S.I.S.) Foundation, and is the innovator behind I.S.I.S. Foundations' award winning Art eNergy Karma Healing (ANKH) programs. She serves on the BOD for the New York State Coalition against Sexual Assault, the first Leadership, Empowerment and Advancement cohort for the Women of Color Network, and the California Coalition against Sexual Assault, and seeks opportunities to forward her mission through art, contemplative thought, and social change. Find her at www.TheISISFoundation.com and catch up with her on twitter @QumykaHowell.

Elizabeth Hoyle is earning her Bachelor's in English and theology from Franciscan University of Steubenville. She is a native of Beckley, West Virginia, and her fiction has been featured in *Origami Journal* and *The Wayfarer*.

A.J. Huffman has published nine solo chapbooks and one joint chapbook, with forthcoming poetry collections, *Another Blood Jet* (Eldritch Press) and *A Few Bullets Short of Home* (mgv2>publishing). A Pushcart Prize nominee, her poetry, fiction, and haiku have appeared in hundreds of national and international journals, including *The James Dickey Review, Bone Orchard, EgoPHobia, Kritya,* and *Offerta Speciale*, in which her work appeared in both English and Italian translation. She is the founding editor of Kind of a Hurricane Press. www.kindofahurricanepress.com.

Lauren Kessler was raised in New York City and now lives in California, where she is pursuing a BA in English and World Literature at Pitzer College. Her poetry has been published in *Neat Magazine* and *Mountain Gazette*.

Ross Knapp is a recent graduate with degrees in philosophy and literature. He has an experimental literary novel forthcoming and poetry publications in *Blue Lake Review, Poetry Pacific Magazine, Indiana Voice Journal, Burningword Literary Journal, Belle Reve Literary Journal, Carcinogenic Poetry,* and others. He lives in Minneapolis.

Page Lambert writes from her mountain home in Colorado. Once, while reading her essay "Porcupine Dusk" at Devils Tower's outdoor amphitheater, a porcupine perched on a ponderosa limb over her head and listened with rapt attention. While reading Mary Oliver's poem "Wild Geese," a flock of wild geese flew overhead. When reading "Turkey Tracks" on a river trip, a wild turkey flew out of the willows, almost snagging her hair. Her award-winning poetry, essays, and stories can be found inside monumental sculptures at the Denver Art Museum, in Huffington Post, *The Writer*, and many Western anthologies. She advocates for organizations such as Clear Creek Land Conservancy, True Nature Journeys, the Aspen Writers' Foundation, Vore Buffalo Jump Foundation, Writing for Peace, and the Children & Nature Network. Go to www.pagelambert.com.

Charles Leggett is a professional actor based in Seattle, WA. Publications include *Clover: A Literary Rag, Frigg, The Worcester Review,* and others. His long poem "Premature Tombeau for John Ashbery" is an e-chapbook in the Barnwood Press "Great Find" series. Other writing projects include a play, The River's Invitation, featured at Seattle's Theatre Off Jackson, and "SPF 1: No Protection!". Twice nominated for the Pushcart Prize, he spent three years as lyricist/frontman for the Seattle blues band Uncle Ed's Molasses Jam, and currently writes, co-arranges and performs blues tunes for the Sandbox Radio Orchestra.

Vicki Lindner is a fiction writer, essayist, journalist, and novelist. She is the author of the novel, *Outlaw Games*, and many short stories, essays, magazine and newspaper articles. She has written about a wide variety of subjects: cooking, bird watching, loneliness, dinosaurs, sculpture, not having children, travel, and medical malpractice. Her work has appeared in journals and anthologies, including *The Paris Review, Kenyon Review, Ploughshares, Fiction, Chick-Lit; Post Feminist Fiction, Witness, the Best of Terrain, Del Sol, The American Literary Review, Gastronomica, New York Stories, In Short: An Anthology of Short Creative Non-Fiction, American Nature Writing, Northern Lights,* and *The Seneca Review.* Her short story about karate, "Barefoot to the Bridge in Winter," was the Fiction Premiere for New York Woman. Most recently, Lindner's essays were published in *Shadowbox* and *Western Humanities Review.*

Cory Lockhart is a teacher, writer, traveler, and aspiring photographer from Louisville, KY. Travels throughout the world opened her eyes and heart to many different cultures, peoples, and injustices. Her encounters sparked a desire to deepen her commitment to nonviolence, specifically by working with Christian Peacemaker Teams. To learn more, visit www.trulylovethyneighbor.com.

Shannon K. Lockhart was born and raised in Louisville, KY. She has a BA in English and Theology and an M.S.W. from Loyola University-Chicago. A human rights advocate, Shannon spent a year in El Salvador and then 12 years in Guatemala. She worked as an accompanier of indigenous returned refugee populations, as a community mental health worker for survivors of massacres, and in the Human Rights Office for the Catholic Church in Guatemala (ODHAG). She also worked as the E.D. of Sister Parish, Inc., an organization promoting long-term ecumenical and cross cultural relationships. Shannon married Luis, a Mexican journalist, and together with their two sons, they moved to the U.S. where both continue to work for peace and justice through music, poetry, teaching, and writing, in order to set an example for their two sons, Liam and Diego.

John C. Mannone has work appearing in *The Southern Poetry Anthology (Volume VII, NC), Still: The Journal, Pine Mountain Sand & Gravel, Split Rock Review, Agave, Tupelo Press, Raven Chronicles, Poetica Magazine, The Baltimore Review, Tipton Poetry Journal, Prairie Wolf Press Review,* and others. His collection, *Flux Lines,* was a semi-finalist for the 2014 Mary Ballard Poetry Chapbook Prize. He's the poetry editor for *Silver Blade* and *Abyss & Apex,* and an adjunct professor of chemistry and physics in east TN. His work has been nominated three times for the Pushcart. Visit *The Art of Poetry:* http://jcmannone.wordpress.com.

Mark Mansfield's poems have appeared in numerous journals, including *The Adirondack Review, Bayou, Blue Mesa Review, The Evansville Review, Fourteen Hills, Gargoyle, The Ledge, Magma, Salt Hill, Scrivener, Tulane Review,* and *Unsplendid.* He holds an MA in Writing from Johns Hopkins. Currently, he lives and teaches in upstate New York.

Jeremy Nathan Marks' poems and photographs have appeared in numerous places including *Lake: a journal of arts and environment, The Blue Hour, Electric Windmill Press, Up The Staircase Quarterly, Right Hand Pointing* and *Wilderness House Literary Review.*

Kevin Patrick McCarthy's early poems were well-received many years ago, but he didn't return to poetry until after the death of a friend in 2011. Since then, his poems have appeared in *Common Ground Review, Written River, Steam Ticket, vox poetica,* and other publications. He is also a dramatist, essayist, geologist, and fourth-generation Coloradan. Please see locuto.com.

Sandra McGarry lived in New Jersey where she was an elementary teacher for 28 years. She moved to be near her family in Colorado. She has published in *Pilgrimage, DoveTales, Paterson Review,* and *Pooled Ink.*

Dean K. Miller is a freelance writer, professional member of Northern Colorado Writers, and Colorado Poets Center. His poetry has appeared in *Torrid Literature Journal* and in other online literary magazines. His creative nonfiction and essays have appeared in *Chicken Soup for the Soul: Parenthood, TROUT Magazine* and won three separate contests at www.midlifecollage.com. Miller's first two books, *Echoes: Reflections Through Poetry and Verse* and *And Then I Smiled: Reflections on a Life Not Yet Complete* were published by Hot Chocolate Press in 2014. For 27 years, Miller has kept the skies safe as an air traffic controller for the FAA and lives in Northern Colorado with his wife Laura and their two dogs.

Mark J. Mitchell studied writing at UC Santa Cruz under Raymond Carver, George Hitchcock and Barbara Hull. His work has appeared in various periodicals and anthologies over the last thirty-five years, and been nominated for both Pushcart Prizes and The Best of the Net. Two full length collections are in the works: *Lent 1999* is coming soon from Leaf Garden Press and *This Twilight World* will be published by Popcorn Press. His chapbook, *Three Visitors* has recently been published by Negative Capability Press. *Artifacts and Relics*, another chapbook, is forthcoming from Folded Word, his novel, *Knight Prisoner*, was recently published by Vagabondage Press, and another novel, *A Book of Lost Songs,* is coming soon from Wild Child Publishing. He lives in San Francisco with his wife, the documentarian and filmmaker Joan Juster.

Roseville Nidea is both a Technical and Literary Writer from the Philippines. Her professional articles are published on different major websites under the company name of her client. Her poetry has appeared in anthologies published in different parts of the world. She is a contributing member of Poets with Voices Strong, Indies in Action, World Peace – World Healing Poetry, and VerseWrights. Words can build as well as can destroy, she states, so when she took the huge responsibility of brushing other's souls, through her poetry, she bound herself to speak only the truth –even dark truth. She believes that creating effective truth creates reconciliations that strengthen peace.

Stephanie Noble lives in Marin County, CA where she served on the BOD of Artists for Social Responsibility and wrote for the *Marin Peace and Justice* newspaper. Her poems have been published in the *Atlanta Review, IthacaLit, Pilgrimage Magazine, Marin Poetry Center Anthology; Unsilenced, the Spirit of Women* and other publications. She was a 2014 Pushcart Prize nominee. She has a BA in Humanities and continues study with Prartho Sereno, Marin County Poet Laureate; Kim Stafford; and Judyth Hill, best known for her poem 'Wage Peace'. Stephanie teaches insight meditation in San Rafael, California and is the author of *Tapping the Wisdom Within, A Guide to Joyous Living*. Visit her at Stephanienoble.com.

Barry W. North is a sixty-nine-year-old retired refrigeration mechanic. Since his retirement in 2007, he has been nominated twice for a Pushcart Prize, won the 2010 A. E. Coppard Prize for Fiction, and, more recently, won Honorable Mention in the 2011 Allen Ginsberg Poetry Awards. His work has appeared or is forthcoming in *The Paterson Literary Review, Slipstream, The Dos Passos Review, Hawaii Pacific Review, Green Hills Literary Lantern, Amoskeag*, and others. His published chapbooks are *Along the Highway* and *Terminally Human*. His new chapbook, *In the Maze*, will be released in August by Finishing Line Press. Visit his website at www.barrynorth.org.

Cheryl Pearson lives in Manchester in the North West of England. Her poems have appeared in publications including *14 Magazine, The Journal, Tincture*, and all three *'Best of Manchester Poets'* anthologies (Puppywolf Press). She is currently working on her first full-length collection, as well as a fiction project.

Adrienne Pine's creative nonfiction has been published in *The Write Place at the Write Time, Tale of Four Cities, The Yale Journal of Humanities in Medicine,* and other venues.

Jeannine Pitas is a writer, teacher and translator living in Toronto. My first poetry chapbook, *Our Lady of the Snow Angels*, was published in 2012 by Lyricalmyrical Press, and my translation of acclaimed Uruguayan writer Marosa di Giorgio's *The History of Violets* was published in 2010 by Brooklyn-based Ugly Duckling Presse.

Jessica Placinto is 18 years old and started writing her freshman year of High school after a close role model of hers took their own life. She went on to publish a poetry book on Lulu.com her Sophomore year. She has found poetry to be the most cleansing self expression for her soul.

David S. Pointer earned an MA in Sociology and later secured a surgical technology diploma. Recent publications include *The Southern Poetry Anthology Series, Volumes V & VI for Georgia and Tennessee*. David serves on the advisory panel at "Writing for Peace."

Laura Pritchett is the author of seven books, most recently the novel *Stars Go Blue*, with two novels forthcoming. Awards for these books include the PEN USA Award for Fiction, the WILLA Award, the Milkweed National Fiction Prize, the Colorado Book Award, and others. She's also published over 100 essays and short stories in numerous magazines, including *The Sun, Salon, Orion, High Country News, OnEarth, Poets & Writers, O Magazine, High Desert Journal*, and others. Four of her stories have been nominated for the Pushcart Prize. More at www.laurapritchett.com.

Claudia Putnam lives in Western Colorado. Her work appears in many journals including *Phoebe, South Dakota Review, Cimarron Review, Roanoke Review, Barrow Street*, and *Poetry East*. A poetry chapbook, *Wild Thing in Our Known World*, is available from Finishing Line Press. In 2011-12 she held the George Bennett Fellowship; in 2015 she'll be at Kimmel Harding Nelson. She hopes that ever more people and peoples will find peace through contact with nature. More at claudiaputnam.com.

Lisa Rizzo is the author of *In the Poem an Ocean,* a chapbook (Big Table Publishing, 2011). Her work also has appeared in such journals as *13th Moon, Earth's Daughters, Calyx Journal, The Fertile Source* and *RiverLit.* Her poems received 1st and 2nd prizes in the 2011 Maggi H. Meyer Poetry Prize competition, and another won the 2014 Poetry Is Contest by Caroline Goodwin, San Mateo Country Poet Laureate. She blogs at Poet Teacher Seeks World and can be reached at www.lisarizzopoetry.com. Lisa is an English/Language Arts Coach for teachers, and lives in the San Francisco Bay Area.

Nicholas Alexander Roos teaches writing, reading and thinking at the University of Northern Iowa. He began delivering newspapers when he was 11, using most of his earnings to buy *Calvin and Hobbes* collections, and has been actively involved in storytelling ever since. He loves the idea of humans reading and writing to experience flashes of emotion and truth.

Sy Roth is a retired school administrator and has finally found the silence and time to think whole thoughts. This has led him to find words and the ability to shape them. He has published in *Visceral Uterus, Amulet, BlogNostics, Every Day Poets, Barefoot Review, Haggard and Halloo, Misfits Miscellany, Mad Swirl, Larks Fiction Magazine, Danse Macabre, Bitchin' Kitch, Bong is Bard, Humber Pie, Poetry Super Highway, Penwood Review, Masque Publications, Foliate Oak, Miller's Pond Poetry* and *The Eloquent Atheist.*

Elizabeth Schultz is constantly writing and thinking about Earthcare. She has written two scholarly books, five books of poetry, a memoir, a collection of short stories, a collection of essays, and her scholarly and creative work appears in numerous journals and reviews.

Tshombe Sekou is a poet whose writings construct meaningful and positive context from the subtext of life. His voice in poetics is unique, yet familiar to that of Kahlil Gibran and Rumi. Tshombe is an American living in Japan where he studies and enhances his poetry.

Alan Semrow lives in Wisconsin and is a graduate of English from the University of Wisconsin-Stevens Point. His poems and fiction have been featured in many publications, including *BlazeVOX14, Red Fez, The Bicycle Review, Earl of Plaid Lit Journal, Potluck Magazine, Blotterature Lit Mag; The Rain, Party, & Disaster Society; The Commonline Journal, Former People: A Journal of Bangs and Whimpers, Golden* and *Wordplay*, and he won the Essayist Award from the University of Wisconsin-Stevens Point English Department for his nonfiction work. In 2015, his stories forthcoming in several journals, including *EAP: The Magazine, The Radvocate, Crack the Spine*, and *Indiana Voice Journal*. Semrow spends the majority of his free time with his boyfriend, friends, family, and Shih Tzu, Remy.

Annette Marie Smith is a freelance journalist, an author, and a poet. Her articles have appeared in print throughout the United States and internationally. Her most recent book is *The Real Reason the Queen Hated Snow* published by Twilight Times Books. She is currently happily at work on a novel of magical realism.

Patty Somlo has been nominated for the Pushcart Prize four times, was a finalist in the Tom Howard Short Story Contest, and has been nominated for the 2013 story South's Million Writers Award. Her essay, "If We Took a Deep Breath," was selected as a Notable Essay of 2013 for Best American Essays 2014. She is the author of From Here to There and Other Stories. Her second book, Hairway to Heaven Stories, is forthcoming in January 2017 from Cherry Castle Publishing. Her work has appeared in numerous journals, including the Los Angeles Review, the Santa Clara Review, Under the Sun, Guernica, The Flagler Review, The Journal of Sustainability Education and WomenArts Quarterly, among others, and in fourteen anthologies, including Solace in So Many Words, which won the Next Generation Indie Book Award for Anthology.

Howard F. Stein, a psychoanalytic, applied, organizational, and medical anthropologist and organizational consultant, is professor emeritus in the Department of Family and Preventive Medicine, University of Oklahoma Health Sciences Center, Oklahoma City, OK, USA, where he taught nearly 35 years. He now serves as group facilitator for the American Indian Diabetes Prevention Center in Oklahoma City. He is author of 27 books, of which 7 are books or chapbooks of poetry. His most recent poetry books are *Raisins and Almonds* (2014) and *In the Shadow of Asclepius: Poems from American Medicine* (2011). He can be reached at howard-stein@ouhsc.edu.

Fred Tarr is a University of Iowa workshop graduate, as well as workshops in NKY and Cincinnati. He has published in European and USA small presses. He has a book of poems published by Owl Oak Press,2006; *Radioroom, Lifeboat, Ship of Fools;* also from Owl Oak, *Anthology of International Poetry*, hard copy, garnered, collected from on-line cullouqies, 2005.

Samantha Terrell has been writing poetry for nearly two decades. Her chapbook *Honesty,* is published six times annually. Her work has been published in various journals, including *DoveTales* and *LaBloga Floricanto*. Samantha resides in Missouri with her husband and two boys.

Jari Thymian volunteers year-round in state and national parks across the United States. She leads a minimalist lifestyle in a 32-foot RV with her husband. Her poetry has appeared in various publications including *tinywords, A Hundred Gourds, The Pedestal, Prune Juice, Ekphrasis, FRiGG, American Tanka,* and in Kent State's traveling art and poetry exhibit *Speak Peace*. Her poetry has been nominated for Best of the Net and a Pushcart Prize.

Debra Lynn Turner's works include short fiction, poetry and a one-act play, *Very Private Party* produced in the 2007 Fringe of Marin Festival. Her short stories have appeared in *Rosebud Magazine, Soundings Review, Trajectory and Edge*, the literary journal of Tahoe Writ-

ers Works. She recently completed her third novel.
Smriti Verma is an adolescent Delhite from India,
whose primary interests are history and philosophy. She
has won seventh position in an international writing
contest organised by Laura Thomas Communications,
received a manuscript consultation from a published
author and is currently in the process of writing her third
novel. Other than that, she is a First Reader for Polyphony
HS and Junior Editor at Siblini Journal. She can be found
burying her head in an Austen novel, watching period
dramas or lecturing a person on social issues.

Wang Ping came to USA from Shanghai in 1986. She is
the founder and director of the Kinship of Rivers project,
a five-year project that builds a sense of kinship among
the people who live along the Mississippi and Yangtze
Rivers through exchanging gifts of art, poetry, stories,
music, dance and food. She paddles along the Mississippi
River and its tributaries, giving poetry and art workshops
along the river communities, making thousands of flags
as gifts and peace ambassadors between the Missis-
sippi and the Yangtze Rivers. Her publications include
Ten Thousand Waves, poetry book from Wings Press,
2014, *American Visa* (short stories, 1994), *Foreign Devil*
(novel, 1996), *Of Flesh and Spirit* (poetry, 1998), *The
Magic Whip* (poetry, 2003), *The Last Communist Virgin*
(stories, 2007), all from Coffee House, *New Generation:
Poetry from China Today,* 1999 from Hanging Loose
Press, *Flash Cards: Poems by Yu Jian,* co-translation
with Ron Padgett, 2010 from Zephyr Press. *Aching for
Beauty: Footbinding in China* (2000, University of Min-
nesota Press, 2002 paperback by Random House) won
the Eugene Kayden Award for the Best Book in Humani-
ties. *The Last Communist Virgin* won 2008 Minnesota
Book Award and Asian American Studies Award, and had
many multi-media exhibitions, including a collaboration
with the British filmmaker Isaac Julien on *Ten Thousand
Waves,* about illegal Chinese immigration in London. She
is the recipient of National Endowment for the Arts, New
York Foundation for the Arts, New York State Council of

the Arts, Minnesota State Arts Board, the Bush Artist Fellowship, Lannan Foundation Fellowship, Vermont Studio Center Fellowship, and the McKnight Artist Fellowship. www.wangping.com and www.kinshipofrivers.org.

Jing M. Wang is an associate professor of Chinese at Colgate University. She earned her MA in English literature and her PhD in Chinese literature. Her first publication, co-authored with Professor Ding Wangdao, is *How to Read English Poetry*(《英诗入门》 Shanghai Translations Publishing House, 1989. Reprints 1994, 1999). *When "I" Was Born: Women's Autobiography in Modern China* (University of Wisconsin Press, 2008) is her recent work on Chinese literary history, examining the emergence of women's autobiography as a genre in China in the 1930s and 1940s, a time when the nation in crises supposedly prioritized collectivistic action over individualistic sentiment.

Mercedes Webb-Pullman earned a IIML from Victoria University, Wellington, New Zealand, and an MA in Creative Writing in 2011. Her work appears in: *Turbine, 4th Floor, Swamp, Reconfigurations, The Electronic Bridge, poetryrepairs, Connotations, The Red Room, and books Numeralla Dreaming, After the Danse, Food 4 Thought, Looking for Kerouac, Ono* and *Bravo Charlie Foxtrot*. www.benchpress.co.nz.

Laura Grace Weldon is an editor and nonviolence educator. She's the author of a poetry collection, *Tending* (Aldrich Press, 2013), and a handbook of alternative education, *Free Range Learning* (Hohm Press, 2010). Laura has written poetry with nursing home residents, used poetry to teach conflict resolution, and painted poems on beehives. Her work appears in such places as *Christian Science Monitor, J Journal, Literary Mama, The Shine Journal, Red River Review, Dressing Room Poetry Journal, Shot Glass Journal, Rose & Thorn Journal, Iodine Poetry Journal*, and *Pudding House.* Connect with her at lauragraceweldon.com.

Art and Photography

Chrystal Berche dabbles and, somewhere in those dabbles, ideas blossom that take shape into images. Many of her current pieces of artwork start out as three minute gesture drawings and eventually get paired with still life photography and a lot of playing in photoshop. She loves to take pictures, especially out in the woods, where she can sit on a rock or a log and wait quietly, jotting notes for stories until something happens by. A free spirit, Chrystal digs in dirt, dances in rain and chases storms, all at the whims of her muses.

Sylvia Freeman is a photographer, writer, singer, and yoga instructor. As a photographer, she is especially interested in the quality of light in nature and through glass. Her images and poems have been published in *When Women Waken,* and her fiction has been published in *Conclave: A Journal of Character.*

Pd Lietz is an award winning and widely published writer, photographer and artist who lives in rural Manitoba, Canada. Lietz has garnered an impressive range of credits working with various publishers and authors, and revels in the creative energy generated within the artistic and literary community. Her writing, art and photography have appeared in and as covers of many publications: *Naugatuck River Review* Summer 2011 & Winter 2013, *MaINtENaNT: Journal of Contemporary DADA Writing and Art*, editions #4, 5 & 6, *Visions, Voices and Verses, In the Company of Women, Sunrise From Blue Thunder, Poet Tree, Reflections of a Blue Planet* 3 1,2,3 & 4, *Uncoil A Night, Origami Poetry Project, Songs of Sandy, Enchanting Verses, International Poetry Journal* to name a few. And her poetry is being placed on billboards around the world due to the wonderful vision of Phantom Billstickers Ltd of New Zealand. You can view works by Pd Lietz here: http://www.pdlietzphotography. com/.

Carl Scharwath's work appears worldwide with over fifty published poems and five short stories. He recently won the National Poetry Contest award on behalf of Writers One Flight Up. The poem was selected and critiqued by Vivian Shipley a Pulitzer Prize nominee. His first poetry book *Journey To Become Forgotten* was published by Kind of a Hurricane Press. His art photography were featured in the *Conclave Journal* and *Edgar Allen Poet*.

Christopher Woods is a writer, teacher and photographer who lives in Texas. He has published a novel, *The Dream Patch*, a prose collection, *Under a Riverbed Sky,* and a book of stage monologues for actors, *Heart Speak*. His photographs can be seen in his online gallery - http://christopherwoods.zenfolio.com/.

Acknowledgements

Writing for Peace would like to acknowledge you, our supporters, and all of our advisers who inspire and guide us, including our young advisers, Lyla June Johnston, Malaka Mohammed, and Nathan Blanc.

We are tremendously grateful to our prestigeous panel of 2015 Young Writers' Contest judges, Antonya Nelson, fiction; Steve Almond, nonfiction; and Stephen Kuusisto, poetry. Thank you for so generously sharing your time, talents and expertise.

Thank you to Adviser Mary Carroll-Hackett (whose work is included in this journal) from Longwood University in Virginia, for the creation, development, and oversight of our first annual Writing for Peace Youth Summit this fall, an event that will invite undergrads and young people to explore peaceful activism through the arts. We are also grateful to Phillip Richards and Colgate University who will help and support participants in the creation of a multi-media journal to commemorate. Keynote speakers include our three young advisers, Lyla June Johnston, from New Mexico; Malaka Mohammed, from Gaza; and Nathan Blanc, from Israel. On the final day, participants will have the opportunity Q&A with Writing for Peace Adviser Dr. Erica Chenoweth, whose research has shown that nonviolence resistance is more effective than violent resistance.

Many thanks to our Board of Directors for their tireless efforts on behalf of Writing for Peace.

Last, but not least, we would like to thank our generous contributors. Special thanks goes to Samantha Peters Terrell, Sandra McGarry, Dean Metcalf, Phillip Richards, Andrea W. Doray, Craig and Carmel Mawle, Willean and Le Hornbeck, Longwood University, and the Colgate University Research Council. This year, Writing for Peace became a 501c3 nonprofit corporation (Federal Tax ID Number, 45-2968027), a development that will allow exciting future growth. Be sure to follow our blog to learn about new developments at www.writingforpeace.org.